Welcome to Rome

Even in a country of exquisite cities like Italy, Rome is special. Epic, hot-blooded and achingly beautiful, it's a heady mix of haunting ruins, awe-inspiring art, iconic monuments and vibrant street life.

Rome's historic cityscape, the result of 3000 years of ad hoc urban development, is an exhilarating spectacle. Ancient icons such as the Colosseum, Roman Forum and Pantheon recall its golden age as *caput mundi* (capital of the world), while barn-storming basilicas testify to its historical role as seat of the Catholic Church.

The city's artistic heritage is also astonishing. Throughout history, Rome has starred in the great upheavals of Western art, drawing the top artists of the day and inspiring them to push the boundaries of creative achievement. The result is a city awash with priceless treasures. Ancient statues adorn world-class museums, Byzantine mosaics and Renaissance frescoes dazzle in art-rich churches, baroque fountains embellish medieval piazzas. Walk around the centre and without even trying you'll come across masterpieces by the likes of Michelangelo, Caravaggio, Raphael and Bernini.

But a trip to Rome is as much about lapping up the dolce vita lifestyle as gorging on art and culture. Whiling away hours at streetside cafes, idling on pretty piazzas, dining in boisterous neighbourhood trattorias – these are all an integral and enjoyable part of the Roman experience.

Rome is special...epic, hot-blooded and achingly beautiful

St Peter's Basilica at dusk
MAPICS/SHUTTERSTOCK ©

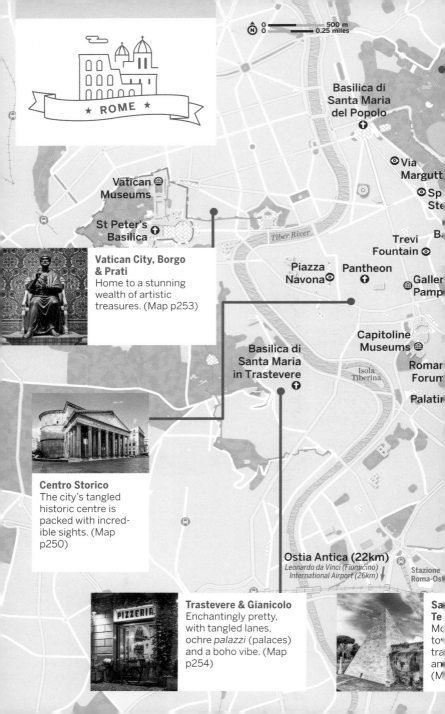

★ ROME ★

Basilica di Santa Maria del Popolo

Via Margutt

Sp Ste

Vatican Museums

St Peter's Basilica

Tiber River

Trevi Fountain

B

Vatican City, Borgo & Prati
Home to a stunning wealth of artistic treasures. (Map p253)

Piazza Navona

Pantheon

Galler Pamp

Basilica di Santa Maria in Trastevere

Capitoline Museums

Roman Forum

Isola Tiberina

Palatin

Centro Storico
The city's tangled historic centre is packed with incredible sights. (Map p250)

Ostia Antica (22km)
Leonardo da Vinci (Fiumicino) International Airport (26km)

Stazione Roma-Ost

Trastevere & Gianicolo
Enchantingly pretty, with tangled lanes, ochre *palazzi* (palaces) and a boho vibe. (Map p254)

Sa Te
Mo to tra an (M

0 / 0 — 500 m / 0.25 miles

Plan Your Trip
This Year in Rome

2019

EMPRESS/SHUTTERSTOCK ©

Rome

From religious processions and neighbourhood parties to fashion shows, food fairs and major arts festivals, Rome's calendar bursts with events. Many are played out against atmospheric outdoor backdrops, adding a wonderful sense of occasion.

From left: Natale di Roma (p9); Primo Maggio (p10); Carnevale Romano (p7)

GLORIA IMBROGNO/SHUTTERSTOCK ©

★ Top Festivals & Events

Carnevale Romano, Feb
Natale di Roma, Apr
Lungo il Tevere, Mid-Jun–Sep
Estate Romana, Jun–Oct
Romaeuropa, Late Sep–Nov

MARIALBA.ITALIA/GETTY IMAGES ©

Plan Your Trip
This Year in Rome

ERNESTO S. RUSCIO/GETTY IMAGES ©

01

January

As New Year celebrations fade, the winter cold digs in. It's a quiet time of year but the winter sales are a welcome diversion.

☆ **Tuffo nel Tevere**　　　1 Jan
By now a New Year's Day tradition, Maurizio Palmulli, a local lifeguard, dives into the icy waters of the Tiber from Ponte Cavour after the Gianicolo cannon sounds at midday.

🛍 **Shopping Sales**　　　Early Jan
Bargain hunters flock to Rome's shops for the winter fashion sales. Running from early January, typically the first Saturday of the month, to mid-February, the eagerly awaited *saldi* offer savings of between 20% and 50%.

🎉 **Epiphany**　　　6 Jan
A witch known as *La Befana* delivers gifts to Italian kids for Epiphany, the last day of the

👁 **Alta Roma**　　　Late Jan
Fashionistas swan in for the winter outing of Rome's top fashion event. Catwalk shows and events, held in venues across town, provide previews of seasonal collections by established designers and emerging talents.

Christmas holidays. To mark the occasion, a costumed procession makes its way down Via della Conciliazione to St Peter's Square.

🎉 **Festa di Sant'Antonio Abate**　　　17 Jan
Animal lovers take their pets to be blessed at the Chiesa di Sant'Eusebio on Piazza Vittorio Emanuele in honour of St Anthony the Abbot, the patron saint of animals.

2019

February

Rome's winter quiet is shattered by high-spirited carnival celebrations and weekend invasions by cheerful rugby fans in town for the annual Six Nations rugby tournament.

☆ Six Nations Rugby 1 Feb –16 Mar
The Stadio Olimpico (pictured above) hosts Italy's home games during the Six Nations rugby tournament. In 2019, Italy's first home game is against Wales on Saturday, 9 February.

❀ Valentine's Day 14 Feb
St Valentine, or San Valentino in Italian, was a 3rd-century martyr who was executed near Ponte Milvio. His saint's day is now widely celebrated – some museums and galleries offer discounted entry, and restaurants prepare romantic menus.

☆ Equilibrio Festival Mid-Feb
Performers from Scandanavia take to the stage at the Auditorium Parco della Musica for the 2019 edition of this contemporary

02

❀ Carnevale Romano Late Feb–Early Mar
Rome goes to town for Carnevale (pictured below), with horse shows, costumed parades, street performers, fireworks and kids in fancy dress. The program changes each year, but the action is often centred on Piazza del Popolo, Via del Corso, Piazza Navona and Piazza del Campidoglio.

dance festival. Past outings have showcased dance from Germany and France.

PCOSTABALDI/GETTY IMAGES ©

MARIALBA.ITALIA/GETTY IMAGES ©

Plan Your Trip
This Year in Rome

March

03

The onset of spring brings blooming flowers, rising temperatures and unpredictable rainfall. The city is fairly subdued, and with Easter not falling until late April low-season prices still apply.

⊙ Festa della Donna   8 Mar

To mark International Women's Day, events are held in museums and cultural sites, many of which offer free admission to women visitors. The traditional Italian gift for the day is a sprig of yellow mimosa flowers.

✿ Festa di Santa Francesca Romana   9 Mar

Devout motorists congregate on Via dei Fori Imperiali to have their cars blessed on the feast day of St Frances of Rome, the patron saint of drivers.

✿ Festa di San Giuseppe   19 Mar

The Feast of St Joseph, which doubles as Father's Day in Italy, is traditionally celebrated by snaffling delicious cream puffs known as *bignè di San Giuseppe (pictured above)*.

⊙ Giornate FAI di Primavera   Late Mar

Palazzi (mansions), churches and archaeological sites that are generally closed to the public open their doors for a weekend of special openings, courtesy of Italy's main conservation body, the Fondo Ambiente Italiano (FAI).

2019

POLIFOTO/SHUTTERSTOCK ©

04

April

April is a great month in Rome, with lovely, sunny weather, fervent Easter celebrations, azaleas on the Spanish Steps and Rome's birthday festivities. Expect high-season prices.

🏃 Maratona di Roma   7 Apr

Sightseeing becomes sport at Rome's annual marathon (pictured above; www.maratonadiroma.it). The 42km route starts and finishes near the Colosseum, taking in many of the city's big sights.

⊙ Mostra delle Azalee   Mid-Apr–Early May

As per an 80-year-old tradition, the Spanish Steps are decorated with hundreds of vases of blooming, brightly coloured azaleas.

🎆 Viaggio nei Fori   Mid-Apr–Mid-Nov

Ancient history is brought to life at the Imperial Forums with multimedia light shows (www.viaggioneifori.it) at the Foro di Augusto and, over the road, the Foro di Cesare.

🎆 Natale di Roma   21 Apr

Rome celebrates its birthday on 21 April with music, free museum entry, historical recreations and firework displays – in 2019 the city will be 2772 years old. Action is centred on Via dei Fori Imperiali and the city's ancient sites.

🎆 Easter   21 Apr

Easter is a big deal in Rome. On Good Friday the pope leads a candlelit procession around the Colosseum, and there are other smaller parades around the city. At noon on Easter Sunday the Pope blesses the crowds in St Peter's Square.

🎆 Festa della Liberazione   25 Apr

Schools, shops and offices shut as Rome commemorates the WWII liberation of Italy by Allied troops and resistance forces in 1945.

Plan Your Trip
This Year in Rome

MICHAEL STEELE/GETTY IMAGES ©

May

May is a busy, high-season month. The weather's perfect – usually warm enough to eat outside – and the city is looking gorgeous with blue skies and spring flowers.

☆ Open House Roma   Early May
Historic and contemporary buildings that are normally closed to the public open their doors for a weekend of visits and guided tours during the Open House Roma event (www.openhouseroma.org), designed to promote Rome's architectural diversity.

☆ Internazionale
BNL d'Italia   Early May
The world's top players slug it out on the red clay courts of the Foro Italico at the Internazionale BNL d'Italia (pictured above; www.internazionalibnlditalia.com), one of Europe's top tennis tournaments.

☆ Piazza di Siena
Show Jumping   Late May
Set in the attractive confines of Villa Borghese, Piazza di Siena stages Rome's

☆ Primo Maggio   1 May
Thousands of music fans troop to Piazza di San Giovanni in Laterano for Rome's free May Day rock concert (www.primomaggio.net). It's a mostly Italian affair with big-name local performers, but you might catch the occasional foreign guest star.

GLORIA IMBROGNO/SHUTTERSTOCK ©

annual international show-jumping event (www.piazzadisiena.it) towards the end of the month.

SALVO77_NA/SHUTTERSTOCK ©

2019

06

June

Summer has arrived and, with it, hot weather and the Italian school holidays. The city's festival season breaks into full stride with a number of outdoor events.

✯ Festa della Repubblica　2 Jun
A big military parade, featuring the President of the Republic, along Via dei Fori Imperiali is the highlight of ceremonial events held to commemorate the birth of the Italian Republic in 1946.

✯ Estate Romana　Jun–Oct
Rome's big summer festival (http://estate romana.comune.roma.it) hosts hundreds of events and cultural activities across the city. Expect everything from concerts and dance performances to book fairs, puppet shows and late-night museum openings.

✯ Gay Village　Jun–Sep
Rome's big annual LGBT event, held in the EUR district, attracts crowds of partygoers and an exuberant cast of DJs, musicians and entertainers. It serves up an eclectic mix of dance music, film screenings, cultural debates and theatrical performances.

☆ Rock in Roma　Jun & Jul
Dust down the denims for Rome's big rock fest (www.rockinroma.com), held at the city's racecourse south of the centre. Recent headline acts include Roger Waters, The Killers and the Chemical Brothers.

☆ Isola del Cinema　Mid-Jun–Sep
The Isola Tiberina sets the picturesque backdrop for this summer open-air film festival (https://isoladelcinema.com). The program runs the gamut from home-grown Italian films to European and Asian arthouse flicks and Hollywood blockbusters.

✯ Festa dei Santi Pietro e Paolo　29 Jun
Rome celebrates its two patron saints, Peter and Paul, with flower displays on St Peter's Square, fireworks at Piazza del Popolo and festivities near the Basilica di San Paolo Fuori-le-Mura (pictured above).

Plan Your Trip
This Year in Rome

STEFANO MONTESI - CORBIS/GETTY IMAGES ©

July

07

Hot summer temperatures make sightseeing a physical endeavour, but come the cool of evening, the city's streets burst into life as locals come out to enjoy the summer festivities.

☆ Luglio Suona Bene — Jul

Music legends, rock stars and crooners take to the outdoor stage at the Auditorium Parco della Musica for this summer concert festival. There are nightly gigs by a range of top international and Italian performers.

☆ Opera at the Terme di Caracalla — Jul

The haunting remains of the Terme di Caracalla, a vast 3rd-century baths complex, provide the spectacular setting for the Teatro dell'Opera's summer season. Between the operas, ballets and even the occasional rock concert are also staged.

☆ Roma Incontro il Mondo — Jul–Mid-Sep

Each summer Villa Ada is transformed into a colourful multi-ethnic village for this popular annual event (www.villaada.org). There's a laid-back party vibe and an excellent program of gigs ranging from rock to reggae, jazz and world music.

☆ Notti Romane al Teatro di Marcello — Late Jul–Mid-Sep

Enjoy classical music in the atmospheric confines of the 1st-century-BC Teatro di Marcello during this summer concert series. Nightly performances are often preceded by a guided tour of the ancient theatre.

Festa de' Noantri — Late Jul

Trastevere celebrates its neighbourhood roots with a raucous street party in the last two weeks of the month. Events (pictured above) kick off with a religious procession and continue with much eating, drinking, dancing and praying.

2019

MARCO IACOBUCCI EPP/SHUTTERSTOCK ©

08

August

Rome melts in the heat as locals flee the city for their summer hols. Many businesses shut down around 15 August, but hoteliers offer discounts and there are loads of summer events to enjoy.

✨ Festa della Madonna della Neve
5 Aug

Artificial snow is showered on celebrants at the Basilica di Santa Maria Maggiore to commemorate a miraculous 4th-century snowfall. Adding to the atmosphere is a sound-and-light show that illuminates the basilica's facade.

✨ Ferragosto
15 Aug

The Festival of the Assumption is celebrated with almost total shutdown as what seems like Rome's entire population decamps to the seaside.

✨ Lungo il Tevere
Mid-Jun–Aug

Nightly crowds converge on the river Tiber for this popular summer-long event. Stalls, clubs, bars, restaurants, cinemas, even dance floors line the river bank between Ponte Sublicio and Ponte Sistio as Rome's nightlife goes alfresco.

☆ Football Season Starts
Late Aug

As the rest of the city sizzles in the summer sun, Rome's footballers return to the grindstone. Italy's Serie A gets underway around 20 August and the city's passionate fans can once more get their weekly fix.

Plan Your Trip
This Year in Rome

September

As summer draws to a close, life returns to the city after the heat-induced August torpor. The kids go back to school and locals return to work, but there's still a relaxed vibe and the weather's perfect.

☆ **Roma Fringe Festival**   Sep

From cabaret and stand-up comedy to performance art, premieres and contemporary takes on classic plays, independent theatre is celebrated at this fringe festival (www.roma fringefestival.it). Performances by Italian and international companies are staged at Villa Merced in the San Lorenzo neighbourhood.

✖ **Taste of Roma**   Mid-Sep

Foodies flock to the Auditorium Parco della Musica to revel in world food. Join Rome's top chefs for four days of tastings, performances, lessons and food-related events (pcitured above; www.tasteofroma.it).

🍷 **Clubbing**   Late Sep

The end of the month is a good time for party-goers as Rome's main clubs return to town after their summer exodus. Curtain-raiser events promise new looks and big nights.

🎭 **Romaeuropa**   Late Sep–Nov

Established international performers join emerging stars at Rome's premier dance and drama festival. Staged across town, events range from avant-garde dance performances to installations, multimedia shows, recitals and readings.

NATTAKIT JEERAPATMAITREE/SHUTTERSTOCK ©

October

Autumn is a good time to visit –
the warm weather is holding,
Romaeuropa ensures plenty of
cultural action and, with the
schools back, there are far fewer
tourists around.

🍷 EurHop Roma
Beer Festival   Early Oct

For three days in early October, aficionados
and enthusiastic quaffers congregate in
EUR to indulge their passion for craft beer.
Brews from around the world fuel three
days of talk, tastings and liquid fun.

☆ Santa Cecilia
Symphony Season   Early Oct

Rome's premier orchestra, the Orchestra
dell'Accademia Nazionale di Santa Cecilia
(www.santacecilia.it) returns to its home
stage at the Auditorium Parco della Musica

☆ Festa del
Cinema di Roma   Late Oct

Held at the Auditorium Parco della Musica (designed by Renzo Piano Building
Workshop), Rome's film festival (www.
romacinemafest.it) rolls out the red car-
pet for Hollywood hotshots and bigwigs
from Italian cinema in late October.

(pictured above) for the inauguration of its
symphony season.

⊙ Night Openings
at the Vatican Museums   Apr–Oct

October is your last chance to spend the
evening at the Vatican Museums, home
of the Sistine Chapel and kilometres of
priceless art treasures. In past years, the
museums have opened on Friday nights
from 7pm to 11pm.

Plan Your Trip
This Year in Rome

ROMAN BABAKIN/SHUTTERSTOCK ©

November

Although the wettest month, November has its compensations – low-season prices, excellent jazz concerts and no queues outside the big sights. It's also a great month for foodies with market stalls full of bumper autumnal produce.

✿ Festa di Ognissanti   1 Nov
Celebrated as a national holiday, All Saints' Day is dedicated to all the saints of the Church. It's followed on 2 November by All Souls' Day when Romans remember their dead by placing flowers on the tombs of loved ones.

☆ Festival Internazionale di Musica e Arte Sacra   Early Nov
Over several days in early November, the Vienna Philharmonic Orchestra and other top ensembles perform a series of classical concerts in Rome's papal basilicas and

☆ Roma Jazz Festival   Nov
The Auditorium Parco della Musica is the place to be in November for jazz fans, as performers from around the world play to appreciative audiences during the three-week Roma Jazz Festival (www.romajazzfestival.it).

other churches. Check the program online: www.festivalmusicaeartesacra.net.

☆ Start of the Opera Season   Mid-Nov
Mid-month, the opera season gets underway at the city's opera house, the Teatro dell'Opera di Roma. The theatre (pictured above) is also home to the city's principal ballet corps whose performance season starts in December.

2019

VVOE/SHUTTERSTOCK ©

12

December

The build-up to Christmas is a festive time – the Christmas lights go on, shopping takes on a new urgency, and presepi (nativity scenes) appear across town, most spectacularly in St Peter's Square.

✿ Festa dell'Immacolate Concezione   8 Dec

The pope, in his capacity as the Bishop of Rome, celebrates the Feast of the Immaculate Conception in Piazza di Spagna. Earlier in the day, Rome's fire brigade places a garland of flowers atop the Colonna dell'Immacolata in adjacent Piazza Mignanelli.

⊙ Piazza Navona Christmas Fair   Dec–6 Jan

Piazza Navona, Rome's showy baroque square, sets the stage for this festive annual market (pictured above). Tradition dictates that the *Befana* (witch) appear on Epiphany (6 January) to hand out sweets to children.

⊙ Christmas Lights   8 Dec

The Mayor of Rome officially starts Rome's festive season by switching on the city's Christmas tree lights in Piazza Venezia. Over the river in the Vatican, a huge tree and life-sized *presepe* adorn St Peter's Square.

VALERIOMEI/SHUTTERSTOCK ©

✿ Capodanno   31 Dec

Rome is a noisy place to be on New Year's Eve as big firework displays usher in the New Year and outdoor concerts are held across town, most notably on the Circo Massimo.

Plan Your Trip
Hotspots for...

HISTORY BUFFS

👁 **Colosseum** Encapsulates the drama of the ancient *caput mundi* (world capital). (p36; pictured above)

👁 **Via Appia Antica** The first great superhighway, built in the 4th century BC. (p74)

☆ **Terme di Caracalla** These 3rd-century baths are a spectacular setting for opera and ballet. (p187)

✘ **La Ciambella** A laid-back eatery over an ancient baths complex. (p124)

🍷 **Antico Caffè Greco** Rome's oldest cafe, a former haunt of Casanova, Goethe, Wagner, Keats, Byron and Shelley. (p126)

ROMANCE

👁 **Pincio Hill Gardens** Take in a glorious sunset from this romantic spot in the Villa Borghese. (p57)

🍫 **Confetteria Moriondo & Gariglio** This historic crimson-walled chocolate shop is sweet decadence. (p148)

🍷 **Stravinskij Bar** Hotel de Russie's courtyard bar exudes effortless dolce vita style. (p170)

✘ **Aroma** Treat yourself to a Michelin-starred dinner and dreamy Colosseum views. (p139)

👁 **Keats-Shelley House** Seek inspiration in the one-time home of Romantic poet John Keats. (p91; pictured below)

GLITZ & GLAMOUR

◉ **Spanish Steps** Scale Rome's iconic steps then head for super-chic Via dei Condotti. (p90)

◉ **Basilica di Santa Maria in Trastevere** Ancient basilica famous for its golden apse mosaics. (p104)

✗ **Pianostrada** Creative cuisine goes with vintage style at this hip eatery. (p124)

🍷 **Zuma Bar** Sophistication on the rooftop terrace of Palazzo Fendi. (p170)

☆ **Teatro dell'Opera di Roma** A plush interior sets the stage for dazzling operas. (p185)

CULTURE VULTURES

◉ **Vatican Museums** Home to the Sistine Chapel and kilometres of art. (p40; pictured above)

◉ **Museo e Galleria Borghese** Little-known gallery with some of Rome's most spectacular artworks. (p54)

✗ **Antonello Colonna Open** New Roman cuisine at Palazzo delle Esposizioni. (p134)

☆ **Auditorium Parco della Musica** Iconic Renzo Piano–designed complex. (p188)

BARGAIN HUNTERS

🛍 **Porta Portese Market** Have a Sunday-morning browse at Rome's busiest flea market. (p159)

◉ **Campo de' Fiori** Enjoy the sights, sounds and smells of this historic market square. (p65; pictured above)

✗ **Pizzarium** Rome's best sliced pizza comes with an array of gourmet toppings. (p129)

✗ **Panella** Enjoy cake and savoury snacks at this treasure-laden cafe-bakery. (p131)

◉ **Trevi Fountain** Throw a coin into this extravagant fountain to ensure your return to Rome. (p84)

Plan Your Trip
Top Days in Rome

BRIAN KINNEY/SHUTTERSTOCK ©

Ancient Rome

The Colosseum is an appropriate high on which to start your odyssey in Rome. Next, head to the nearby crumbling scenic ruins of the Palatino, followed by the Roman Forum. After lunch enjoy 360-degree views from Il Vittoriano and classical art at the Capitoline Museums.

Day
01

❶ Colosseum

More than any other monument, it's the Colosseum (pictured above) that symbolises the power and glory of ancient Rome. Visit its broken interior and imagine the roar of the 50,000-strong crowd as the gladiators fought for their entertainment.

➲ Colosseum to Palatino

🚶 Head south down the Via di San Gregorio to the Palatino.

❷ Palatino

The gardens and ruins of the Palatino (included with the Colosseum ticket) are an atmospheric place to explore, with great views across the Roman Forum. The Palatino was the most exclusive part of ancient Rome, home of the imperial palace, and is still today a hauntingly beautiful site.

➲ Palatino to Roman Forum

🚶 Still in the Palatino, follow the path down past the Vigna Barberino to enter the Roman Forum near the Arco di Tito.

BELY944/SHUTTERSTOCK ©

❸ Roman Forum

Sprawled beneath the Palatino, the Forum was the empire's nerve centre, a teeming hive of law courts, temples, piazzas and shops. See where the vestal virgins lived and senators debated matters of state in the Curia.

⊙ Roman Forum to Terre e Domus

🏃 Exit the Forum onto Via dei Fori Imperiali and head up past the Imperial Forums to Terre e Domus near Trajan's Column.

❹ Lunch at Terre e Domus

Lunch on earthy Lazio food at this bright, modern restaurant just off Piazza Venezia.

⊙ Terre e Domus to Il Vittoriano

🏃 Return to Piazza Venezia and follow it up to the mountainous monument Il Vittoriano.

❺ Il Vittoriano

Il Vittoriano (pictured above) is an ostentatious, overpowering mountain of white marble; love it or hate it, it's an impressive sight. For an even more mind-blowing vista, take the glass lift to the top and you'll be rewarded with 360-degree views across the whole of Rome.

⊙ Il Vittoriano to the Capitoline Museums

🏃 Descend from Il Vittoriano and head left to the sweeping staircase, La Cordonata. Climb the stairs to reach Piazza del Campidoglio and the Capitoline Museums.

❻ Capitoline Museums

Marking the summit of the Capitoline Hill (Campidoglio), Piazza del Campidoglio was designed by Michelangelo and is flanked by the world's oldest national museums. The Capitoline Museums harbour some of Rome's most iconic ancient art, including the iconic depiction of Romulus and Remus sat under the *Lupa capitolina* (Capitoline Wolf).

From left: Colosseum; Il Vittoriano

Plan Your Trip
Top Days in Rome

KIEV.VICTOR/SHUTTERSTOCK ©

Vatican City & Centro Storico

With some ancient monuments under your belt, it's time to hit the Vatican. Blow your mind at the Sistine Chapel and Vatican Museums, then complete your tour at St Peter's Basilica. Dedicate the afternoon to exploring the historic centre, including Piazza Navona and the Pantheon.

❶ Vatican Museums

There are about 7km of exhibits, so you'll never see everything, but try to take in the Pinacoteca, Museo Pio-Clementino, Galleria delle Carte Geografiche, Stanze di Raffaello (Raphael Rooms) and the Sistine Chapel at the Vatican Museums (pictured above).

⭕ Vatican Museums to Fa-Bìo

🏃 From the Vatican Museums entrance, turn downhill and follow the walls towards Piazza del Risorgimento. Take a left down Via Vespasiano and then the first right to Via Germanico and Fa-Bìo.

❷ Lunch at Fa-Bìo

Grab a light lunch bite at this tiny takeaway. It's very popular so you'll need to squeeze through to the counter to order your *panino,* salad or smoothie, all made with quality organic ingredients.

⭕ Fa-Bìo to St Peter's Basilica

🏃 Double back to Piazza del Risorgimento, then follow the crowds to reach St Peter's Basilica.

Day
02

BLUE PLANET STUDIO/SHUTTERSTOCK ©

❸ St Peter's Basilica

Approaching St Peter's Square from the side, you'll see it as Bernini intended: a surprise. At the head of the piazza, the basilica is home to many artistic masterpieces including Michelangelo's *Pietà*. Up above, its breathtaking dome offers magical views.

⟳ St Peter's Basilica to Castel Sant'Angelo

🚶 From St Peter's Square, head down the monumental Via della Conciliazione to Castel Sant'Angelo.

❹ Castel Sant'Angelo

If you've still more energy for sightseeing, visit this landmark castle (pictured above) set around an ancient Roman tomb.

⟳ Castel Sant'Angelo to Piazza Navona

🚶 Cross the river via Ponte Sant'Angelo, then follow the river eastwards for around 300m before turning right down Via G Zanardelli to reach Piazza Navona.

❺ Piazza Navona

This vast baroque square is a showpiece of the *centro storico* (historic centre), and is full of vibrant life. The lozenge-shaped space is an echo of its ancient origins as the site of a stadium.

⟳ Piazza Navona to the Pantheon

🚶 It's a short walk eastwards from Piazza Navona to Piazza della Rotonda, where you'll find the Pantheon.

❻ Pantheon

This 2000-year-old temple, now a church, is an extraordinary building; its innovative design has served to inspire generations of architects and engineers.

⟳ Pantheon to Casa Coppelle

🚶 Take Via del Pantheon and Via della Maddalena, then bear left to Piazza delle Coppelle and Casa Coppelle.

❼ Dinner at Casa Coppelle

Savour an evening at Casa Coppelle, with its plush furnishings and gorgeous Gallic-Roman cuisine.

From left: Museo Pio-Clementino, Vatican Museums; Castel Sant'Angelo

Plan Your Trip
Top Days in Rome

WJAREK/SHUTTERSTOCK ©

Villa Borghese, Tridente, Trevi & Trastevere

Start your day at the brilliant Museo e Galleria Borghese before a ramble through the shady avenues of Villa Borghese. Next, explore the Tridente neighbourhood, stopping off at the Spanish Steps en route to the Trevi Fountain and an evening in Trastevere.

Day
03

❶ Museo e Galleria Borghese

Book ahead and start your day at the Museo e Galleria Borghese (pictured above), one of Rome's best art museums. The highlight is a series of astonishing sculptures by baroque genius Gian Lorenzo Bernini.

○ Museo e Galleria Borghese to Villa Borghese

🚶 Work your way through the leafy paths of Villa Borghese.

❷ Villa Borghese

Meander through the lovely, rambling park of Villa Borghese, formerly the playground of the mighty Borghese family. Make your way past Piazza di Siena and along tree-shaded lanes to the Pincio, a panoramic terrace offering great views across Rome.

○ Villa Borghese to Piazza del Popolo

🚶 From the Pincio terrace take the ramps and stairs down to Piazza del Popolo.

BRIAN KINNEY/SHUTTERSTOCK ©

❸ Piazza del Popolo

With its towering Egyptian obelisk, the monumental Piazza del Popolo dates from the 16th century. Nearby, Chiesa di Santa Maria del Popolo is home to remarkable art.

➲ Piazza del Popolo to Fiaschetteria Beltramme

🚶 Head along Via del Corso, then turn left up Via della Croce to No 39.

❹ Lunch at Fiaschetteria Beltramme

Recharge the batteries with genuine Roman food at this classic trattoria. Traditionally cooked dishes such as spaghetti carbonara are reassuringly filling.

➲ Fiaschetteria Beltramme to Spanish Steps

🚶 Continue up Via della Croce and you'll emerge onto Piazza di Spagna.

❺ Spanish Steps

This glorious flight of ornamental rococo steps (pictured above) looks over Piazza di Spagna and glittering designer district Tridente.

➲ Spanish Steps to Trevi Fountain

🚶 Take Via dei due Macelli to Via del Tritone. Cross over to Via in Arcione until it becomes Via del Lavatore.

❻ Trevi Fountain

Join the crowds at this fantastical baroque fountain, where you can toss in a coin to ensure your return to Rome.

➲ Trevi Fountain to Trastevere

🚶 Pick up Via del Corso and continue on to Piazza Venezia. Take tram 8 over the river to Trastevere.

❼ Trastevere

Spend the evening wandering Trastevere's charismatic streets, as popular with locals as it is with visitors. It's a beguiling place for a stroll before dinner.

From left: *Rape of Proserpine* by Gian Lorenzo Bernini in Museo Borghese; Spanish Steps

Plan Your Trip
Top Days in Rome

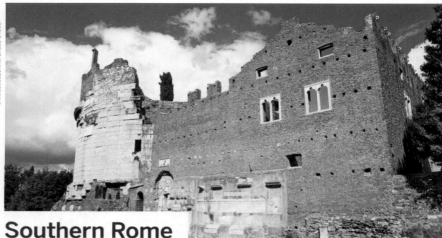

PABLO DEBAT/SHUTTERSTOCK ©

Southern Rome & Monti

On your fourth day, venture out to Via Appia Antica and the catacombs. Start the afternoon by visiting the Museo Nazionale Romano: Palazzo Massimo alle Terme, then drop by the Basilica di Santa Maria Maggiore before seeing the day out in boho Monti.

Day
04

❶ Catacombe di San Sebastiano

Start your day underground on a tour of one of the three networks of catacombs open to the public. It's a fascinating and chilling experience to see the tunnels where early Christians buried their dead.

○ Catacombe di San Sebastiano to Villa di Massenzio

⚵ Head south about 100m along Via Appia and you'll see Villa di Massenzio on your left.

❷ Villa di Massenzio

The best-preserved part of Maxentius' 4th-century ruined palace is the Circo di Massenzio, once a racetrack boasting arena space for 10,000 people.

○ Villa di Massenzio to Mausoleo di Cecilia Metella

⚵ Carry on 50m or so along Via Appia to the tomb of Cecilia Metella.

❸ Mausoleo di Cecilia Metella

With travertine walls and an interior decorated with a sculpted frieze bearing Gaelic shields, ox skulls and festoons, this great,

rotund tomb (pictured above left) is an imposing sight.

⊙ Mausoleo di Cecilia to Qui Nun Se More Mai

🏃 From the tomb, continue up the road for a few metres to Qui Nun Se More Mai.

❹ Lunch at Qui Nun Se More Mai

Fortify yourself for the afternoon ahead with a lunch of hearty Roman pasta and expertly grilled meat at this rustic restaurant.

⊙ Qui Nun Se More Mai to Palazzo Massimo alle Terme

🚌 After lunch, hop on a bus to Termini station to visit the Palazzo Massimo alle Terme.

❺ Palazzo Massimo alle Terme

This light-filled museum holds part of the Museo Nazionale Romano collection, including some superb classical sculpture and an unparalleled collection of ancient Roman frescoes.

⊙ Palazzo Massimo alle Terme to Basilica di Santa Maria Maggiore

🏃 From near the museum, pick up Via Cavour and head downhill to reach Santa Maria Maggiore.

❻ Basilica di Santa Maria Maggiore

One of Rome's four patriarchal basilicas, this monumental church (pictured above) stands on the summit of the Esquiline Hill, on the spot where snow is said to have miraculously fallen in the summer of AD 358.

⊙ Basilica di Santa Maria Maggiore to Monti

🚌 From Piazza Esquilino by the back of the basilica, pick up Via Urbana, which runs down to the Monti neighbourhood.

❼ Monti

There's plenty of evening action in Monti. Take your pick from the wine bars, cafes and restaurants that line its trendy cobbled streets.

From left: Mausoleo di Cecilia Metella; Basilica di Santa Maria Maggiore

Plan Your Trip
Need to Know

Daily Costs

Budget: Less than €110

○ Dorm bed: €20–35

○ Double room in a budget hotel: €60–130

○ Pizza plus beer: €15

Midrange: €110–250

○ Double room in a hotel: €110–200

○ Local restaurant meal: €25–45

○ Admission to museum: €5–16

○ Roma Pass, a 72-hour card covering museum entry and public transport: €38.50

Top end: More than €250

○ Double room in a four- or five-star hotel: €200–450

○ Top restaurant dinner: €45–150

○ City-centre taxi ride: €10–15

○ Auditorium concert tickets: €25–90

Advance Planning

Two months before Book high-season accommodation.

One month before Check for concerts at www.auditorium.com and www.operaroma.it.

One to two weeks before Reserve tables at A-list restaurants; sort tickets for Museo e Galleria Borghese, Palazzo Farnese and the pope's weekly audience at St Peter's.

A few days before Book tickets for the Vatican Museums and Colosseum (advisable, to avoid queues).

Useful Websites

060608 (www.060608.it) Has practical details on sights, transport, upcoming events.

Coopculture (www.coopculture.it) Ticket booking for Rome's monuments.

Lonely Planet (www.lonelyplanet.com/rome) Destination information, hotel bookings, and traveller forum.

Turismo Roma (www.turismoroma.it) Official tourist website.

Vatican Museums (www.museivaticani.va) Book tickets and guided tours.

Arriving in Rome

Leonardo da Vinci (Fiumicino) Airport Leonardo Express trains to Stazione Termini 6.23am to 11.23pm, €14; slower FL1 trains to Trastevere, Ostiense and Tiburtina stations 5.57am to 10.42pm, €8; buses to Stazione Termini 6.05am to 12.30am, €6; private transfers from €22 per person; taxis €48 (fixed fare to within the Aurelian walls).

Ciampino Airport Buses to Stazione Termini 4am to 11.59pm, €5; private transfers

When to Go

Spring and early autumn are the best times – the weather's good and there are many festivals and outdoor events on. But it's also busy and peak rates apply.

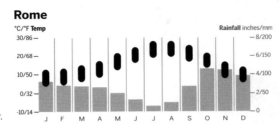

Rome

€25 per person; taxis €30 (fixed fare to within the Aurelian walls).

Stazione Termini Airport buses and trains, and international trains, arrive at Stazione Termini. From here, continue by bus, metro or taxi.

Getting Around

Walking is the best way of getting around the *centro storico* (historic centre). Public transport includes buses, trams, metro and a suburban train network. The main hub is Stazione Termini. Tickets, which come in various forms, are valid for all forms of transport. Children under 10 years travel free.

Metro The metro is quicker than surface transport but the network is limited. There are two main lines, A (orange) and B (blue), which cross at Stazione Termini. Trains run between 5.30am and 11.30pm

(to 1.30am on Fridays and Saturdays).

Buses Most routes pass through Stazione Termini. Buses run from approximately 5.30am until midnight, with limited services throughout the night.

Sleeping

Rome is expensive and busy; book ahead to secure the best deal. Accommodation ranges from palatial five-star hotels to hostels, B&Bs, *pensioni* and private rooms. Hostels are the cheapest, with dorm beds and private rooms: around Stazione Termini several budget hotels also offer 'dorm beds', meaning you can book a bed in a shared double, triple or quad hotel room. B&Bs and hotels cover every style and price range.

What to Pack

○ Trainers or comfy walking shoes – cobbled streets can be murder on the feet

○ Smart-casual evening clothes – Romans dress up to go out

○ Purse with strap – petty theft can be a problem

○ Water bottle – refill it at drinking water fountains

○ Electrical adapter and phone charger

What to Wear

Appearances matter in Rome. That said, you'll need to dress comfortably because you'll be walking a lot. Suitable wear for men is generally trousers (pants) and shirts or polo shirts, and for women, skirts, trousers or dresses. Shorts, T-shirts and sandals are fine in summer but bear in mind that strict dress codes are enforced at St Peter's Basilica and the Vatican Museums. For evening wear, smart casual is the norm. A light sweater or waterproof jacket is useful in spring and autumn.

Plan Your Trip
What's New

The Cloud

Contemporary architecture buffs can now have a field day exploring the city's brand-new congress centre (p101), aka La Nuvola (Cloud), designed by Massimiliano Fuksas, in EUR.

Fendi

Rome's home-grown haute-couture fashion house continues to turn heads with the opening of a boutique hotel, the uber-chic rooftop bar Zuma (p170) in the Palazzo Fendi, and a contemporary-art exhibition space at the Palazzo della Civiltà Italiana (p101).

Roscioli Caffè

The name Roscioli is always a guarantee of good things to come. Its deli and bakery have long set the standards, and the recent Roscioli Caffè (p123) fits the bill perfectly with smooth coffee and artfully crafted pastries.

Speakeasies

From Spirito (p171), reminiscent of 1920s Prohibition-era New York and hidden in a Pigneto sandwich shop, to hard-to-find Keyhole (p175) in a Trastevere backstreet, underground speakeasies serving superbly mixed craft cocktails are Rome's hottest drinking trend right now.

Testaccio Food Stalls

This covered market is an increasingly fashionable foodie hang-out. Recent new-comer Cups (p138), a takeaway backed by top city chef Cristina Bowerman, specialis-es in soups and freshly prepared sauces.

Piazza Vittorio Emanuele

Brilliant new openings are kick-starting the piazza's gentrification. Leading the way is Gatsby Café (p172), a cool bar serving craft cocktails in a vintage hat shop.

Above: Cosmopolitan cocktail

Plan Your Trip
For Free

STEFANO_VALERI/SHUTTERSTOCK ©

Need to Know

Transport Holders of the Roma Pass (p231) are entitled to free public transport.

Wi-fi Free wi-fi is available in many hostels, hotels, bars and cafes.

Tours To take a free tour, check out www.newrome freetour.com.

Free Art

Churches Rome's churches are all free to enter and many contain priceless treasures. Major art churches include St Peter's Basilica (p46), Basilica di San Pietro in Vincoli (p103), Chiesa di San Luigi dei Francesi (p65) and Basilica di Santa Maria del Popolo (p86).

Vatican Museums The Vatican Museums (p40) are free on the last Sunday of the month.

State Museums All state-run museums are gratis on the first Sunday of the month.

Free Monuments

Trevi Fountain You don't have to spend a thing to admire the Trevi Fountain (p84), although most people throw a coin into the water to ensure their return to Rome.

Bocca della Verità According to legend, if you tell a lie with your hand placed in the Bocca della Verità (Mouth of Truth; p73), it'll bite it off.

Spanish Steps The ideal perch for a sightseeing time-out, the Spanish Steps (p90) have long been a favourite visitor hang-out.

Piazzas & Parks

Piazzas People-watching on Rome's piazzas is a signature city experience. Top spots include Piazza Navona (p62), Campo de' Fiori (p65), Piazza di Spagna (p91) and Piazza del Popolo (p87).

Parks It doesn't cost a thing to enjoy parks such as Villa Borghese (p56) and Villa Celimontana (p97).

Above: Basilica di San Pietro in Vincoli

Plan Your Trip
Family Travel

SORIN COLAC/SHUTTERSTOCK ©

Need to Know

Getting Around Cobbled streets make getting around with a pram or pushchair difficult.

Eating Out In a restaurant ask for a *mezza porzione* (child's portion) and *seggiolone* (high chair).

Supplies Buy baby formula and sterilising solutions at pharmacies. Disposable nappies (diapers; *pannolini*) are available from supermarkets and pharmacies.

Discounts Under 18-year-olds get in free at state-run museums, while city-run museums are free for children under six years, and discounted for six- to 25-year-olds.

Transport Children under 10 years travel free on all public transport in the city.

History for Kids

Everyone wants to see the **Colosseum** (p36) and it doesn't disappoint, especially if accompanied by tales of bloodthirsty gladiators and hungry lions. For maximum effect, prep your kids beforehand with a Rome-based film.

To the south of the city centre, the catacombs on **Via Appia Antica** (p74) will spook teens and adults alike. These creepy tunnels, full of tombs and ancient burial chambers, are fascinating, but not suitable for children less than about seven years old.

Parents and older kids will enjoy the multimedia tour of Roman excavations beneath **Palazzo Valentini** (☎06 2276 1280; www.palazzovalentini.it; Via Foro Traiano 85; adult/reduced €12/8, advance booking fee €1.50; ⊙9.30am-6.30pm Wed-Mon; 🚻; MBarberini).

Hands-on Activities

Kids love throwing things so they'll enjoy tossing coins into the **Trevi Fountain** (p84). And if they ask, an average of about €3000 is thrown in daily.

Another favourite is putting your hand in the **Bocca della Verità** (Mouth of Truth; p73). Local legend has it that if you tell a fib, the mouth will slam shut and bite your hand off.

TOMASZ WOZNIAK/SHUTTERSTOCK ©

Run in the Park

When the time comes to let the kids off the leash, head to **Villa Borghese** (p56), the most central of Rome's main parks. There's plenty of space to run around in – though it's not absolutely car-free – and you can hire bicycles, including four-seater family bikes.

Family Day Trips

Many of Rome's ancient sites can be hard work for families with young children, but at **Ostia Antica** (p93) kids can run along the ancient town's streets, among shops, and all over its impressive amphitheatre. There's even an ancient public toilet to check out.

At Tivoli, east of Rome, kids will enjoy exploring the gardens at **Villa d'Este** (p110) with their water-spouting fountains and grim-faced gargoyles. Nearby, the extensive ruins of **Villa Adriana** (p111) provide ample opportunity for hide-and-seek.

Best Snack Joints

Pizzarium (p129)

Trapizzino (p137)

La Ciambella (p123)

Supplizio (p124)

Fatamorgana (p87)

Food for Kids

Keep your little ones happy with some Roman-style fast food. Pizza *al taglio* (sliced pizza) is a favourite local snack and a saviour for parents. It's cheap (about €1 buys two small slices of pizza *bianca* – with salt and olive oil), easy to get hold of (there are hundreds of takeaways around town), and works wonders on flagging spirits.

Ice cream is another guaranteed winner, served in *coppette* (tubs) or *coni* (cones).

From left: Bocca della Verità (p73); Villa Borghese (p56)

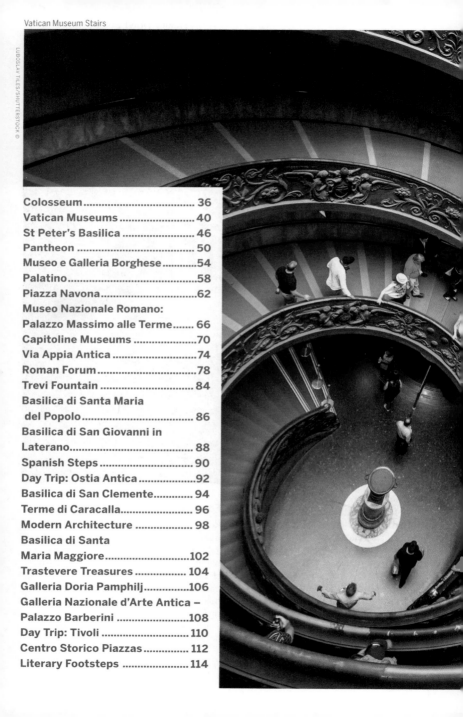

Vatican Museum Stairs

LUBOSLAV TILES/SHUTTERSTOCK ©

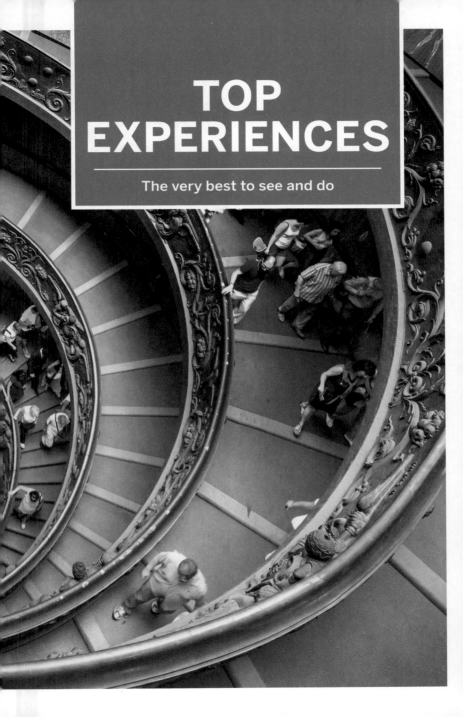

TOP EXPERIENCES

The very best to see and do

Colosseum

A monument to raw, merciless power, the Colosseum is the most thrilling of Rome's ancient sights. It was here that gladiators met in mortal combat and condemned prisoners fought off wild beasts in front of baying, bloodthirsty crowds. Two thousand years on and it's Italy's top tourist attraction, drawing more than six million visitors a year.

Great for...

ⓘ **Need to Know**

Map p246; ☎ 06 3996 7700; www.coopculture. it; Piazza del Colosseo; adult/reduced incl Roman Forum & Palatino €12/7.50; ⏰ 8.30am-1hr before sunset; Ⓜ Colosseo

★ **Top Tip**

Beat the queues by buying your ticket at the Palatino (p58; Via di San Gregorio 30).

VIACHESLAV LOPATIN/SHUTTERSTOCK

Built by Vespasian (r AD 69–79) in the grounds of Nero's vast Domus Aurea complex, the arena was inaugurated in AD 80, eight years after it had been commissioned. To mark the occasion, Vespasian's son and successor Titus (r AD 79–81) staged games that lasted 100 days and nights, during which 5000 animals were slaughtered. Trajan (r AD 98–117) later topped this, holding a marathon 117-day killing spree involving 9000 gladiators and 10,000 animals.

The 50,000-seat arena was originally known as the Flavian Amphitheatre, and although it was Rome's most fearsome arena it wasn't the biggest – the Circo Massimo could hold up to 250,000 people. The name Colosseum, when introduced in medieval times, was a reference not to its size but to the Colosso di Nerone, a giant statue of Nero that stood nearby.

With the fall of the Roman Empire in the 5th century, the Colosseum was abandoned and gradually became overgrown. In the Middle Ages it served as a fortress for two of the city's warrior families, the Frangipani and the Annibaldi. Later, during the Renaissance and baroque periods, it was plundered of its precious travertine, and the marble stripped from it was used to make huge palaces such as Palazzo Venezia, Palazzo Barberini and Palazzo Cancelleria.

More recently, pollution and vibrations caused by traffic and the metro have taken a toll. To help counter this, it was recently given a major clean-up, the first in its 2000-year history, as part of a €25-million

Interior of the Colosseum

restoration project sponsored by the luxury shoemaker Tod's.

Exterior

The outer walls have three levels of arches, framed by Ionic, Doric and Corinthian columns. These were originally covered in travertine, and marble statues filled the niches on the 2nd and 3rd storeys. The upper level, punctuated with windows and slender Corinthian pilasters, had supports for 240 masts that held up a huge canvas awning over the arena, shielding spectators from sun and rain.

> ☑ **Don't Miss**
>
> The Belvedere (top three tiers) and the hypogeum's network of dank tunnels beneath the main arena. Visits require advance booking and cost an extra €9.

BY PIOTR JACZEWSKI/GETTY IMAGES ©

The 80 entrance arches, known as *vomitoria*, allowed the spectators to enter and be seated in a matter of minutes.

Arena

The stadium originally had a wooden floor covered in sand – *harena* in Latin, hence the word 'arena' – to prevent combatants from slipping and to soak up spilt blood.

From the floor, trapdoors led down to the hypogeum, a subterranean complex of corridors, cages and lifts beneath the arena floor.

Stands

The *cavea,* for spectator seating, was divided into three tiers: magistrates and senior officials sat in the lowest tier, wealthy citizens in the middle, and the plebeians in the highest tier. Women (except for vestal virgins) were relegated to the cheapest sections at the top. As in modern stadiums, tickets were numbered and spectators assigned a seat in a specific sector – in 2015, restorers uncovered traces of red numerals on the arches, indicating how the sectors were numbered. The podium, a broad terrace in front of the tiers of seats, was reserved for the emperor, senators and VIPs.

Hypogeum

The hypogeum served as the stadium's backstage area. Sets for the various battle scenes were prepared here and hoisted up to the arena by a complicated system of pulleys. Caged animals were also kept here and gladiators would gather here before showtime, having come in through an underground corridor from the nearby Ludus Magnus (gladiator school).

> ✕ **Take a Break**
>
> Cafè Cafè (p138) is the perfect venue for a post-arena break of tea and cake or a light meal.

Galleria delle Carte Geografiche

Vatican Museums

Founded in the 16th century, the Vatican Museums boast one of the world's greatest art collections. Highlights include spectacular classical statuary, rooms frescoed by Raphael, and the Michelangelo-decorated Sistine Chapel.

Housing the museums are the lavishly decorated halls and galleries of the Palazzo Apostolico Vaticano. This vast 5.5-hectare complex consists of two palaces – the Vatican palace (nearer to St Peter's) and the Palazzetto di Belvedere – joined by two long galleries. Inside are three courtyards: the Cortile della Pigna, the Cortile della Biblioteca and, to the south, the Cortile del Belvedere. You'll never cover it all in one day, so it pays to be selective.

Pinacoteca

Often overlooked by visitors, the papal picture gallery contains Raphael's last work, *La Trasfigurazione* (1517–20), and paintings by Giotto, Fra Angelico, Filippo Lippi, Perugino, Titian, Guido Reni, Guercino, Pietro da Cortona, Caravaggio and Leonardo da

Great for...

☑ **Don't Miss**

Raphael's last painting, *La Trasfigurazione* (Transfiguration), in the Pinacoteca.

Apollo Belvedere

ⓘ Need to Know

Map p253 ☎06 6988 4676; www.museivaticani.va; Viale Vaticano; adult/reduced €17/8; ⏰9am-6pm Mon-Sat, 9am-2pm last Sun of month, last entry 2hr before close; 🚌Piazza del Risorgimento, Ⓜ️Ottaviano-San Pietro

✕ Take a Break

Snack on scissor-cut squares of gourmet pizza at Pizzarium (p129).

★ Top Tip

To avoid queues, book tickets online (http://biglietteriamusei.vatican.va/musei/tickets/do; plus €4 booking fee).

Vinci, whose haunting *San Gerolamo* (St Jerome; c 1480) was never finished.

Museo Chiaramonti & Braccio Nuovo

The Museo Chiaramonti is effectively the long corridor that runs down the eastern side of the Palazzetto di Belvedere. Its walls are lined with thousands of statues and busts representing everything from immortal gods to playful cherubs and unattractive Roman patricians. Near the end of the hall, off to the right, is the Braccio Nuovo (New Wing), which contains a famous statue of the Nile as a reclining god covered by 16 babies.

Museo Pio-Clementino

This stunning museum contains some of the Vatican Museums' finest classical statuary, including the peerless *Apollo Belvedere*

and the 1st-century *Laocoön,* both in the **Cortile Ottagono** (Octagonal Courtyard). Before you go into the courtyard, take a moment to admire the 1st-century *Apoxyomenos,* one of the earliest-known sculptures to depict a figure with a raised arm.

To the left as you enter the courtyard, the *Apollo Belvedere* is a 2nd-century Roman copy of a 4th-century-BC Greek bronze. A beautifully proportioned representation of the sun god Apollo, it's considered one of the great masterpieces of classical sculpture. Nearby, the *Laocoön* depicts a muscular Trojan priest and his two sons in mortal struggle with two sea serpents.

Back inside, the **Sala degli Animali** is filled with sculpted creatures and some magnificent 4th-century mosaics. Continuing on, you come to the **Sala delle Muse**, centred on the *Torso Belvedere*, another of the museum's must-sees. A fragment of a muscular 1st-century-BC Greek sculpture, it was found in Campo de' Fiori and used by Michelangelo as a model for his *ignudi* (male nudes) in the Sistine Chapel.

The next room, the **Sala Rotonda**, contains a number of colossal statues, including a gilded-bronze *Ercole* (Hercules) and an exquisite floor mosaic. The enormous basin in the centre of the room was found at Nero's Domus Aurea and is made out of a single piece of red porphyry stone.

Museo Gregoriano Egizio

Founded by Gregory XVI in 1839, this museum contains pieces taken from Egypt in Roman times. The collection is small but there are fascinating exhibits, including a fragmented statue of the pharaoh Ramses II on his throne, vividly painted sarcophagi dating from around 1000 BC, and a macabre mummy.

Museo Gregoriano Etrusco

At the top of the 18th-century Simonetti staircase, the Museo Gregoriano Etrusco contains artefacts unearthed in the Etruscan tombs of northern Lazio, as well as a superb collection of vases and Roman antiquities. Of particular interest is the *Marte di Todi* (Mars of Todi), a black bronze of a warrior dating to the late 5th century BC.

Galleria delle Carte Geografiche & Sala Sobieski

The last of three galleries on the upper floor – the other two are the **Galleria dei Candelabri** (Gallery of the Candelabra) and the **Galleria degli Arazzi** (Tapestry Gallery) – this 120m-long corridor is hung with 40 huge topographical maps. These were created between 1580 and 1583 for Pope Gregory

Museo Pio-Clementino

XIII based on drafts by Ignazio Danti, one of the leading cartographers of his day.

Beyond the gallery, the **Sala Sobieski** is named after an enormous 19th-century painting depicting the victory of the Polish king John III Sobieski over the Turks in 1683.

Stanze di Raffaello

These four frescoed chambers, currently undergoing partial restoration, were part of Pope Julius II's private apartments. Raphael himself painted the Stanza della Segnatura (1508–11) and the Stanza d'Eliodoro (1512–14), while

> ★ **Local Knowledge**
>
> Tuesdays and Thursdays are the quietest days to visit. Wednesday mornings are also good; afternoons are better than mornings. Avoid Mondays, when many other museums are shut.

the Stanza dell'Incendio (1514–17) and Sala di Costantino (1517–24) were decorated by students following his designs.

The first room you come to is the **Sala di Costantino**, which features a huge fresco depicting Constantine's defeat of Maxentius at the battle of Milvian Bridge.

The **Stanza d'Eliodoro**, which was used for private audiences, takes its name from the *Cacciata d'Eliodoro* (Expulsion of Heliodorus from the Temple), an allegorical work reflecting Pope Julius II's policy of forcing foreign powers off Church lands. To its right, the *Messa di Bolsena* (Mass of Bolsena) shows Julius paying homage to the relic of a 13th-century miracle at the lakeside town of Bolsena. Next is the *Incontro di Leone Magno con Attila* (Encounter of Leo the Great with Attila) by Raphael and his school, and, on the fourth wall, the *Liberazione di San Pietro* (Liberation of St Peter), a brilliant work illustrating Raphael's masterful ability to depict light.

The **Stanza della Segnatura**, Julius' study and library, was the first room that Raphael painted, and it's here that you'll find his great masterpiece, *La Scuola di Atene* (The School of Athens), featuring philosophers and scholars gathered around Plato and Aristotle. The seated figure in front of the steps is believed to be Michelangelo, while the figure of Plato is said to be a portrait of Leonardo da Vinci, and Euclide (the bald man bending over) is Bramante. Raphael also included a self-portrait in the lower right corner – he's the second figure from the right.

The most famous work in the **Stanza dell'Incendio di Borgo** is the *Incendio di Borgo* (Fire in the Borgo), which depicts Pope Leo IV extinguishing a fire by making the sign of the cross. The ceiling was painted by Raphael's master, Perugino.

> ★ **Top Tip**
>
> Most exhibits are not well-labelled. Consider hiring an audio guide (€7) or buying the excellent *Guide to the Vatican Museums and City* (€14).

Sistine Chapel

The jewel in the Vatican's crown, the Sistine Chapel (Cappella Sistina) is home to two of the world's most famous works of art: Michelangelo's ceiling frescoes and his *Giudizio Universale* (Last Judgment).

The chapel was originally built for Pope Sixtus IV, after whom it's named, and was consecrated on 15 August 1483. However, apart from the wall frescoes and floor, little remains of the original decor, which was sacrificed to make way for Michelangelo's two masterpieces. The first, the ceiling, was commissioned by Pope Julius II and painted between 1508 and 1512; the second, the spectacular *Giudizio Universale* was painted between 1535 and 1541.

Michelangelo's ceiling design, which is best viewed from the chapel's main entrance in the far east wall, covers the entire 800-sq-m surface. With painted architectural features and a cast of colourful biblical characters, it's centred on nine panels depicting stories from the book of Genesis.

As you look up from the east wall, the first panel is the *Drunkenness of Noah,* followed by *The Flood* and the *Sacrifice of Noah.* Next, *Original Sin and Banishment from the Garden of Eden* famously depicts Adam and Eve being sent packing after accepting the forbidden fruit from Satan, represented by a snake with the body of a woman coiled around a tree. The *Creation of Eve* is then followed by the *Creation of Adam.* This, one of the most famous images in Western art, shows a bearded God pointing his finger at Adam, thus bringing him to life. Completing the sequence are the *Separation of Land from Sea;* the *Creation of the Sun, Moon and Plants;* and the *Separation of Light from Darkness,* featuring a fearsome

Stanza della Segnatura

God reaching out to touch the sun. Set around the central panels are 20 athletic male nudes, known as *ignudi.*

Opposite, on the west wall is Michelangelo's mesmeric *Giudizio Universale,* showing Christ – in the centre near the top – passing sentence over the souls of the dead as they are torn from their graves to face him. The saved get to stay in heaven (in the upper right); the damned are sent down to face the demons in hell (in the bottom right).

Near the bottom, on the right, you'll see a man with donkey ears and a snake wrapped around him. This is Biagio de Cesena, the papal master of ceremonies, who was a fierce critic of Michelangelo's composition. Another famous figure is St Bartholomew, just beneath Christ, holding his own flayed skin. The face in the skin is said to be a self-portrait of Michelangelo, its anguished look reflecting the artist's tormented faith.

The chapel's walls also boast superb frescoes. Painted between 1481 and 1482 by a crack team of Renaissance artists, including Botticelli, Ghirlandaio, Pinturicchio, Perugino and Luca Signorelli, they represent events in the lives of Moses (to the left looking at the *Giudizio Universale*) and Christ (to the right). Highlights include Botticelli's *Temptations of Christ* and Perugino's *Handing over of the Keys*.

As well as providing a showcase for priceless art, the Sistine Chapel serves an important religious function as the place where the conclave meets to elect a new pope.

★ Did You Know?

A popular Sistine Chapel myth is that Michelangelo painted the ceilings lying down. In fact, he designed a curved scaffolding that allowed him to work standing up.

Interior of St Peter's Basilica

St Peter's Basilica

In this city of outstanding churches, none can hold a candle to St Peter's, Italy's largest, richest and most spectacular basilica.

Great for...

☑ Don't Miss

Climbing the (numerous, steep and tiring but worth it) steps of the dome for views over Rome.

The original church was commissioned by the Emperor Constantine and built around 349 on the site where St Peter is said to have been buried between AD 64 and 67. But like many medieval churches, it eventually fell into disrepair and it wasn't until the mid-15th century that efforts were made to restore it, first by Pope Nicholas V and then, rather more successfully, by Julius II.

In 1506 construction began on a design by Bramante, but building ground to a halt when the architect died in 1514. In 1547 Michelangelo stepped in to take on the project. He simplified Bramante's plans and drew up designs for what was to become his greatest architectural achievement: the dome. He didn't live to see it built, though, and it was left to Giacomo della Porta, Domenico Fontana and Carlo Maderno to complete the basilica, which was finally consecrated in 1626.

Nuns resting at St Peter's Square

JUSTIN FOULKES/LONELY PLANET ©

ℹ Need to Know

Basilica di San Pietro; Map p253; ☑06 6988 3731; www.vatican.va; St Peter's Square; ⊘7am-7pm summer, to 6.30pm winter; ☲Piazza del Risorgimento, Ⓜ Ottaviano-San Pietro; `FREE`

✕ Take a Break

Head to the Borgo for a pit-stop *panino* at Cotto Crudo (p130).

★ Top Tip

Strict dress codes are enforced, so no shorts, miniskirts or bare shoulders.

Facade

Built between 1608 and 1612, Maderno's immense facade is 48m high and 115m wide. Eight 27m-high columns support the upper attic on which 13 statues stand, representing Christ the Redeemer, St John the Baptist and the 11 apostles. The central balcony, the **Loggia della Benedizione**, is where the pope stands to deliver his *Urbi et Orbi* blessing at Christmas and Easter.

Interior

At the beginning of the right aisle is Michelangelo's hauntingly beautiful *Pietà*. Sculpted when the artist was 25 (in 1499), it's the only work he ever signed; his signature is etched into the sash across the Madonna's breast.

On a pillar just beyond the *Pietà*, Carlo Fontana's gilt and bronze **monument to**

Queen Christina of Sweden commemorates the far-from-holy Swedish monarch who converted to Catholicism in 1655.

Moving on, you'll come to the **Cappella di San Sebastiano**, home of Pope John Paul II's tomb, and the **Cappella del Santissimo Sacramento**, a sumptuously decorated baroque chapel.

Dominating the centre of the basilica is Bernini's 29m-high **baldachin**. Supported by four spiral columns and made with bronze taken from the Pantheon, it stands over the **papal altar**, which itself stands over St Peter's original grave.

Above the baldachin, Michelangelo's **dome** soars to a height of 119m. Based on Brunelleschi's cupola in Florence, it's supported by four massive stone **piers** named after the saints whose statues adorn the Bernini-designed niches – Longinus, Helena, Veronica and Andrew.

At the base of the **Pier of St Longinus** is Arnolfo di Cambio's much-loved 13th-century bronze **statue of St Peter**, whose right foot has been worn down by centuries of caresses.

Dominating the tribune behind the altar is Bernini's extraordinary **Cattedra di San Pietro**, centred on a wooden seat that was once thought to have been St Peter's, but in fact dates to the 9th century.

To the right of the throne, Bernini's **monument to Urban VIII** depicts the pope flanked by the figures of Charity and Justice.

Near the head of the left aisle are the so-called **Stuart monuments**. On the right is the monument to Clementina Sobieska, wife of James Stuart, by Filippo Barigioni, and on the left is Canova's vaguely erotic monument to the last three members of the Stuart clan, the pretenders to the English throne who died in exile in Rome.

Dome

From the **dome** (with/without lift €10/8; ⊗8am-6pm summer, to 5pm winter) entrance on the right of the basilica's main portico, you can walk the 551 steps to the top or take a small lift halfway and then follow on foot for the last 320 steps. Either way, it's a long, steep climb. But make it to the top, and you're rewarded with stunning views.

Museo Storico Artistico

Accessed from the left nave, the **Museo Storico Artistico** (Tesoro, Treasury; ☏06 6988 1840; adult/reduced €8/7; ⊗8am-6.40pm summer, to 5.40pm winter) sparkles with sacred relics. Highlights include a tabernacle by Donatello and the 6th-century *Crux Vaticana* (Vatican Cross).

Michelangelo Dome

Vatican Grottoes

Extending beneath the basilica, the **Vatican Grottoes** (⊙8am-6pm summer, to 5.30pm winter) `FREE` contain the tombs and sarcophagi of numerous popes, as well as several columns from the original 4th-century basilica. The entrance is in the Pier of St Andrew.

St Peter's Tomb

Excavations beneath the basilica have uncovered part of the original church and what archaeologists believe is the **Tomb of St Peter** (☑06 6988 5318; www.scavi.va; €13).

The excavations can only be visited by guided tour. To book a spot, see the website of the Ufficio Scavi (www.scavi.va).

What's Nearby?

St Peter's Square　　　Piazza

(Piazza San Pietro; 🚊Piazza del Risorgimento, MOttaviano-San Pietro) Overlooked by St Peter's Basilica, the Vatican's central square was laid out between 1656 and 1667 to a design by Gian Lorenzo Bernini. Seen from above, it resembles a giant keyhole with two semicircular colonnades, each consisting of four rows of Doric columns, encircling a giant ellipse that straightens out to funnel believers into the basilica. The effect was deliberate – Bernini described the colonnades as representing 'the motherly arms of the church'.

Castel Sant'Angelo　Museum, Castle

(☑06 681 91 11; www.castelsantangelo. beniculturali.it; Lungotevere Castello 50; adult/reduced €14/7; ⊙9am-7.30pm, ticket office to 6.30pm; 🚊Piazza Pia) With its chunky round keep, this castle is an instantly recognisable landmark. Built as a mausoleum for the emperor Hadrian, it was converted into a papal fortress in the 6th century and named after an angelic vision that Pope Gregory the Great had in 590. Nowadays, it houses the **Museo Nazionale di Castel Sant'Angelo** and its eclectic collection of paintings, sculpture, military memorabilia and medieval firearms.

⭐**Free Tours**

Between October and late May, free English-language tours of the basilica are run by seminarians from the Pontifical North American College, usually departing 2.15pm Monday to Friday from the Ufficio Pellegrini e Turisti.

BILL PERRY/SHUTTERSTOCK ©

⭐ **Local Knowledge**

Near the main entrance of St Peter's, a red floor disk marks the spot where Charlemagne and later Holy Roman Emperors were crowned by the pope.

Pantheon

A striking 2000-year-old temple, now a church, the Pantheon is Rome's best-preserved ancient monument and one of the most influential buildings in the Western world. Its greying, pockmarked exterior may look its age, but inside it's a different story, and it's a unique and exhilarating experience to pass through its vast bronze doors and gaze up at the largest unreinforced concrete dome ever built.

Great for...

❶ Need to Know

Map p250; www.pantheonroma.com; Piazza della Rotonda; €2; ⊘8.30am-7.15pm Mon-Sat, 9am-5.45pm Sun; ☒Largo di Torre Argentina

★ **Top Tip**

Mass is celebrated at the Pantheon at 5pm on Saturday and 10.30am on Sunday.

In its current form the Pantheon dates to around AD 125. The original temple, built by Marcus Agrippa in 27 BC, burnt down in AD 80, and although it was rebuilt by Domitian, it was struck by lightning and destroyed for a second time in AD 110. The emperor Hadrian had it reconstructed between AD 118 and 125, and it's this version that you see today.

Hadrian's temple was dedicated to the classical gods – the name Pantheon is a derivation of the Greek words *pan* (all) and *theos* (god) – but in 608 it was consecrated as a Christian church and it's now officially known as Basilica di Santa Maria ad Martyres.

Thanks to this consecration, it was spared the worst of the medieval plundering that reduced many of Rome's ancient buildings to near dereliction. But it didn't

escape entirely unscathed – gilded-bronze roof tiles were removed and bronze from the portico was used by Bernini for the baldachin at St Peter's Basilica.

Exterior

The dark-grey pitted exterior faces onto busy, cafe-lined Piazza della Rotonda. And while its facade is somewhat the worse for wear, it's still an imposing sight. The monumental entrance **portico** consists of 16 Corinthian columns, each 11.8m high and made of Egyptian granite, supporting a triangular **pediment**. Behind the columns, two 20-tonne **bronze doors**, 16th-century restorations of the original portal, give onto the central rotunda. Rivets and holes in the building's brickwork indicate where marble-veneer panels were originally placed.

Oculus in the Pantheon's dome

Inscription

For centuries the inscription under the pediment – 'M:AGRIPPA.L.F.COS.TERTIUM. FECIT' or 'Marcus Agrippa, son of Lucius, in his third consulate built this' – led scholars to think that the current building was Agrippa's original temple. However, 19th-century excavations revealed traces of an earlier temple and historians realised that Hadrian had simply kept Agrippa's original inscription.

Interior

Although impressive from outside, it's only when you get inside that you can really appreciate the Pantheon's full size. With light streaming in through the **oculus** (the 8.7m-diameter hole in the centre of the dome), the cylindrical marble-clad interior seems vast.

Opposite the entrance is the church's main **altar**, over which hangs a 7th-century icon of the *Madonna col Bambino* (Madonna and Child). To the left are the tombs of the artist Raphael, King Umberto I and Margherita of Savoy. Over on the opposite side of the rotunda is the tomb of King Vittorio Emanuele II.

Dome

The Pantheon's dome, considered to be the Romans' most important architectural achievement, was the largest dome in the world until the 15th century when Brunelleschi beat it with his Florentine cupola. Its harmonious appearance is due to a precisely calibrated symmetry – its diameter is exactly equal to the building's interior height of 43.3m. At its centre, the oculus, which symbolically connected the temple with the gods, plays a vital structural role by absorbing and redistributing the dome's huge tensile forces.

What's Nearby?

Basilica di Santa Maria Sopra Minerva · Basilica

(www.santamariasopraminerva.it; Piazza della Minerva 42; ⊘6.55am-7pm Mon-Fri, 10am-12.30pm & 3.30-7pm Sat, 8.10am-12.30pm & 3.30-7pm Sun; ⊒Largo di Torre Argentina) Built on the site of three pagan temples, including one dedicated to the goddess Minerva, the Dominican Basilica di Santa Maria Sopra Minerva is Rome's only Gothic church. However, little remains of the original 13th-century structure and these days the main drawcard is a minor Michelangelo sculpture and the magisterial, art-rich interior.

> ☑ **Don't Miss**
> The 7m-high bronze doors provide a suitably grand entrance to the rotunda.

CEDRIC WEBER/SHUTTERSTOCK ©

> ✕ **Take a Break**
> Grab a shot of Rome's best coffee at Caffè Sant'Eustachio (p122).

DFLC PRINTS/SHUTTERSTOCK ©

Museo e Galleria Borghese

Housing what's often referred to as the 'queen of all private art collections', this spectacular gallery boasts some of the city's finest art treasures.

Great for...

☑ **Don't Miss**

Canova's *Venere Vincitrice*, his sensual portrayal of Paolina Bonaparte Borghese.

Including a series of sensational sculptures by Gian Lorenzo Bernini and important paintings by the likes of Caravaggio, Titian, Raphael and Rubens, the museum's collection was formed by Cardinal Scipione Borghese (1579–1633), the most knowledgeable and ruthless art collector of his day. It was originally housed in his residence near St Peter's, but in the 1620s he had it transferred to his new villa just outside Porta Pinciana. And it's in the villa's central building, the Casino Borghese, that you'll see it today.

Over the centuries the villa has undergone several overhauls, most notably in the late 1700s when Prince Marcantonio Borghese added much of the lavish neoclassical decor.

The villa is divided into two parts: the ground-floor museum and the upstairs picture gallery.

David by Gian Lorenzo Bernini in Galleria Borghese

Museo e Galleria Borghese

❶ Need to Know

Map p256; ✆06 3 28 10; http://galleria borghese.beniculturali.it; Piazzale del Museo Borghese 5; adult/child €15/8.50; ⏰9am-7pm Tue-Sun; 🚋Via Pinciana

✗ Take a Break

Stroll through Villa Borghese for a cocktail at Hotel de Russie's Stravinskij Bar (p170).

★ Top Tip

Remember to prebook your ticket, and take ID when you pick it up.

Entrance & Ground Floor

From the basement entrance, stairs lead up to **Sala IV**, home of Bernini's *Ratto di Proserpina* (1621–22). This flamboyant sculpture, one of a series depicting pagan myths, brilliantly reveals the artist's virtuosity – just look at Pluto's hand pressing into the seemingly soft flesh of Persephone's thigh. Further on, in **Sala III**, he captures the exact moment Daphne's hands start morphing into leaves in *Apollo e Dafne* (1622–25).

Another scene-stealer is Antonio Canova's depiction of Napoleon's sister, Paolina Bonaparte Borghese, reclining topless as *Venere Vincitrice* (1805–08) in **Sala I**. Its suggestive pose and technical virtuosity is typical of Canova's elegant, mildly erotic neoclassical style.

Caravaggio dominates **Sala VIII** with a dissipated *Bacchino Malato* (Young Sick Bacchus; 1593–94), the strangely beautiful *La Madonna dei Palafrenieri* (Madonna of the Palafrenieri; 1605–06), and *San Giovanni Battista* (St John the Baptist; 1609–10), probably the artist's last work.

Beyond Sala VIII, the grand **entrance hall** features 4th-century floor mosaics of fighting gladiators and 2nd-century *Satiro Combattente* (Fighting Satyr). High on the wall is a gravity-defying bas-relief of a horse and rider falling into the void *(Marco Curzio a Cavallo)* by Pietro Bernini (Gian Lorenzo's father).

Pinacoteca

Upstairs, the picture gallery offers a wonderful snapshot of Renaissance art.

Don't miss Raphael's extraordinary *La Deposizione di Cristo* (The Deposition; 1507) in **Sala IX**, and his *Dama con Liocorno* (Lady with a Unicorn; 1506). In the same room is Fra Bartolomeo's superb *Adorazione del Bambino* (Adoration of the Christ Child; 1495) and Perugino's *Madonna con Bambino* (Madonna and Child; first quarter of the 16th century).

WJAREK/SHUTTERSTOCK ©

Next door, Correggio's *Danäe* (1530–31) shares the room with a willowy Venus, as portrayed by Cranach in his *Venere e Amore che Reca Il Favo do Miele* (Venus and Cupid with Honeycomb; 1531).

Other highlights include Bernini's self-portraits in **Sala XIV**, and Titian's early masterpiece, *Amor Sacro e Amor Profano* (Sacred and Profane Love; 1514) in **Sala XX**.

What's Nearby?

Villa Borghese   Park

(entrances at Piazzale San Paolo del Brasile, Piazzale Flaminio, Via Pinciana, Via Raimondo, Largo Pablo Picasso; ☉sunrise-sunset; ☐Via Pinciana) Locals, lovers, tourists, joggers – no one can resist the lure of Rome's most celebrated park. Originally the 17th-century estate of Cardinal Scipione Borghese, it covers about 80 hectares of wooded glades, gardens and grassy banks. Among its attractions are several excellent museums, the landscaped **Giardino del Lago** (boat hire per 20min €3; ☉7am-9pm summer, to 6pm winter), **Piazza di Siena**, a dusty arena used for Rome's top equestrian event in May, and a panoramic terrace on the Pincio Hill (p57).

Museo Nazionale
Etrusco di Villa Giulia   Museum

(☏06 322 65 71; www.villagiulia.beniculturali.it; Piazzale di Villa Giulia; adult/reduced €8/4; ☉9am-8pm Tue-Sun; ☐Via delle Belle Arti) Pope Julius III's 16th-century villa provides the charming setting for Italy's finest collection of Etruscan and pre-Roman treasures. Exhibits, many of which came from tombs in the surrounding Lazio region, range from bronze figurines and black *bucchero* tableware to temple

Villa Borghese

decorations, terracotta vases and a dazzling display of sophisticated jewellery.

Must-sees include a polychrome terracotta statue of Apollo from a temple in Veio, and the 6th-century-BC *Sarcofago degli Sposi* (Sarcophagus of the Betrothed), found in 1881 in Cerveteri.

La Galleria Nazionale   Gallery

(Galleria Nazionale d'Arte Moderna e Contemporanea; ☎06 3229 8221; http://lagallerianazionale. com; Viale delle Belle Arti 131, accessible entrance Via Antonio Gramsci 71; adult/reduced €10/5; ☉8.30am-7.30pm Tue-Sun; ☐Piazza Thorvaldsen)

> ### ★ Top Tip
>
> Monday is not a good time for exploring Villa Borghese. Sure, you can walk in the park, but its museums and galleries are all shut – they are only open Tuesday to Sunday.

PHANT/GETTY IMAGES ©

Housed in a vast belle-époque palace, this oft-overlooked modern art gallery, known locally as GNAM, is an unsung gem. Its superlative collection runs the gamut from neoclassical sculpture to abstract expressionism, with works by many of the most important exponents of 19th- and 20th-century art.

Pincio Hill Gardens   Gardens

(Ⓜ️Flaminio) Overlooking Piazza del Popolo, 19th-century Pincio Hill is named after the Pinci family, who owned this part of Rome in the 4th century. It's quite a climb up from the piazza, but at the top you're rewarded with lovely views over to St Peter's and the Gianicolo Hill. Alternatively, approach from the top of the Spanish Steps. From the gardens, strike out to explore Villa Borghese, **Villa Medici** (☎06 676 13 11; www.villamedici.it; Viale Trinità dei Monti 1; 1½hr guided tour adult/reduced €12/6; ☉ticket office 9.30am-7pm Tue-Sun; Ⓜ️Spagna) or Chiesa della Trinità dei Monti (p91) at the top of the Spanish Steps.

Museo d'Arte Contemporanea di Roma   Gallery

(MACRO; ☎06 69 62 71; www.museomacro. org; Via Nizza 138, cnr Via Cagliari; admission price depends on exhibition; ☉9am-9pm; ☐Via Nizza) Along with MAXXI, this is Rome's most important contemporary art gallery. Occupying a converted Peroni brewery, it hosts exhibitions by international artists such as Anish Kapoor, and displays works from its permanent collection of post-1960s Italian art.

Vying with the exhibits for your attention is the museum's sleek black-and-red interior design. The work of French architect Odile Decq, this retains much of the building's original structure while also incorporating a sophisticated steel-and-glass finish.

> ### ★ Local Knowledge
>
> For unforgettable views over Rome's rooftops and domes, make your way to the Pincio Hill Gardens in the southwest of Villa Borghese.

Stadio

Palatino

Rising above the Roman Forum, the Palatino (Palatine Hill) is an atmospheric area of towering pine trees, majestic ruins and memorable views. According to legend, this is where Romulus and Remus were saved by a wolf and where Romulus founded Rome in 753 BC. Archaeological evidence can't prove the myth, but it has dated human habitation here to the 8th century BC.

Great for...

❶ Need to Know

Map p246; Palatine Hill; ☑06 3996 7700; www.coopculture.it; Via di San Gregorio 30, Piazza di Santa Maria Nova; adult/reduced incl Colosseum & Roman Forum €12/7.50; ☉8.30am-1hr before sunset; Ⓜ︎Colosseo

★ **Top Tip**

The best spot for a picnic is the grassy Vigna Barberini near the Orti Farnesiani.

The Palatino was ancient Rome's most exclusive neighbourhood. The emperor Augustus lived here all his life and successive emperors built increasingly opulent palaces. But after Rome's fall, it fell into disrepair, and in the Middle Ages churches and castles were built over the ruins. Later, wealthy Renaissance families had landscaped gardens laid out on the site.

Most of the Palatino as it appears today is covered by the ruins of the emperor Domitian's 1st-century complex, which served as the main imperial palace for 300 years.

Stadio

On entering the Palatino from Via di San Gregorio, head uphill until you come to the first recognisable construction, the

stadio. This sunken area, which was part of the main imperial palace, was used by the emperor for private games. A path to the side of the *stadio* leads to the remains of a complex built by Septimius Severus, comprising baths (**Terme di Settimio Severo**) and a palace (**Domus Severiana**) where, if they're open, you can visit the **Arcate Severiane** (Severian Arches; admission incl in Palatino ticket; ⊘8.30am-6.45pm Tue & Fri summer, shorter hours Tue & Fri winter), a series of arches built to facilitate further development.

Domus Augustana, Museo Palatino & Domus Flavia

Next to the *stadio* are the ruins of the **Domus Augustana**, the emperor's private quarters in the imperial palace. This was built on two levels, with rooms leading off

Domus Augustana

a *peristilio* (porticoed courtyard) on each floor. You can't get to the lower level, but from above you can see the basin of a fountain.

The grey building next to the Domus houses the **Museo Palatino** (admission incl in Palatino ticket; ☉8.30am-1½hr before sunset), a small museum dedicated to the history of the area. Archaeological artefacts on show include a beautiful 1st-century bronze, the *Erma di Canefora*, and a celebrated 3rd-century graffito depicting a man with a donkey's head being crucified.

North of the museum is the **Domus Flavia**, the public part of the palace. This was centred on a grand columned peristyle – the grassy area with the base of an octagonal fountain – off which the main halls led.

Casa di Livia & Casa di Augusto

Among the best-preserved buildings on the Palatino is the **Casa di Livia** (✆06 3996 7700; www.coopculture.it; incl Casa di Augusto visit/guided tour €4/9; ☉visits 12.45pm daily, reservations necessary), northwest of the Domus Flavia. Home to Augustus' wife Livia, it was built around an atrium leading onto what were once frescoed reception rooms. Nearby, the **Casa di Augusto**, Augustus' private residence, features some superb frescoes in vivid reds, yellows and blues.

Criptoportico Neroniano

Northeast of the Casa di Livia lies the **Criptoportico**, a 130m tunnel where Caligula is said to have been murdered, and which Nero used to connect his Domus Aurea with the Palatino.

Orti Farnesiani

Covering the Domus Tiberiana (Tiberius' palace) in the northwest of the Palatino, the **Orti Farnesiani** is one of Europe's earliest botanical gardens. Named after Cardinal Alessandro Farnese, who had it laid out in the mid-16th century, it commands breathtaking views over the Roman Forum.

> ☑ **Don't Miss**
>
> The sight of the Roman Forum laid out beneath you from the balcony in the Orti Farnesiani is spectacular.

MARCPO/GETTY IMAGES ©

> ✕ **Take a Break**
>
> Located on the Circo Massimo, the welcoming bar 0.75 (p168) is an attractive spot for an evening *aperitivo*.

Fontana del Moro

Piazza Navona

With its ornate fountains, exuberant baroque palazzi (mansions) and pavement cafes, Piazza Navona is central Rome's elegant showcase square. Long a hub of local life, it hosted Rome's main market for close on 300 years, and today attracts a colourful daily circus of street performers, hawkers, artists, tourists, fortune-tellers and pigeons.

Great for...

Via dei Coronari

Piazza Navona ◎

Corso del Rinascimento

Corso Vittorio Emanuele II

ⓘ Need to Know

Map p250; 🚊 Corso del Rinascimento

★ **Top Tip**
Each December the piazza hosts a traditional Christmas market.

Stadio di Domiziano

Like many of Rome's landmarks, the piazza sits over an ancient monument, in this case the 1st-century-AD **Stadio di Domiziano** (Domitian's Stadium; ☎06 6880 5311; www. stadiodomiziano.com; adult/reduced €8/6; ☉10am-7pm Sun-Fri, to 8pm Sat). This 30,000-seat stadium, whose subterranean remains can be accessed from Via di Tor Sanguigna, used to host athletic meets – hence, the name Navona, a corruption of the Greek word *agon*, meaning public games.

Fountains

The piazza's grand centrepiece is Bernini's **Fontana dei Quattro Fiumi**, a showy fountain featuring four muscular personifications of the rivers Nile, Ganges, Danube and Plate.

The **Fontana del Moro** at the southern end of the square was designed by Giacomo della Porta in 1576.

At the northern end of the piazza, the 19th-century **Fontana del Nettuno** depicts Neptune fighting with a sea monster, surrounded by sea nymphs.

Main Buildings

Overlooking Bernini's Fontana dei Quattro Fiumi, is the **Chiesa di Sant'Agnese in Agone** (☎06 6819 2134; www.santagneseinagone. org;; ☉9am-1pm & 3-7pm Tue-Fri, to 8pm Sat & Sun), an elaborate baroque church designed by Francesco Borromini.

Further down, the 17th-century **Palazzo Pamphilj** (http://roma.itamaraty.gov.br/it; Piazza Navona 10; ☉by reservation only) was built for Pope Innocent X and now houses the Brazilian Embassy.

Fontana dei Quattro Fiumi

What's Nearby?

Chiesa di San Luigi dei Francesi   Church

(☏06 68 82 71; http://saintlouis-rome.net; Piazza di San Luigi dei Francesi 5; ⊘9.30am-12.45 Mon-Fri, 9.30am-12.15pm Sat, 11.30am-12.45pm Sun, 2.30-6.30pm daily; ▣Corso del Rinascimento) Church to Rome's French community since 1589, this opulent baroque *chiesa* is home to a celebrated trio of Caravaggio paintings: the *Vocazione di San Matteo* (The Calling of Saint Matthew), the *Martirio di San Matteo* (The Martyrdom of Saint Matthew) and *San Matteo e l'Angelo* (Saint Matthew and the Angel), known collectively as the St Matthew cycle.

> ☑**Don't Miss**
>
> Bernini's Fontana dei Quattro Fiumi, the piazza's high-camp central fountain.

Museo Nazionale Romano: Palazzo Altemps   Museum

(☏06 3996 7700; www.coopculture.it; Piazza Sant'Apollinare 46; adult/reduced €10/5, incl Palazzo Massimo alle Terme, Crypta Balbi & Terme di Diocleziano €12/6; ⊘9am-7.45pm Tue-Sun; ▣Corso del Rinascimento) Just north of Piazza Navona, Palazzo Altemps is a beautiful late-15th-century *palazzo*, housing the best of the Museo Nazionale Romano's formidable collection of classical sculpture. Many pieces come from the celebrated Ludovisi collection, amassed by Cardinal Ludovico Ludovisi in the 17th century.

Basilica di Sant'Agostino   Basilica

(Piazza di Sant'Agostino 80; ⊘7.30am-noon & 4-7.30pm; ▣Corso del Rinascimento) The plain white facade of this early Renaissance church, built in the 15th century and renovated in the late 1700s, gives no indication of the impressive art inside. The most famous work is Caravaggio's *Madonna dei Pellegrini* (Madonna of the Pilgrims), in the first chapel on the left, but you'll also find a fresco by Raphael and a much-venerated sculpture by Jacopo Sansovino.

Campo de' Fiori   Piazza

(▣Corso Vittorio Emanuele II) Noisy, colourful 'Il Campo' is a major focus of Roman life: by day it hosts one of Rome's best-known markets, while at night it morphs into a raucous open-air pub as drinkers spill out from its many bars and eateries. For centuries the square was the site of public executions, and it was here that philosopher Giordano Bruno was burned for heresy in 1600. The spot is marked by a sinister statue of the hooded monk, which was created by Ettore Ferrari in 1889.

> ✗ **Take a Break**
>
> A short stroll to the south, Emma Pizzeria (p124) serves excellent pizzas and craft beer.

BELENOS/SHUTTERSTOCK ©

Museo Nazionale Romano

Museo Nazionale Romano: Palazzo Massimo alle Terme

Every day, thousands of passers-by hurry past this towering neo-Renaissance palazzo without giving it a second glance. They don't know what they're missing. This is one of Rome's finest museums, a light-filled treasure trove packed with spectacular classical art. The sculpture is truly impressive, but what really takes the breath away is its collection of vibrantly coloured frescoes and mosaics.

Great for...

Piazza della Repubblica
Repubblica
Via Torino
Viale Enrico de Nicola
Piazza dei Cinquecento
Museo Nazionale Romano: Palazzo Massimo alle Terme
Stazione Termini
Termini
Via del Viminale

❶ Need to Know

Map p252; ☑06 3996 7700; www.coopculture. it; Largo di Villa Peretti 1; adult/reduced €10/5, incl Palazzo Altemps, Crypta Balbi & Terme di Diocleziano €12/6; ⊗9am-7.45pm Tue-Sun; Ⓜ Termini

★ **Top Tip**

For an extra euro or two, you can buy a ticket that also covers admission to the Terme di Diocleziano, Palazzo Altemps and the Crypta Balbi (valid for three days).

Sculpture

The ground and 1st floors are devoted to sculpture, examining imperial portraiture as propaganda and including some breathtaking works of art, including the 2nd-century-BC Greek bronzes, the *Boxer* and the *Prince,* a crouching *Aphrodite* from Villa Adriana, the 2nd-century-BC *Sleeping Hermaphrodite,* and the idealised vision of the *Discus Thrower.* Also fascinating are the elaborate bronze fittings that belonged to Caligula's ceremonial ships.

Frescoes & Mosaics

On the 2nd floor, magnificent and vibrantly coloured frescoes include scenes from nature, mythology, and domestic and sensual life, using rich, vivid (and expensive) colours. These magnificent panels, originally used as interior decor, give a more complete picture of the inside of an ancient Roman villa than you'll see anywhere else in the world.

Particularly breathtaking are the frescoes (dating from 30 BC to 20 BC) from Villa Livia, one of the homes of Augustus' wife Livia Drusilla. These cover an entire room and depict a paradisiacal garden full of a wild tangle of roses, pomegranates, irises and camomile under a deep-blue sky. They once decorated a summer *triclinium*, a large living and dining area built half underground to provide protection from the heat.

The 2nd floor also features some exquisitely fine floor mosaics and rare inlay work.

Basement

The basement contains an absorbing coin collection tracing the Roman Empire's use of coins for propaganda purposes. There's

Fresco depicting scenes of a garden from Villa Livia

also jewellery dating back several millennia, and the disturbing remains of a mummified eight-year-old girl, the only known example of mummification dating from the Roman Empire.

What's Nearby?

Museo Nazionale Romano: Terme di Diocleziano
Museum

(☑06 3996 7700; www.coopculture.it; Viale Enrico de Nicola 78; adult/reduced €10/5, incl Palazzo Massimo alle Terme, Palazzo Altemps & Crypta Balbi €12/6; ⊘9am-7.30pm Tue-Sun; Ⓜ Termini) The Terme di Diocleziano was ancient Rome's largest bath complex, covering about 13 hectares and able to accommodate some 3000 people. Today its ruins house a branch of the impressive Museo Nazionale Romano. Exhibits, which include memorial inscriptions, bas-reliefs and archaeological artefacts, provide a fascinating insight into Roman life. Outside, the vast cloister, constructed from drawings by Michelangelo, is lined with classical sarcophagi, headless statues and huge sculpted animal heads, thought to have come from the Foro di Traiano.

Chiesa di Santa Maria della Vittoria
Church

(☑06 4274 0571; Via XX Settembre 17; ⊘8.30am-noon & 3.30-6pm; Ⓜ Repubblica) This modest church is an unlikely setting for an extraordinary work of art – Bernini's extravagant and sexually charged *Santa Teresa trafitta dall'amore di Dio* (Ecstasy of St Teresa). This daring sculpture depicts Teresa, engulfed in the folds of a flowing cloak, floating in ecstasy on a cloud while a teasing angel pierces her repeatedly with a golden arrow.

Palazzo delle Esposizioni
Cultural Centre

(☑06 3996 7500; www.palazzoesposizioni.it; Via Nazionale 194; ⊘10am-8pm Tue-Thu & Sun, to 10.30pm Fri & Sat; ☐ Via Nazionale) This huge neoclassical palace was built in 1882 as an exhibition centre, though it has since served as headquarters for the Italian Communist Party, a mess hall for Allied servicemen, a polling station and even a public loo. Nowadays it's a splendid cultural hub, with cathedral-scale spaces hosting blockbuster art exhibitions and sleekly designed art labs, as well as a bookshop, cafe and Michelin-starred restaurant (p134) serving a bargain lunch or brunch beneath a dazzling all-glass roof. Occasional concerts, performances and film screenings are also held here.

> ☑ **Don't Miss**
> The athletic pose of the discus thrower, *Il Discobolo*, a stirring homage to the male physique.

ADAM EASTLAND/ALAMY STOCK PHOTO ©

> ✕ **Take a Break**
> Head to the Mercato Centrale (p128) at Termini station for a range of tempting food stalls.

Capitoline Museums

Dating to 1471, the Capitoline Museums are the world's oldest public museums. Their collection of classical sculpture is one of Italy's finest, including crowd-pleasers such as the iconic Lupa Capitolina (Capitoline Wolf), and the formidable picture gallery includes masterpieces by the likes of Titian, Tintoretto, Rubens and Caravaggio.

Great for...

ℹ Need to Know

Map p250; ☎06 06 08; www.museicapitolini. org; Piazza del Campidoglio 1; adult/reduced €11.50/9.50; ⊗9.30am-7.30pm, last admission 6.30pm; ⊞Piazza Venezia

★ **Top Tip**

In a tunnel between the two *palazzi*, the Tabularium commands inspiring views over the Roman Forum.

The museums occupy two stately *palazzi* on **Piazza del Campidoglio**. The entrance is in **Palazzo dei Conservatori**, where you'll find the original core of the sculptural collection and the Pinacoteca (picture gallery).

Palazzo dei Conservatori: 1st Floor

Before you start on the sculpture collection proper, check out the marble body parts littered around the ground-floor **courtyard**. The mammoth head, hand and feet all belonged to a 12m-high statue of Constantine that once stood in the Basilica di Massenzio in the Roman Forum.

Of the sculpture on the 1st floor, the Etruscan *Lupa Capitolina* (Capitoline Wolf) is the most famous. Dating to the 5th century BC, the bronze wolf stands over her suckling wards, Romulus and Remus, who were added in 1471.

Other highlights include the *Spinario*, a delicate 1st-century-BC bronze of a boy removing a thorn from his foot, and Gian Lorenzo Bernini's *Medusa* bust.

Also on this floor, in the modern **Esedra di Marco Aurelio**, is the original of the equestrian statue that stands outside in Piazza del Campidoglio.

Palazzo dei Conservatori: 2nd Floor

The 2nd floor is given over to the **Pinacoteca**, the museum's picture gallery. Each room harbours masterpieces, but two stand out: the **Sala Pietro da Cortona**, which features Pietro da Cortona's famous depiction of the *Ratto delle Sabine* (Rape of the Sabine Women; 1630), and the **Sala di Santa Petronilla**, named after Guercino's huge canvas *Seppellimento di Santa Petronilla*

(The Burial of St Petronilla; 1621–23). This airy hall also boasts two works by Caravaggio: *La Buona Ventura* (The Fortune Teller; 1595) and *San Giovanni Battista* (John the Baptist; 1602).

Tabularium

A tunnel links Palazzo dei Conservatori to Palazzo Nuovo via the Tabularium, ancient Rome's central archive, beneath **Palazzo Senatorio**.

Palazzo Nuovo

Palazzo Nuovo contains some unforgettable show-stoppers. Chief among them is the *Ga-*

☑ Don't Miss

The Sala degli Orazi e Curiazi where the 1957 Treaty of Rome was signed, establishing the European Economic Community, precursor of the European Union.

JUSTIN FOULKES/LONELY PLANET ©

lata Morente (Dying Gaul), a Roman copy of a 3rd-century-BC Greek original that movingly depicts the anguish of a dying Gaul warrior. Another superb figurative piece is the *Venere capitolina* (Capitoline Venus), a sensual yet demure portrayal of the nude goddess.

What's Nearby?

Vittoriano   Monument

(Victor Emanuel Monument; Piazza Venezia; ☺9.30am-5.30pm summer, to 4.30pm winter; 🚇Piazza Venezia) **FREE** Love it or loathe it (as many Romans do), you can't ignore the Vittoriano (aka the Altare della Patria, Altar of the Fatherland), the massive mountain of white marble that towers over Piazza Venezia. Begun in 1885 to honour Italy's first king, Vittorio Emanuele II – who's immortalised in its vast equestrian statue – it incorporates the **Museo Centrale del Risorgimento** (☎06 679 35 98; www.risorgimento.it; adult/reduced €5/2.50; ☺9.30am-6.30pm), a small museum documenting Italian unification, and the **Tomb of the Unknown Soldier**.

For Rome's best 360-degree views, take the **Roma dal Cielo** (adult/reduced €7/3.50; ☺9.30am-7.30pm, last admission 6.45pm) lift to the top.

Bocca della Verità   Monument

(Mouth of Truth; Piazza Bocca della Verità 18; ☺9.30am-5.50pm summer, to 4.50pm winter; 🚇Piazza Bocca della Verità) A bearded face carved into a giant marble disc, the Bocca della Verità is one of Rome's most popular curiosities. Legend has it that if you put your hand in the mouth and tell a lie, the Bocca will slam shut and bite your hand off.

The mouth, which was originally part of a fountain, or possibly an ancient manhole cover, now lives in the portico of the **Chiesa di Santa Maria in Cosmedin**, a handsome medieval church.

✕ Take a Break

Head up to the 2nd floor of Palazzo dei Conservatori for a coffee at the panoramic Terrazza Caffarelli (p122).

Via Appia Antica

Ancient Rome's regina viarum (queen of roads) is now one of Rome's most exclusive addresses, a beautiful cobbled thoroughfare flanked by grassy fields, ancient ruins and towering pine trees. But it has a dark history – it was here that Spartacus and 6000 of his slave rebels were crucified, and the early Christians buried their dead in the underground catacombs.

Great for...

ⓘ Need to Know

06 513 53 16; www.parcoappiaantica.it; Info Point 9.30am-1pm & 2-6.30pm Mon-Fri, 9.30am-7.30pm Sat & Sun summer, 9.30am-1pm & 2-5.30pm Mon-Fri, 9.30am-5.30pm Sat & Sun winter; Via Appia Antica

★ **Top Tip**

Rent bikes and pick up maps at **Info Point Appia Antica**.

Heading southeast from Porta San Sebastiano, Via Appia Antica was named after Appius Claudius Caecus, who laid the first 90km section in 312 BC. It was later extended in 190 BC to reach Brindisi, some 540km away on the southern Adriatic coast.

Catacombe di San Sebastiano

The **Catacombe di San Sebastiano** (☏06 785 03 50; www.catacombe.org; Via Appia Antica 136; adult/reduced €8/5; ⊙10am-5pm Mon-Sat Jan-Nov; ☐Via Appia Antica) were the first burial chambers to be called catacombs – the name was derived from the Greek *kata* (near) and *kymbas* (cavity), because they were located near a cave. They were heavily developed from the 1st century, and during the persecutory reign of Vespasian they provided a safe haven for the remains of Saints Peter and Paul.

The 1st level is now almost completely destroyed, but frescoes, stucco work and epigraphs can be seen on the 2nd level. There are also three perfectly preserved mausoleums and a plastered wall with hundreds of invocations to Peter and Paul, engraved by worshippers in the 3rd and 4th centuries.

Above the catacombs, the **Basilica di San Sebastiano** preserves one of the arrows allegedly used to kill St Sebastian, and the column to which he was tied.

Catacombe di San Callisto

These are the largest and busiest of Rome's catacombs. Founded at the end of the 2nd century and named after Pope Calixtus I, the **Catacombe di San Callisto** (☏06 513 01 51;

Bas relief along Via Appia Antica

www.catacombe.roma.it; Via Appia Antica 110-126; adult/reduced €8/5; ⏰9am-noon & 2-5pm Thu-Tue Mar-Jan; 🚇Via Appia Antica) became the official cemetery of the newly established Roman Church. In the 20km of tunnels explored to date, archaeologists have found the tombs of 16 popes, dozens of martyrs and thousands upon thousands of Christians.

The patron saint of music, St Cecilia, was also buried here, though her body was later removed to the Basilica di Santa Cecilia in Trastevere. When her body was exhumed in 1599, more than a thousand years after her death, it was apparently perfectly preserved.

> ☑**Don't Miss**
>
> The ruins of Villa di Massenzio, which litter the green fields by the side of the cobbled road.

ALESSANDRO0770/GETTY IMAGES ©

Catacombe di Santa Domitilla

Among Rome's largest and oldest, the **Catacombe di Santa Domitilla** (🔗06 511 03 42; www.domitilla.info; Via delle Sette Chiese 282; adult/reduced €8/5; ⏰9am-noon & 2-5pm Wed-Mon mid-Jan–mid-Dec; 🚇Via Appia Antica) contains Christian wall paintings and the haunting underground **Chiesa di SS Nereus e Achilleus**, a 4th-century church dedicated to two Roman soldiers martyred by Diocletian.

What's Nearby?

Mausoleo di Cecilia Metella   Ruins
(🔗06 3996 7700; www.coopculture.it; Via Appia Antica 161; adult/reduced €5/2.50, incl Villa dei Quintili & Complesso di Santa Maria Nova €10; ⏰9am-1hr before sunset Tue-Sun; 🚇Via Appia Antica) Dating to the 1st century BC, this great drum of a mausoleum encloses a burial chamber, now roofless. In the 14th century it was converted into a fort by the Caetani family, who were related to Pope Boniface VIII and used to frighten passing traffic into paying a toll.

Villa di Massenzio   Ruins
(🔗06 06 08; www.villadimassenzio.it; Via Appia Antica 153; ⏰10am-4pm Tue-Sun; 🚇Via Appia Antica) **FREE** The outstanding feature of Maxentius' enormous 4th-century palace complex is the **Circo di Massenzio** Rome's best-preserved ancient racetrack – you can still make out the starting stalls used for chariot races. The 10,000-seat arena was built by Maxentius around 309, but he died before ever seeing a race here. Above the arena are the ruins of Maxentius' imperial residence. Near the racetrack, the **Mausoleo di Romolo** was built by Maxentius for his 17-year-old son Romulus.

> ✕ **Take a Break**
>
> For an atmospheric lunch adjourn to L'Archeologia Ristorante (p141), housed in a 19th-century inn.

Roman Forum

The Roman Forum was ancient Rome's showpiece centre, a grandiose district of temples, basilicas and vibrant public spaces. Nowadays, it's a collection of impressive, if sketchily labelled, ruins that can leave you drained and confused. But if you can get your imagination going, there's something wonderfully compelling about walking in the footsteps of Julius Caesar and other legendary figures of Roman history.

Great for...

ℹ Need to Know

Foro Romano; Map p246; ☑06 3996 7700; www.coopculture.it; Largo della Salara Vecchia, Piazza di Santa Maria Nova; adult/reduced incl Colosseum & Palatino €12/7.50; ⊗8.30am-1hr before sunset; ☐Via dei Fori Imperiali

★ **Top Tip**

Orientate yourself by viewing the Forum from the balcony on the Palatino.

Originally an Etruscan burial ground, the Forum was first developed in the 7th century BC, growing over time to become the social, political and commercial hub of the Roman Empire. But like many of ancient Rome's great urban developments, it fell into disrepair after the fall of the Roman Empire until eventually it was used as pasture land. In the Middle Ages it was known as the Campo Vaccino ('Cow Field') and extensively plundered for its stone and marble. The area was systematically excavated in the 18th and 19th centuries, and excavations continue to this day.

Via Sacra to Campidoglio

Entering the Forum from Largo della Salara Vecchia, you'll see the **Tempio di Antonino e Faustina** ahead to your left. Erected in AD 141, this was transformed into a church in the 8th century, the **Chiesa di San Lorenzo in Miranda**. To your right is the 179 BC **Basilica Fulvia Aemilia**.

At the end of the path, you'll come to **Via Sacra**, the Forum's main thoroughfare, and the **Tempio di Giulio Cesare**, which stands on the spot where Julius Caesar was cremated.

Heading right brings you to the **Curia**, the original seat of the Roman Senate, though what you see today is a reconstruction of how it looked in the reign of Diocletian (r 284–305).

At the end of Via Sacra, the **Arco di Settimio Severo** is dedicated to the eponymous emperor and his sons, Caracalla and Geta. Close by, the **Colonna di Foca** rises above what was once the Forum's main square, **Piazza del Foro**.

The eight granite columns that rise behind the Colonna are all that survive of the **Tempio**

di Saturno, an important temple that doubled as the state treasury.

Tempio di Castore e Polluce & Casa delle Vestali

From the path that runs parallel to Via Sacra, you'll pass the stubby ruins of the **Basilica Giulia**. At the end of the basilica, three columns remain from the 5th-century-BC **Tempio di Castore e Polluce**.

Nearby, the 6th-century **Chiesa di Santa Maria Antiqua** is the oldest church in the Forum, a veritable treasure trove of early Christian art. Accessible from in front of the church is the **Rampa Imperiale**, a passageway that linked the Forum to the Palatine.

> **☑ Don't Miss**
> It's not always open, but if it is, the frescoed Chiesa di Santa Maria Antiqua is a real highlight.

VIACHESLAV LOPATIN/SHUTTERSTOCK ©

Back towards Via Sacra is the **Casa delle Vestali**, home of the virgins who tended the flame in the adjoining **Tempio di Vesta**.

Via Sacra Towards the Colosseum

Heading up Via Sacra past the **Tempio di Romolo**, you'll come to the **Basilica di Massenzio**, the largest building in the Forum.

Beyond the basilica, the **Arco di Tito** was built in AD 81 to celebrate Vespasian and Titus' victories against rebels in Jerusalem.

What's Nearby?

Imperial Forums   Archaeological Site
(Fori Imperiali; ☑06 06 08; Piazza Santa Maria di Loreto; guided tours adult/reduced €4/3; ☐Via dei Fori Imperiali) Visible from Via dei Fori Imperiali and, when it's open, Via Alessandrina, the forums of Trajan, Augustus, Nerva and Caesar are known collectively as the Imperial Forums. These were largely buried when Mussolini bulldozed Via dei Fori Imperiali through the area in 1933, but excavations have since unearthed much of them. The standout sights are the **Mercati di Traiano** (Trajan's Markets), accessible through the Museo dei Fori Imperiali, and the landmark **Colonna Traiana** (Trajan's Column).

Mercati di Traiano Museo dei Fori Imperiali   Museum
(☑06 06 08; www.mercatiditraiano.it; Via IV Novembre 94; adult/reduced €11.50/9.50; ☺9.30am-7.30pm, last admission 6.30pm; ☐Via IV Novembre) This striking museum brings to life the **Mercati di Traiano**, Emperor Trajan's great 2nd-century complex, while also providing a fascinating introduction to the Imperial Forums with multimedia displays, explanatory panels and a smattering of archaeological artefacts.

> **✕ Take a Break**
> Alongside its views of the Colonna di Traiano, Terre e Domus (p122) offers regional dishes and Lazio wines.

Roman Forum

A HISTORICAL TOUR

In ancient times, a forum was a market place, civic centre and religious complex all rolled into one, and the greatest of all was the Roman Forum (Foro Romano). Situated between the Palatino (Palatine Hill), ancient Rome's most exclusive neighbourhood, and the Campidoglio (Capitoline Hill), it was the city's busy, bustling centre. On any given day it teemed with activity. Senators debated affairs of state in the **❶ Curia**, shoppers thronged the squares and traffic-free streets and crowds gathered under the **❷ Colonna di Foca** to listen to politicians holding forth from the **❷ Rostri**. Elsewhere, lawyers worked the courts in basilicas including the **❸ Basilica di Massenzio**, while the Vestal Virgins quietly went about their business in the **❹ Casa delle Vestali**.

Special occasions were also celebrated in the Forum: religious holidays were marked with ceremonies at temples such as **❺ Tempio di Saturno** and **❻ Tempio di Castore e Polluce**, and military victories were honoured with dramatic processions up Via Sacra and the building of monumental arches like **❼ Arco di Settimio Severo** and **❽ Arco di Tito**.

The ruins you see today are impressive but they can be confusing without a clear picture of what the Forum once looked like. This spread shows the Forum in its heyday, complete with temples, civic buildings and towering monuments to heroes of the Roman Empire.

TOP TIPS

➡ Get grandstand views of the Forum from the Palatino and Campidoglio.

➡ Visit first thing in the morning or late afternoon; crowds are worst between 11am and 2pm.

➡ In summer it gets hot in the Forum and there's little shade, so take a hat and plenty of water.

Colonna di Foca & Rostri
The free-standing, 13.5m-high Column of Phocus is the Forum's youngest monument, dating to AD 608. Behind it, the Rostri provided a suitably grandiose platform for pontificating public speakers.

Campidoglio (Capitoline Hill)

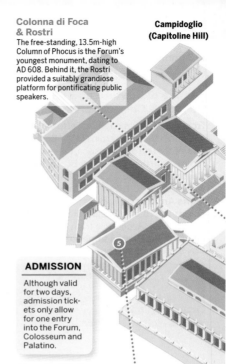

ADMISSION

Although valid for two days, admission tickets only allow for one entry into the Forum, Colosseum and Palatino.

Tempio di Saturno
Ancient Rome's Fort Knox, the Temple of Saturn was the city treasury. In Caesar's day it housed 13 tonnes of gold, 114 tonnes of silver and 30 million sestertii worth of silver coins.

IASDIC/SHUTTERSTOCK©

VIACHESLAV LOPATIN/SHUTTERSTOCK©

Tempio di Castore e Polluce
Only three columns of the Temple of Castor and Pollux remain. The temple was dedicated to the Heavenly Twins after they supposedly led the Romans to victory over the Latin League in 496 BC.

Arco di Settimio Severo
One of the Forum's signature monuments, this imposing triumphal arch commemorates the military victories of Septimius Severus. Relief panels depict his campaigns against the Parthians.

Curia
This big barn-like building was the official seat of the Roman Senate. Most of what you see is a reconstruction, but the interior marble floor dates to the 3rd-century reign of Diocletian.

Basilica di Massenzio
Marvel at the scale of this vast 4th-century basilica. In its original form the central hall was divided into enormous naves; now only part of the northern nave survives.

JULIUS CAESAR
Julius Caesar was cremated on the site where the Tempio di Giulio Cesare now stands.

Via Sacra

Tempio di Giulio Cesare

Arco di Tito
Said to be the inspiration for the Arc de Triomphe in Paris, the well-preserved Arch of Titus was built by the emperor Domitian to honour his elder brother Titus.

Casa delle Vestali
White statues line the grassy atrium of what was once the luxurious 50-room home of the Vestal Virgins. The virgins played an important role in Roman religion, serving the goddess Vesta.

BELENOS/SHUTTERSTOCK ©

Trevi Fountain

The Fontana di Trevi is Rome's largest and most celebrated fountain. A foaming ensemble of mythical figures, wild horses and cascading rock falls, it takes up the entire side of the 17th-century Palazzo Poli.

Immortalised by Federico Fellini's film *La Dolce Vita* – apparently Anita Ekberg wore waders under her iconic black ballgown when she took her famous dip – the Trevi Fountain is one of Rome's must-see sights. It was completed in 1762 and named Trevi in reference to the *tre vie* (three roads) that converge on it.

The water comes from the Aqua Virgo, an underground aqueduct that was built 2000 years ago, during the reign of Augustus, to bring water in from the Salone springs around 19km away.

The Design

The fountain's design, conceived by Nicola Salvi in 1732, depicts Neptune, the god of the sea, in a shell-shaped chariot being led by Tritons and two sea horses. In the niche

Great for...

☑ Don't Miss

The contrasting horses – one tempestuous, one calm – which depict the moods of the sea.

Neptune

KOCHMANSKI/BUDGET TRAVEL ©

❶ Need to Know

Fontana di Trevi; Piazza di Trevi; Map p252; Ⓜ Barberini

✕ Take a Break

For a great value brunch or aperitif, make for Bistro del Quirino (p126).

★ Top Tip

Come at dawn to avoid the crowds, or in the evening when the fountain is beautifully lit.

to the left of Neptune, a statue represents Abundance; to the right is Salubrity.

On the eastern side is a strange conical urn. Known as the *Assso di coppe* (Ace of Cups), this was supposedly placed by Nicola Salvi to block the view of a busybody barber who had been a vocal critic of Salvi's design during the fountain's construction.

Throw In Your Money

The famous tradition (since the 1954 film *Three Coins in the Fountain*) is to toss a coin into the water and thus ensure you'll one day return to Rome. About €3000 is thrown in on an average day. For years much of this was scooped up by local thieves, but in 2012 the city authorities clamped down, making it illegal to remove coins from the water. The money is now collected daily and handed over to the Catholic charity Caritas.

What's Nearby?

Palazzo del Quirinale   Palace

(☑ 06 3996 7557; www.quirinale.it; Piazza del Quirinale; 1¼hr tour €1.50, 2½hr tour adult/reduced €10/5; ◷ 9.30am-4pm Tue, Wed & Fri-Sun, closed Aug; Ⓜ Barberini) Overlooking Piazza del Quirinale, this immense palace is the official residence of Italy's head of state, the President of the Republic. For almost three centuries it was the pope's summer residence, but in 1870 Pope Pius IX begrudgingly handed the keys over to Italy's new king. Later, in 1948, it was given to the Italian state. Visits, by guided tour only, should be booked at least five days ahead by telephone (collect tour tickets at the nearby **Infopoint** at Salita di Montecavallo 15) or buy online at www.coopculture.it.

Caravaggio and Carracci paintings in Cerasi Chapel

SALAJEAN/GETTY IMAGES ©

Basilica di Santa Maria del Popolo

A magnificent repository of art, this is one of Rome's earliest and richest Renaissance churches, with lavish chapels decorated by artists including Caravaggio, Bernini, Raphael and Pinturicchio.

Great for...

☑ Don't Miss

As all eyes are turned on Caravaggio's canvases, don't miss Pinturicchio's wonderful frescoes.

The first chapel was built here in 1099 to exorcise the ghost of Nero, who was secretly buried on this spot and whose malicious spirit was thought to haunt the area. There were subsequent overhauls, but the church's most important makeover came when Bramante renovated the presbytery and choir in the early 16th century and Pinturicchio added a series of frescoes. Bernini further reworked the church in the 17th century.

Cerasi Chapel

The church's dazzling highlight is the Cappella Cerasi, which has two works by Caravaggio: the *Conversion of Saul* (1601) and the *Crucifixion of St Peter* (1601), dramatically spotlit via the artist's use of light and shade. The former is the second version, as the first was rejected by the patron. The central altarpiece painting is the *Assumption* (1590) by Annibale Carracci.

Habakkuk and the Angel by Lorenzo Bernini, Chigi chapel

ZVONIMIR ATLETIC/SHUTTERSTOCK ©

ⓘ Need to Know

Map p252; ☑392 3612243; www.smaria
delpopolo.com; Piazza del Popolo 12; ⊘7.30am-
noon & 4-7pm Mon-Fri, 7.30am-7pm Sat, 4.30-
6.30pm Sun; Ⓜ Flaminio

✕ Take a Break

Treat yourself to a sublime ice cream
from the magnificent **Fatamorgana** (☑06
3265 2238; www.gelateria.com; Via Laurina 10;
2/3/4/5 scoops €2.50/3.50/4.50/5; ⊘noon-
11pm; Ⓜ Flaminio).

★ Top Tip

Look out for the oldest stained-glass
windows in Rome.

Chigi Chapel

Raphael designed the Cappella Chigi,
dedicated to his patron Agostino Chigi,
but never lived to see it completed. Bernini
finished the job more than 100 years
later, contributing statues of Daniel and
Habakkuk to the altarpiece. Only the floor
mosaics were retained from Raphael's
original design, including that of a kneeling
skeleton, placed there to remind the living
of the inevitable.

Delle Rovere Chapel

This 15th-century chapel features works
by Pinturicchio and his school. Frescoes in
the *lunettes* (half-moon-shaped recesses)
depict episodes from the life of St Jerome,
while the main altarpiece shows the Nativity with St Jerome.

What's Nearby?

Piazza del Popolo   Piazza

(Ⓜ Flaminio) This dazzling piazza was laid out
in 1538 to provide a grandiose entrance to
what was then Rome's main northern gate-
way. It has since been remodelled several
times, most recently by Giuseppe Valadier
in 1823. Guarding its southern approach are
Carlo Rainaldi's twin 17th-century churches,
Chiesa di Santa Maria dei Miracoli and
Chiesa di Santa Maria in Montesanto.
In the centre, the 36m-high **obelisk** (Piazza
del Popolo) was brought by Augustus from
ancient Egypt; it originally stood in Circo
Massimo.

Via Margutta   Street

(Ⓜ Spagna) Small independent antiques
shops, art galleries and boutiques pepper Via
Margutta, one of Rome's prettiest pedestrian
cobbled lanes strung with ivy-laced *palazzi*,
decorative potted plants, marble-engraved
shop plaques and the odd monumental
fountain.

Facade

S TATIANA/SHUTTERSTOCK ©

Basilica di San Giovanni in Laterano

Dating to the 4th century, this monumental cathedral was the first Christian basilica built in the city, and until the late 14th century it was the pope's main place of worship.

Great for...

☑ Don't Miss

The Giotto fresco on the first column in the right-hand aisle.

The oldest of Rome's four papal basilicas was commissioned by Emperor Constantine and consecrated by Pope Sylvester I in 324. From then until 1309, when the papacy moved to Avignon, it was the principal pontifical church, and the adjacent Palazzo Laterano was the pope's official residence. Both buildings fell into disrepair during the papacy's French interlude, and when Pope Gregory XI returned to Rome in 1377 he preferred to decamp to the fortified Vatican rather than stay in the official papal digs.

The basilica has been revamped several times over the centuries, most notably by Borromini in the 17th century, and by Alessandro Galilei, who added the immense white facade in 1735.

Mosaic floor

❶ Need to Know

Piazza di San Giovanni in Laterano 4; Map p255 basilica free, cloister €3; ⏱7am-6.30pm, cloister 9am-6pm; Ⓜ San Giovanni

✕ Take a Break

Head south of the basilica for fabulous pizza at Sbanco (p138).

★ Top Tip

Look down as well as up – the basilica has a beautiful inlaid marble floor.

The Facade

Surmounted by 15 7m-high statues – Christ with St John the Baptist, John the Evangelist and the 12 Apostles – Galilei's huge facade is an imposing work of late-baroque classicism. The **central bronze doors** were moved here from the Curia in the Roman Forum, while, on the far right, the **Holy Door** is only opened in Jubilee years.

The Interior

The cavernous interior owes much of its present look to Francesco Borromini, who styled it for the 1650 Jubilee. It's a breathtaking sight with a golden gilt **ceiling**, a 15th-century **mosaic floor**, and a wide **nave** lined with 18th-century sculptures of the apostles, each 4.6m high and each set in its own dramatic niche.

At the end of the nave, an elaborate Gothic **baldachin** stands over the papal altar. Dating to the 14th century, this is said to contain the relics of the heads of Sts Peter and Paul. In front, a double staircase leads down to the **confessio** and the Renaissance tomb of Pope Martin V.

Behind the altar, the massive **apse** is decorated with sparkling mosaics. Parts of these date to the 4th century, but most were added in the 1800s.

At the other end of the basilica, on the first pillar in the right-hand aisle, is an incomplete Giotto fresco.

The Cloister

To the left of the altar, the basilica's 13th-century cloister is a lovely, peaceful place with graceful twisted columns set around a central garden. Lining the ambulatories are marble fragments from the original church, including the remains of a 5th-century papal throne and inscriptions of two papal bulls.

Spanish Steps

Rising above Piazza di Spagna, the Spanish Steps provide a perfect people-watching perch, and you'll almost certainly find yourself taking stock here at some point in your visit to Rome.

Great for...

☑ Don't Miss

The sweeping rooftop views from the top of the steps.

The area around the steps has long been a magnet for foreigners. In the late 1700s, it was much loved by English travellers on the Grand Tour, and was known locally as *'er ghetto de l'inglesi'* (the English ghetto). Poet John Keats lived for a short time in some rooms overlooking the Spanish Steps, and died here of tuberculosis at the age of 25. Later, in the 19th century, Charles Dickens visited, noting how artists' models would hang around in the hope of being hired to sit for a painting.

The Steps

Piazza di Spagna was named after the Spanish Embassy to the Holy See, but the 135-step staircase – known in Italian as the *Scalinata della Trinità dei Monti* – was designed by an Italian, Francesco de Sanctis, and built in 1725 with money bequeathed by the French.

ⓘ Need to Know

Map p252; Ⓜ Spagna

✕ Take a Break

Watch the sun set over the steps from the terrace of cocktail bar Il Palazzetto (p170).

★ Top Tip

Visit in late April or early May to see the steps ablaze with brightly coloured azaleas.

aqueduct, represent the Barberini family who commissioned the fountain.

Opposite the fountain, **Via dei Condotti** is Rome's most exclusive shopping strip, while to the southeast, Piazza Mignanelli is dominated by the **Colonna dell'Immacolata**, built in 1857 to celebrate Pope Pius IX's declaration of the Immaculate Conception.

What's Nearby?

Keats-Shelley House   Museum

(☏06 678 42 35; www.keats-shelley-house. org; Piazza di Spagna 26; adult/reduced €5/4; ◷10am-1pm & 2-6pm Mon-Sat; Ⓜ Spagna) The Keats-Shelley House is where Romantic poet John Keats died of tuberculosis at the age of 25, in February 1821. Keats came to Rome in 1820 to try to improve his health in the Italian climate, and rented two rooms on the 3rd floor of a townhouse next to the Spanish Steps, with painter companion Joseph Severn (1793–1879). Watch a film on the 1st floor about the Romantics, then head upstairs to see where Keats and Severn lived and worked.

Chiesa della Trinità dei Monti

The **Chiesa della Trinità dei Monti** (☏06 679 41 79; Piazza Trinità dei Monti 3; ◷7.30am-7pm Tue-Thu, noon-7pm Fri, 10am-5pm Sat & Sun; Ⓜ Spagna) was commissioned by King Louis XII of France and consecrated in 1585. As well as great rooftop views, it boasts some wonderful frescoes by Daniele da Volterra. His *Deposizione* (Deposition), in the second chapel on the left, is regarded as a masterpiece of mannerist painting.

Piazza di Spagna

At the foot of the steps, the fountain of a sinking boat, the **Barcaccia** (1627), is believed to be by Pietro Bernini, father of the more famous Giani Lorenzo. The bees and suns that decorate the structure, which is sunken to compensate for the low pressure of the feeder

Terme di Nettuno

BILL PERRY/SHUTTERSTOCK ©

Day Trip: Ostia Antica

Rome's answer to Pompeii, the Scavi Archeologici di Ostia Antica is one of Italy's most under-appreciated archaeological sites. The amazingly preserved ruins of Rome's main seaport provide a thrilling glimpse into the workings of an ancient town.

Great for...

☑ Don't Miss

The views over the site from atop the Terme di Nettuno.

Founded in the 4th century BC, the city started life as a fortified military camp guarding the mouth of the Tiber – hence the name: Ostia is a derivation of the Latin word *ostium* (mouth). It quickly grew, and by the 2nd century AD was a thriving port with a population of around 50,000.

Decline set in after the fall of the Roman Empire, and by the 9th century the city had largely been abandoned, its citizens driven off by barbarian raids and outbreaks of malaria. Over subsequent centuries, it was plundered of marble and building materials and its ruins were gradually buried in river silt, hence their survival.

To get to the site from Rome, take the Ostia Lido train from Stazione Porta San Paolo (next to Piramide metro station) and get off at Ostia Antica.

Marble mask ornaments

❶ Need to Know

☑06 5635 0215; www.ostiaantica.beniculturali.
it; Viale dei Romagnoli 717; adult/reduced €10/5;
⊙8.30am-6.15pm Tue-Sun summer, shorter
hours winter

✕ Take a Break

Lunch at the **Ristorante Monumento**
(☑06 565 00 21; www.ristorantemonumento.
it; Piazza Umberto I 8; meals €30-35; ⊙12.30-
2.45pm & 8-10pm Tue-Sun) in the picturesque *borgo* near the Scavi entrance.

★ Top Tip

Come on a weekday when it's much
quieter.

The Ruins

Near the entrance, **Porta Romana** gives
onto the **Decumanus Maximus**, the site's
central strip, which runs over 1km to Porta
Marina, the city's original sea-facing gate.

On the Decumanus, the **Terme di Nettuno** is a must-see. This baths complex, one
of 20 that originally stood in town, dates to
the 2nd century and boasts some superb
mosaics, including one of Neptune driving
his sea-horse chariot. In the centre of the
complex are the remains of an arcaded
palestra (gym).

Next to the Terme is the 1st-century BC
Teatro, an amphitheatre built by Agrippa
and later enlarged to hold 4000 people.

The grassy area behind the amphitheatre
is the **Piazzale delle Corporazioni** (Forum
of the Corporations), home to the offices
of Ostia's merchant guilds. The mosaics
that line the perimeter – ships, dolphins, a
lighthouse and an elephant – are thought
to represent the businesses housed on the
square: ships and dolphins indicated ship-
ping agencies, while the elephant probably
referred to a business involved in the ivory
trade.

The **Forum**, Ostia's main square, is overlooked by what remains of the **Capitolium**,
a temple built by Hadrian and dedicated to
Jupiter, Juno and Minerva.

Nearby is another highlight: the **Ther-
mopolium**, an ancient cafe, complete with
a bar, frescoed menu, kitchen and small
courtyard where customers would have
relaxed by a fountain.

Across the road are the remains of the
2nd-century **Terme del Foro**, originally
the city's largest baths complex. Here, in
the *forica* (public toilet), you can see 20
well-preserved latrines set sociably into a
long stone bench.

STEFANO_VALERI/SHUTTERSTOCK ©

Basilica di San Clemente

Nowhere better illustrates the various stages of Rome's turbulent past than this fascinating, multilayered church in the shadow of the Colosseum.

This fascinating basilica is in fact a series of buildings laid over each other: a 12th-century basilica sits atop a 4th-century church, which in turn stands over a 2nd-century pagan temple and a 1st-century Roman house.

Basilica Superiore

The street-level *basilica superiore* contains some glorious works of medieval art. These include a golden 12th-century apse mosaic, the *Trionfo della Croce* (Triumph of the Cross), showing the Madonna and St John the Baptist standing by a cross on which Christ is represented by 12 white doves. Also impressive are Masolino's 15th-century frescoes in the **Cappella di Santa Caterina**, depicting a crucifixion scene and episodes from the life of St Catherine.

Great for...

☑**Don't Miss**

The temple to Mithras, deep in the bowels of the basilica.

PARIS JEFFERSON/GETTY IMAGES ©

ℹ **Need to Know**

Map p255; ☏06 774 00 21; www.basilicasan clemente.com; Piazza di San Clemente; excavations adult/reduced €10/5; ⊙9am-12.30pm & 3-6pm Mon-Sat, 12.15-6pm Sun; 🚇Via Labicana

✕ **Take a Break**

Choose a daily special from laid-back **Il Bocconcino** (☏06 7707 9175; www.ilbocconcino.com; Via Ostilia 23; meals €30-35; ⊙12.30-3.30pm & 7.30-11.30pm Thu-Tue; 🚇Via Labicana).

★ **Top Tip**

Bring a sweater: the temperature drops underground.

Basilica Inferiore

Steps lead down to the 4th-century *basilica inferiore*. This was mostly destroyed by Norman invaders in 1084, but some faded 11th-century frescoes remain, illustrating the life of San Clemente.

Follow the steps down another level and you'll come to a 1st-century Roman house and a dark, 2nd-century **temple to Mithras**, with an altar showing the god slaying a bull. Beneath it all, you can hear the eerie sound of a subterranean river flowing through a Republic-era drain.

What's Nearby?
Basilica dei SS Quattro Coronati   Basilica

(☏335 495248; Via dei Santi Quattro 20; cloisters €2, Oratorio di San Silvestro €1; ⊙9.45am-11.45am & 3.45-5.45pm, cloisters closed Sun; 🚇Via di San

Giovanni in Laterano) This brooding fortified church harbours some lovely 13th-century frescoes and a delightful hidden **cloister**, accessible from the left-hand aisle. The frescoes, in the **Oratorio di San Silvestro**, depict the story of Constantine and Pope Sylvester I and the so-called Donation of Constantine, a notorious forged document with which the emperor supposedly ceded control of Rome and the Western Roman Empire to the papacy.

To access the Oratorio, ring the bell in the entrance courtyard.

Chiesa di Santo Stefano Rotondo   Church

(www.santo-stefano-rotondo.it; Via di Santo Stefano Rotondo 7; ⊙10am-1pm & 2.30-5.30pm winter, 10am-1pm & 3.30-6.30pm summer; 🚇Via Claudia) Set in its own secluded grounds, this haunting church boasts a porticoed facade and a round, columned interior. But what really gets the heart racing is the graphic wall decor – a cycle of 16th-century frescoes depicting the tortures suffered by many early Christian martyrs.

ALESSANDROCALZOLARO/GETTY IMAGES ©

Terme di Caracalla

The remains of the emperor Caracalla's vast baths complex are among Rome's most awe-inspiring ruins. Inaugurated in AD 216, the original 10-hectare complex comprised baths, gyms, libraries, shops and gardens.

Great for...

☑ **Don't Miss**

The white marble slab that was once part of an ancient board game.

The baths remained in continuous use until AD 537, when the invading Visigoths cut off Rome's water supply. Excavations in the 16th and 17th centuries unearthed a number of important sculptures, many of which found their way into the Farnese family's art collection.

In its heyday, the complex attracted up to 8000 people daily, while hundreds of slaves sweated in a 9.5km tunnel network, tending to the complex plumbing systems.

The Ruins

Most of the ruins are what's left of the central bath house. This was a huge rectangular edifice bookended by two **palestre** (gyms) and centred on a **frigidarium** (cold room), where bathers would stop after spells in the warmer **tepidarium** and dome-capped **caldarium** (hot room). As you traverse the ruins towards the *palestra orientale,* look out

❶ Need to Know

📞06 3996 7700; www.coopculture.it; Viale delle Terme di Caracalla 52; adult/reduced €8/4; ⊘9am-1hr before sunset Tue-Sun, 9am-2pm Mon; 🚌Viale delle Terme di Caracalla

✕ Take a Break

Pop by Casa Manfredi (p138) for an artisanal gelato or light lunch.

★ Top Tip

The Terme's virtual-reality video guide allows you to see how the original complex looked.

for a slab of white, pockmarked marble on your right. This is a board from an ancient game called *tropa* ('the hole game').

In summer the ruins are used to stage opera and ballet performances.

What's Nearby?

Villa Celimontana   Park

(Via della Navicella 12; ⊘7am-sunset; 🚌Via della Navicella) With its grassy banks and colourful flower beds, this leafy park is a wonderful place to escape the crowds and enjoy a summer picnic. At its centre is a 16th-century villa housing the Italian Geographical Society, while to the south stands a 12m-plus Egyptian obelisk.

Basilica di Santa Sabina   Basilica

(📞06 57 94 01; Piazza Pietro d'Illiria 1; ⊘8.15am-12.30pm & 3.30-6pm; 🚌Lungotevere Aventino) This solemn basilica, one of Rome's most beautiful early Christian churches, was founded by Peter of Illyria around AD 422. It was enlarged in the 9th century and again in 1216, just before it was given to the newly founded Dominican order – note the tombstone of Muñoz de Zamora, one of the order's founding fathers, in the nave floor. A 20th-century restoration returned it to its original look.

Villa del Priorato di Malta   Historic Building

(Villa Magistrale; Piazza dei Cavalieri di Malta; 🚌Lungotevere Aventino) Fronting an ornate cypress-shaded piazza, the Roman headquarters of the Sovereign Order of Malta, aka the Cavalieri di Malta (Knights of Malta), boasts one of Rome's most celebrated views. It's not immediately apparent, but look through the keyhole in the villa's green door and you'll see the dome of St Peter's Basilica perfectly aligned at the end of a hedge-lined avenue.

Palazzo della Civiltà Italiana

Modern Architecture

Rome is best known for its classical architecture, but the city also boasts a string of striking modern buildings, many created and designed by the 21st-century's top 'starchitects'.

Great for...

ⓘ **Need to Know**

The Auditorium and MAXXI can be accessed by tram 2 from Piazzale Flaminio.

★ **Top Tip**

Take in a gig at the Auditorium Parco della Musica (p188) to experience its perfect acoustics.

Auditorium Parco della Musica · Cultural Centre

(📞06 8024 1281; www.auditorium.com; Viale Pietro de Coubertin; guided tours adult/reduced €9/5; ⏱11am-8pm Mon-Sat, 10am-8pm Sun summer, to 6pm winter; 🚃Viale Tiziano) Designed by archistar Renzo Piano and inaugurated in 2002, Rome's flagship cultural centre is an audacious work of architecture consisting of three grey pod-like concert halls set round a 3000-seat amphitheatre.

Excavations during its construction revealed remains of an ancient Roman villa, which are now on show in the Auditorium's small **Museo Archeologico** `FREE`.

Guided tours of the Auditorium (for a minimum of 10 people) depart hourly between 11.30am and 4.30pm Saturday and Sunday, and by arrangement from Monday to Friday.

Museo Nazionale delle Arti del XXI Secolo · Gallery

(MAXXI; 📞06 320 19 54; www.maxxi.art; Via Guido Reni 4a; adult/reduced €12/8, permanent collection Tue-Fri & 1st Sun of month free; ⏱11am-7pm Tue-Fri & Sun, to 10pm Sat; 🚃Viale Tiziano) As much as the exhibitions, the highlight of Rome's leading contemporary art gallery is the Zaha Hadid–designed building it occupies. Formerly a barracks, the curved concrete structure is striking inside and out with a multilayered geometric facade and a cavernous light-filled interior full of snaking walkways and suspended staircases.

The gallery has a permanent collection of 20th- and 21st-century works, of which a selection are on free display in Gallery 4, but more interesting are its international exhibitions.

Museo dell'Ara Pacis

Museo dell'Ara Pacis   Museum

(📞06 06 08; www.arapacis.it; Lungotevere in Augusta; adult/reduced €10.50/8.50; 🕤9.30am-7.30pm; Ⓜ Flaminio) The first modern construction in Rome's historic centre since WWII, Richard Meier's controversial and widely detested glass-and-marble pavilion houses the *Ara Pacis Augustae* (Altar of Peace), Augustus' great monument to peace. One of the most important works of ancient Roman sculpture, the vast marble altar – measuring 11.6m by 10.6m by 3.6m – was completed in 13 BC.

> ☑ **Don't Miss**
>
> The outlying EUR district, which is home to some impressive rationalist architecture.

4KCLIPS/SHUTTERSTOCK

Palazzo della Civiltà Italiana   Historic Building

(Palace of Italian Civilisation; 📞06 3345 0970; www.fendi.com; Quadrato della Concordia; 🕤depends on exhibition; Ⓜ EUR Magliana) **FREE** Also known more prosaically as the Square Colosseum, this iconic building in the EUR district is a masterpiece of rationalist architecture with its symmetrical rows of 216 arches and gleaming white travertine marble. For much of its 72-year history – it was completed in 1943 – it has remained unoccupied, but in 2015 the Fendi fashion house transferred its global headquarters here. Watch for some dazzling contemporary-art exhibitions, hosted by the Italian fashion house, on the ground floor of the striking Fendi palace.

Rome Convention Centre La Nuvola   Architecture

(📞06 5451 3710; www.romaconventiongroup. it; Viale Asia, entrance cnr Via Cristoforo Colombo; Ⓜ EUR Fermi) Contemporary architecture buffs will appreciate Rome's brand-new congress centre, designed by Italian architects Massimiliano and Doriana Fuksas, and unveiled with much pomp and ceremony in late 2016. The striking building comprises a transparent, glass-and-steel box (40m high, 70m wide and 175m long) called **Le Theca** ('The Shrine'), inside of which hangs organically shaped **La Nuvola** ('The Cloud') containing an auditorium and conference rooms seating up to 8000 people. A separate black skyscraper called **La Luma** ('The Blade'), with a 439-room hotel, spa and restaurant, completes the ambitious €270 million ensemble.

> ✕ **Take a Break**
>
> Tucked away behind MAXXI, Neve di Latte (p139) serves scoops of near-perfect gelato.

PEN_85/SHUTTERSTOCK©

Basilica di Santa Maria Maggiore

One of Rome's four patriarchal basilicas, this monumental church stands on the summit of the Esquilino Hill, on the site of a miraculous snowfall in the summer of AD 358.

Great for...

☑ **Don't Miss**

The luminous 13th-century apse mosaics by Jacopo Torriti.

Much altered over the centuries, the basilica is something of an architectural hybrid, with a 14th-century Romanesque belfry, an 18th-century baroque facade, a largely baroque interior, and a series of glorious 5th-century mosaics.

Exterior

The basilica's exterior is decorated with glimmering 13th-century mosaics, protected by Ferdinand Fuga's baroque porch (1741). Rising behind, the 75m-high belfry is Rome's highest.

In front of the church, the 18.78m-high column originally stood in the Basilica of Massenzio in the Roman Forum.

Interior

The vast interior retains its original structure, despite the basilica's many overhauls.

ℹ **Need to Know**

Map p252; ☎06 6988 6800; Piazza Santa Maria Maggiore; basilica free, adult/reduced museum €3/2, museum & loggia €5/4; ⊙7am-6.45pm, loggia guided tours 9.30am-5.45pm; ☐Piazza Santa Maria Maggiore

✕ **Take a Break**

Decamp to Trattoria Monti (p133) for a taste of traditional cuisine from the Marches region.

★ **Top Tip**

Come on 5 August to see a magical recreation of the historic snowfall.

Particularly spectacular are the **5th-century mosaics** in the triumphal arch and nave, depicting Old Testament scenes. The central image in the apse, signed by Jacopo Torriti, dates from the 13th century and represents the coronation of the Virgin Mary. Beneath your feet, the nave floor is a fine example of 12th-century Cosmati paving.

The **baldachin** over the high altar is heavy with gilt cherubs; the altar itself is a porphyry sarcophagus, which is said to contain the relics of St Matthew and other martyrs.

A simple stone plaque embedded in the floor to the right of the altar marks the spot where Gian Lorenzo Bernini and his father Pietro are buried. Steps lead down to the **confessio** where a statue of Pope Pius IX kneels before a reliquary containing a fragment of Jesus' manger.

Through the souvenir shop on the right-hand side of the church is the **Museo del Tesoro** with a glittering collection of religious artefacts. Most interesting, however, is Ferdinando Fuga's **Loggia delle Benedizioni** (upper loggia; accessible only by guided tours). Here you can get a close look at the facade's iridescent 13th-century mosaics created by Filippo Rusuti, and Bernini's magnificent helical staircase.

What's Nearby?
Basilica di San
Pietro in Vincoli   Basilica

(☎06 9784 4950; Piazza di San Pietro in Vincoli 4a; ⊙8am-12.30pm & 3-7pm summer, to 6pm winter; ⓜCavour) Pilgrims and art lovers flock to this 5th-century basilica for two reasons: to marvel at Michelangelo's colossal *Moses* (1505) sculpture and to see the chains that supposedly bound St Peter when he was imprisoned in the Carcere Mamertino (near the Roman Forum). Access to the church is via a flight of steps through a low arch that leads up from Via Cavour.

Basilica di Santa Maria in Trastevere

PHOTOSHOOTER2015/SHUTTERSTOCK ©

Trastevere Treasures

On the left-bank of the Tiber, boho Trastevere is one of Rome's most vivacious neighbourhoods, its medieval lanes studded with art-rich churches and villas, bars, cafes and popular trattorias.

Great for...

☑**Don't Miss**

The golden mosaics in the Basilica di Santa Maria in Trastevere (p104).

Basilica di Santa Maria in Trastevere   Basilica

(☏06 581 48 02; Piazza Santa Maria in Trastevere; ⏱7.30am-9pm Sep-Jul, 8am-noon & 4-9pm Aug; ▣Viale di Trastevere, ▣Viale di Trastevere)
Nestled in a quiet corner of Trastevere's focal square, this is said to be the oldest church dedicated to the Virgin Mary in Rome. In its original form, it dates to the early 3rd century, but a major 12th-century makeover saw the addition of a Romanesque bell tower and glittering facade. The portico came later, added by Carlo Fontana in 1702. Inside, the 12th-century mosaics are the headline feature.

In the apse, look out for Christ and his mother flanked by various saints and, on the far left, Pope Innocent II holding a model of the church. Beneath this are six

Street dining in Trastevere

BORIS B/SHUTTERSTOCK ©

ⓘ Need to Know

To get to Trastevere, take tram 8 from Largo di Torre Argentina.

✕ Take a Break

A meal at Da Augusto (p134) offers an authentic trattoria experience.

★ Top Tip

Swing by the neighbourhood for an evening of aperitifs and lively drinking.

On the 1st floor, Peruzzi's dazzling frescoes in the Salone delle Prospettive are a superb illusionary perspective of a colonnade and panorama of 16th-century Rome.

mosaics by Pietro Cavallini illustrating the life of the Virgin (c 1291).

According to legend, the church stands on the spot where a fountain of oil miraculously sprang from the ground. It incorporates 21 ancient Roman columns, some plundered from the Terme di Caracalla, and boasts a 17th-century wooden ceiling.

Villa Farnesina   Historic Building
(📞06 6802 7268; www.villafarnesina.it; Via della Lungara 230; adult/reduced €6/5, guided tour €4; ⊘9am-2pm Mon-Sat, to 5pm 2nd Sun of the month; 🚋Lungotevere della Farnesina) The interior of this gorgeous 16th-century villa is fantastically frescoed from top to bottom. Several paintings in the Loggia of Cupid and Psyche and the Loggia of Galatea, both on the ground floor, are attributed to Raphael.

**Basilica di Santa
Cecilia in Trastevere**   Basilica
(📞06 589 92 89; www.benedettinesantacecilia. it; Piazza di Santa Cecilia 22; fresco & crypt each €2.50; ⊘basilica & crypt 9.30am-12.30pm & 4-6.30pm Mon-Sat, 11.30am-12.30pm & 4-6.30pm Sun, fresco 10am-12.30pm Mon-Sat, 11.30am-12.30pm Sun; 🚋Viale di Trastevere, 🚋Viale di Trastevere) The last resting place of the patron saint of music features Pietro Cavallini's stunning 13th-century fresco, in the nuns' choir of the hushed convent adjoining the church. Inside the church itself, Stefano Maderno's mysterious sculpture depicts St Cecilia's miraculously preserved body, unearthed in the Catacombs of San Callisto in 1599. You can also visit the excavations of Roman houses, one of which was possibly that of Cecilia.

PHOTOGOLFER/SHUTTERSTOCK ©

Galleria Doria Pamphilj

Hidden behind the grimy grey exterior of Palazzo Doria Pamphilj, this wonderful gallery boasts one of Rome's richest private art collections, with works by Raphael, Tintoretto, Brueghel, Titian, Caravaggio, Bernini and Velázquez.

Great for...

☑ Don't Miss

The *Ritratto di papa Innocenzo X* is generally considered the gallery's greatest masterpiece.

Palazzo Doria Pamphilj dates to the mid-15th century, but its current look was largely the work of the current owners, the Doria Pamphilj family, who acquired it in the 18th century. The Pamphilj's golden age, during which the family collection was started, came during the papacy of one of their own, Innocent X (r 1644–55).

The picture galleries are hung with floor-to-ceiling paintings, all ordered chronologically. Masterpieces abound but look out for Titian's *Salomè con la testa del Battista* (Salome with the Head of John the Baptist) and two early Caravaggio's: *Riposo durante la fuga in Egitto* (Rest During the Flight into Egypt) and *Maddalene Penitente* (Penitent Magdalen). Also of note is Alessandro Algardi's bust of Donna Olimpia, the formidable woman calling the shots behind

Innocent X's papacy. The star painting,
though, is Velázquez' portrait of Pope Innocent X, who grumbled that the depiction
was 'too real'. For a comparison, check out
Bernini's sculptural interpretation of the
same subject.

The excellent free audio guide, narrated
by Jonathan Pamphilj, brings the gallery
alive with family anecdotes and background information.

What's Nearby?
Chiesa del Gesù   Church

(☏06 69 70 01; www.chiesadelgesu.org; Piazza
del Gesù; ⊙7am-12.30pm & 4-7.45pm, St Ignatius
rooms 4-6pm Mon-Sat, 10am-noon Sun; 🚇Largo
di Torre Argentina) An imposing example of
Counter-Reformation architecture, Rome's
most important Jesuit church is a fabulous

treasure trove of baroque art. Headline
works include a swirling vault fresco by
Giovanni Battista Gaulli (aka Il Baciccia),
and Andrea del Pozzo's (1642–1709)
opulent tomb for Ignatius Loyola, the
Spanish soldier and saint who founded
the Jesuits in 1540. St Ignatius lived in the
church from 1544 until his death in 1556
and you can visit his private rooms to the
right of the main building in the Cappella di
Sant'Ignazio.

Chiesa di Sant'Ignazio
di Loyola   Church

(☏06 679 44 06; https://santignazio.gesuiti.it;
Piazza di Sant'Ignazio; ⊙7.30am-7pm Mon-Sat,
9am-7pm Sun; 🚇Via del Corso) Flanking a
delightful rococo piazza, this important
Jesuit church boasts a Carlo Maderno
facade and two celebrated *trompe l'oeil*
frescoes by Andrea Pozzo. One cleverly
depicts a fake dome, while the other, on
the nave ceiling, shows St Ignatius Loyola
being welcomed into paradise by Christ
and the Madonna.

Ceiling fresco by Pietro de Cortona

PHOTOGOLFER/SHUTTERSTOCK ©

Galleria Nazionale d'Arte Antica – Palazzo Barberini

Palazzo Barberini, one of Rome's grandest palaces, provides the sumptuous setting for a riveting collection of Old Masters and baroque masterpieces.

Great for...

☑ **Don't Miss**

Hans Holbein's celebrated depiction of King Henry VIII.

The *palazzo*, commissioned to celebrate the Barberini family's rise to papal power, impresses even before you clap eyes on the breathtaking art inside. Many of the 17th century's top architects worked on it, including Bernini, who designed a large square-shafted staircase, and Borromini, his hated rival who added a monumental helicoidal stairway.

Amid the artistic treasures on show, don't miss Pietro da Cortona's mind-blowing ceiling fresco, *Il Trionfo della Divina Provvidenza* (Triumph of Divine Providence; 1632–39), in the 1st-floor main salon. Other must-sees include Hans Holbein's famous portrait of a pugnacious Henry VIII (c 1540); Filippo Lippi's luminous *Annunciazione* (Annunciation); and Raphael's *La Fornarina* (The Baker's Girl), a portrait of his mistress, who worked in a bakery in Trastevere.

VINICIO TULLIO/SHUTTERSTOCK ©

Piazza Barberini
Via delle Quattro Fontane
Via Barberini
Barberini
Ⓜ
🅟 **Palazzo Barberini**
Via XX Settembre
Giardino del Quirinale

❶ Need to Know

Map p256; 📞06 481 45 91; www.barberinicors ini.org; Via delle Quattro Fontane 13; adult/re-duced incl Galleria Corsini €12/6; ⏱8.30am-7pm Tue-Sun; ⓂBarberini

✕ Take a Break

Treat yourself to fabulous regional cuisine from Emilia-Romagna at nearby Colline Emiliane (p128).

★ Top Tip

The **Galleria Corsini** (Palazzo Corsini; 📞06 6880 2323; www.barberinicorsini.org; Via della Lungara 10; adult/reduced incl Palaz-zo Barberini €12/6; ⏱8.30am-7pm Wed-Mon; 🚌Lungotevere della Farnesina) in Trastevere displays the rest of the Galleria Nazion-ale d'Arte Antica's collection.

Works by Caravaggio (1571-1610) include *San Francesco d'Assisi in meditazione* (St Francis in Meditation), *Narciso* (Narcissus) and the mesmerisingly horrific *Giuditta e Oloferne* (Judith Beheading Holophernes; c 1597–1600).

What's Nearby?

Chiesa di San Carlino alle Quattro Fontane
Church

(📞06 488 32 61; Via del Quirinale 23; ⏱10am-1pm Mon-Sat, noon-1pm Sun; 🚌Via Nazionale) This tiny church is a masterpiece of Roman baroque. It was Borromini's first church, and the play of convex and concave surfaces and the dome illuminated by hidden windows cleverly transform the small space into a place of light and beauty. The church, completed in 1641, stands at the intersection known as the **Quattro Fontane**, named after the late-16th-century fountains on its four corners, representing Fidelity, Strength and the rivers Arno and Tiber.

Convento dei Cappuccini
Museum

(📞06 8880 3695; www.cappucciniviaveneto.it; Via Vittorio Veneto 27; adult/reduced €8.50/5; ⏱9am-7pm; ⓂBarberini) This church and convent complex safeguards what is pos-sibly Rome's strangest sight: crypt chapels where everything from the picture frames to the light fittings is made of human bones. Between 1732 and 1775 resident Capuchin monks used the bones of 3700 of their departed brothers to create this ma-cabre *memento mori* (reminder of death) – a 30m-long passageway ensnaring six crypts, each named after the type of bone used to decorate it (skulls, shin bones, pelvises etc).

Avenue of the Hundred Fountains

Day Trip: Tivoli

A summer retreat for ancient Romans and the Renaissance rich, the hilltop town of Tivoli is home to two Unesco World Heritage Sites: sprawling Villa Adriana and the 16th-century Villa d'Este.

Great for...

☑ Don't Miss

Admire the rich mannerist frescoes of Villa d'Este before heading into the gardens.

Villa d'Este

In Tivoli's hilltop centre, the steeply terraced grounds of **Villa d'Este** (☎0774 33 29 20; www.villadestetivoli.info; Piazza Trento 5; adult/reduced €8/4; ☺8.30am-7.45pm Tue-Sun, 2-7.45pm Mon, gardens close 5pm, ticket office closes 6.45pm) are a superlative example of a Renaissance garden, complete with monumental fountains, elegant tree-lined avenues and landscaped grottoes. The villa, originally a Benedictine convent, was converted into a luxury retreat by Lucrezia Borgia's son, Cardinal Ippolito d'Este, in the late 16th century. It provided inspiration for composer Franz Liszt who stayed here between 1865 and 1886, and immortalised it in his 1877 piano composition *The Fountains of the Villa d'Este*.

Villa d'Este

In the gardens, look out for the Bernini-designed **Fountain of the Organ**, which uses water pressure to play music through a concealed organ, and the 130m-long **Avenue of the Hundred Fountains**.

Villa Adriana

The ruins of Emperor Hadrian's vast country **villa** (☏0774 38 27 33; www.villaadriana.benic ulturali.it; Largo Marguerite Yourcenar 1; adult/reduced €8/4; ☺9am-1hr before sunset), 5km outside Tivoli proper, are quite magnificent, easily on a par with anything you'll see in Rome. Built between AD 118 and 138, the villa was one of the largest in the ancient world, encompassing more than 120 hectares – of which about 40 are now open to the public. You'll need several hours to explore.

ⓘ Need to Know

Information is available from the **tourist information point** (☏0774 31 35 36; Piazzale delle Nazioni Unite; ☺10am-1pm & 4-6pm Tue-Sun) near where the bus arrives.

✕ Take a Break

Enjoy a meal with a view at **Sibilla** (☏0774 33 52 81; www.ristorantesibilla.com; Via della Sibilla 50; meals €40-50; ☺12.30-3pm & 7.30-10.30pm Tue-Sun) in the hilltop centre.

★ Top Tip

Tivoli makes an excellent day trip from Rome, but to cover its two main sites you'll have to start early.

Must-see sights include the **canopo**, a landscaped canal overlooked by a *nymphaeum* (shrine to the water nymph), and the **Teatro Marittimo**, Hadrian's personal refuge. To the east, **Piazza d'Oro** makes for a memorable picture, particularly in spring when its grassy centre is cloaked in yellow wildflowers.

There are also several bath complexes, temples and barracks.

Getting There & Around

Tivoli lies 30km east of Rome. It's accessible by Cotral bus (€1.30, 50 minutes, at least twice hourly) from Ponte Mammolo metro station. By car, take Via Tiburtina or the quicker Rome–L'Aquila autostrada (A24). Trains run from Rome's Stazione Tiburtina to Tivoli (€2.60, one hour, at least hourly).

The best way to see both main sites is to visit Villa d'Este first, then have lunch up in the centre, before heading down to Villa Adriana. To get to the villa from the centre, take local CAT bus 4 or 4X (€1.30, 10 minutes, half-hourly) from Piazza Garibaldi. After you've visited Villa Adriana, pick up the Cotral bus back to Rome.

Centro Storico Piazzas

Rome's historic centre boasts some of the city's most celebrated piazzas, and several lovely but lesser-known squares. Each has its own character but together they encapsulate much of the city's beauty, history and drama.

Start Piazza Colonna
Distance 1.5km
Duration 3.5 hours

Classic Photo Pantheon

4 It's a short walk along Via del Seminario to **Piazza della Rotonda**, where the **Pantheon** (p50) needs no introduction.

5 Piazza Navona (p112) is Rome's great showpiece square, where you can compare the two giants of Roman baroque – Gian Lorenzo Bernini and Francesco Borromini.

Piazza Navona

Corso del Rinascimento

Salita dei Crescenzi

Via degli Staderari

Via della Rotonda

Via del Canestrari

Via Monterone

Piazza di San Pantaleo

Via dei Cappellari

Corso Vittorio Emanuele II

Via dei Baullari

Via del Monserrato

Lgt dei Tebaldi

Via dei Farnesi

Via dei Giubbonari

FINISH

Take a Break...

Those in the know head to **Forno di Campo de' Fiori** (www.fornocampo defiori.com; pizza slices around €3) for some of Rome's best *pizza bianca* ('white' pizza with olive oil and salt).

7 Just beyond the Campo, the more sober **Piazza Farnese** is looked over by the austere facade of the Renaissance Palazzo Farnese.

1 Piazza Colonna is dominated by the 30m-high Colonna di Marco Aurelio and flanked by Palazzo Chigi, the official residence of the Italian PM.

2 Follow Via dei Bergamaschi to **Piazza di Pietra**, a refined space overlooked by the 2nd-century Tempio di Adriano.

3 Continue down Via de' Burro to **Piazza di Sant'Ignazio Loyola**, a small piazza with a **church** (p107) boasting celebrated *trompe l'œil* frescoes.

6 On the other side of Corso Vittorio Emanuele II, **Campo de' Fiori** (p65) hosts a noisy market and boisterous drinking scene.

START

Piazza di Montecitorio

Via di Pietra

Via dei Pastini

Via del Seminario

Via del Caravita

Via della Minerva

Via di Sant'Ignazio

1 GRINCHENKOVA ANZHELA/SHUTTERSTOCK © 4 KAMIRA/SHUTTERSTOCK © 5 IAKOV KALININ/SHUTTERSTOCK © 6 MATEJ KASTELIC/SHUTTERSTOCK ©

Literary Footsteps

This walk through the Tridente district explores the literary haunts, both real and fictional, that litter the area. Discover the cafe where Casanova drank, the hotel that inspired Cocteau and the house where Keats breathed his last.

Start Pincio Hill Gardens
Distance 1km
Duration 2 hours

2 Dan Brown's *Angels and Demons* made use of the art-rich **Basilica di Santa Maria del Popolo** (p86) in its convoluted plot.

3 Jean Cocteau stayed at the **Hotel de Russie** (p170) with Picasso, and wrote a letter home describing picking oranges from outside his window.

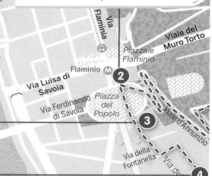

4 Cobbled **Via Margutta** (p87) is where Truman Capote wrote his short story *Lola*. Fellini, Picasso, Stravinsky and Puccini all lived here at some point.

TRIDENTE

COLONNA

N 0 ————— 500 m
   0 ————— 0.25 miles

1 Begin your walk in the panoramic **Pincio Hill Gardens** (p57), where Henry James' Daisy Miller walked with Frederick Winterborne.

VILLA BORGHESE

Viale dell' Obelisco

Viale delle Magnolie

1 START

Galoppatoio

Viale del Muro Torto

Viale Trinità dei Monti

Via Margutta

Via Alibert

CAMPO MARZIO

M Spagna

Via di Porta Pinciana

Piazza di Spagna

Via delle Carrozze

Via dei Condotti

5

6

7

FINISH Piazza Mignanelli

Via Sistina

Via Mario de' Fi

Via dei Due Mace

Classic Photo Spanish Steps

6 Leaving the cafe, you're almost at the **Spanish Steps** (p90), which Dickens described in his *Pictures from Italy*. Byron stayed at 25 Piazza di Spagna in 1817.

Take a Break Compose your own whimsical tale in the Hassler Hotel's romantic rooftop restaurant, **Imàgo** (p128).

7 Overlooking the Spanish Steps, the **Keats-Shelley House** (p91) is now a small museum devoted to the Romantic poets.

5 Head to Via dei Condotti, where William Thackeray stayed, and stop at **Antico Caffè Greco** (p126), a former haunt of Casanova, Goethe, Keats, Byron and Shelley.

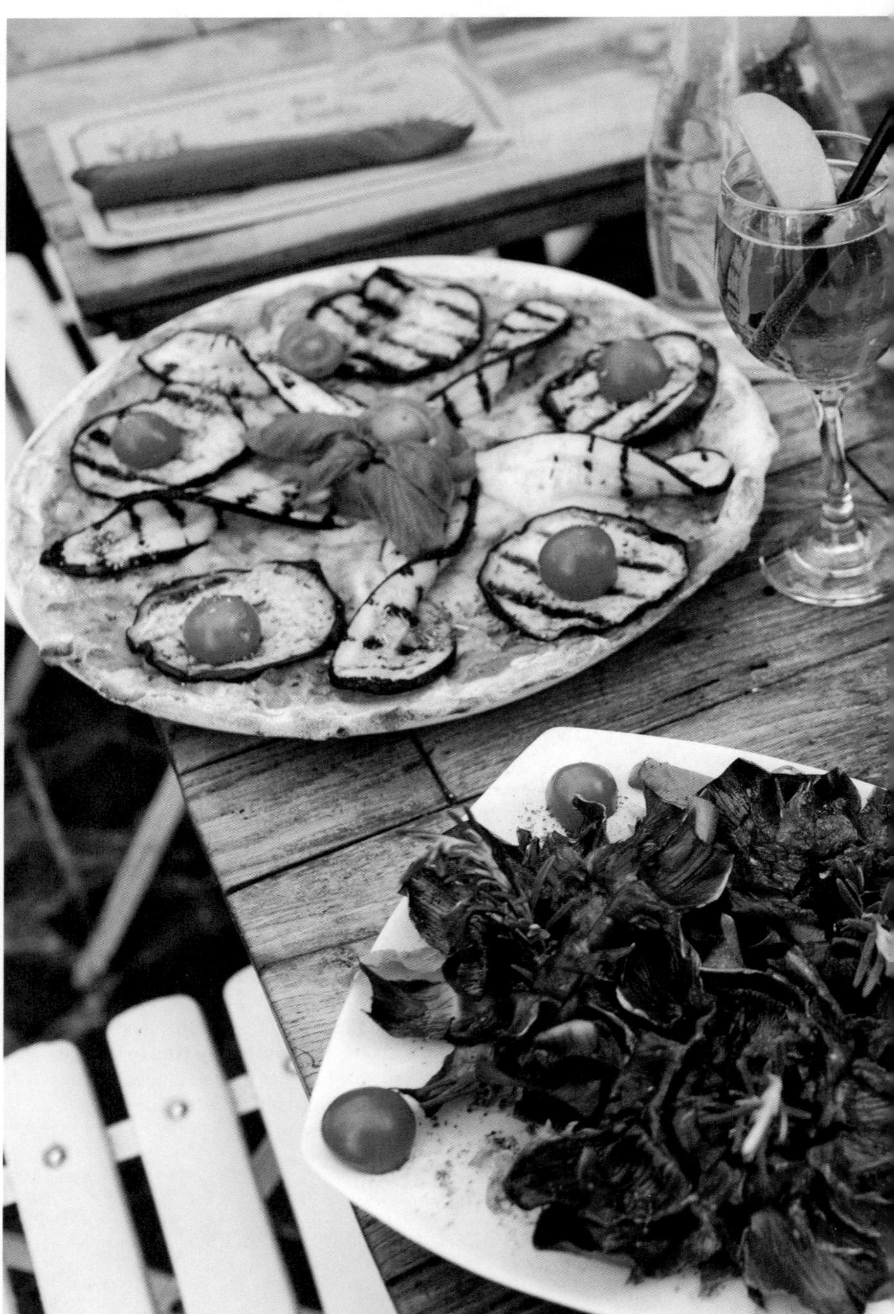

CHRISTINE WEHRMEIER/GETTY IMAGES ©

DINING OUT

Pizza, pasta and delicious gelato

Dining Out

This is a city that lives to eat. Food feeds the Roman soul, and a social occasion would be nothing without it.

In recent years, Rome's foodscape has undergone something of a transformation. Trends for all-day dining and street-food have led to new openings, and fine dining has blossomed, fuelling a taste for contemporary Roman cuisine. But the city hasn't lost sight of its culinary roots and you'll still find legions of family-run trattorias dotted around its streets and piazzas. These humble eateries have fed visitors for centuries and still provide some of the city's most memorable dining experiences.

In This Section

Price Ranges

The following price ranges refer to a meal that includes *primo* (first course), *secondo* (second course) and *dolce* (dessert), plus a glass of wine.

€ less than €25

€€ €25–€45

€€€ more than €45

Tipping

Although service is included, leave a tip: anything from 5% in a pizzeria to 10% in a more upmarket place. At least round up the bill.

Vatican City, Borgo & Prati
Sophisticated restaurants, delicious takeaways, heavenly gelaterie (p129)

Villa Borghese & Northern Rome
Park cafes and smart, fashionable restaurants (p139)

Tridente, Trevi & the Quirinale
Classy neighbourhood eateries, great gelaterie and upmarket cafes (p126)

Centro Storico
Romantic hideaways, old-school trattorias, top pizzerias (p122)

Monti, Esquilino & San Lorenzo
Ethnic eats, cool bars, boho restaurants (p131)

Ancient Rome
Hidden gems among the tourist traps (p122)

Trastevere & Gianicolo
Touristy but terrific trattorias, gelaterie, bars and pizzerias (p134)

San Giovanni & Testaccio
Traditional Roman cuisine, good cheap eats (p137)

Southern Rome
Trend-setting foodie venues in ex-industrial Ostiense district (p140)

Useful Phrases

I'd like to reserve a table for... Vorrei prenotare un tavolo per... (Vo.*ray* pre. no.*ta*.re oon *ta*.vo.lo per...)

two people due persone (*doo*.e per. *so*.ne)

eight o'clock le otto (le *o*.to)

What would you recommend? Cosa mi consiglia? (*ko*.za mee kon.*see*.lya)

Can I have the bill please? Mi porta il conto, per favore? (mee *por*.taeel *kon*.to per fa.vo.re)

Must Try

Bucatini all'amatriciana Thick spaghetti with a tomato pancetta sauce spiked with chilli.

Cacio e pepe Pasta with *pecorino romano* (sheep's milk cheese), black pepper and olive oil.

Carciofi alla giudia Deep-fried 'Jewish-style' artichokes.

Pizza bianca Sliced pizza with no tomato topping, just salt and olive oil.

The Best...

Experience Rome's top restaurants and cafes

See & Be Seen

Said (p134) Hipster all-rounder in a 1920s chocolate factory in San Lorenzo.

Il Sorpasso (p130) Vintage-styled bar restaurant, haunt of trendy Prati crowd.

Temakinho (p133) Hip, Brazilian-sushi hybrid in Monti.

Gelateria

Fatamorgana (p129) Rome's finest artisanal flavours in multiple locations.

Gelateria del Teatro (p123) Around 40 delicious choices, all made on site.

Gelateria Dei Gracchi (p127) A taste of heaven in several locations.

Fior di Luna (p135) Great artisan ice cream in Trastevere.

Neve di Latte (p139) Classic flavours near MAXXI art museum.

Local Hangouts

Da Felice (p139) Traditional Roman cooking in Testaccio.

Da Teo (p137) Popular trattoria on a pretty Trastevere piazza.

Pizza Ostiense (p141) Fabulous thin-crust pizza in hip Ostiense neighbourhood.

Hostaria Romana (p127) Buzzing trattoria, footsteps from the Trevi Fountain.

Modern Roman

Glass Hostaria (p139) Innovative cuisine by celebrity chef Cristina Bowerman.

Antonello Colonna Open (p134) Antonello Colonna's creative takes on Roman classics.

Ristorante L'Arcangelo (p131) Updated takes on classic Roman dishes at this Prati hotspot.

Pianostrada (p124) Uberfashionable, bistro-and-bar dining.

Settings

Aroma (p139) Michelin-starred rooftop restaurant with 'marry-me' Colosseum views.

Casa Bleve (p125) Gracious colonnaded wine bar with a stained-glass ceiling.

Caffetteria Chiostro del Bramante (p123) Hidden cafe overlooking Bramante's graceful Renaissance cloister.

Pizzerias

Sbanco (p138) Creative pizzas, craft beer, casual bar-like setting.

Romeo e Giulietta (p138) Sensational pizzas and contemporary design at Testaccio newcomer.

Emma Pizzeria (p124) Excellent wood-fired pizzas in the historic centre.

Pizzeria Da Remo (p138) Spartan but stunning: for the frenetic Roman pizzeria experience.

Fast Food

Trapizzino (p137) Trend-setting home of the *trapizzino* snack.

Mercato Centrale (p128) For gourmet food fast at Termini station.

Supplizio (p124) Creative versions of fried rice balls, *supplì*.

Fa-Bio (p129) Popular organic takeaway near the Vatican.

Mordi e Vai (p138) Classic Roman street food at acclaimed food stall.

★ Lonely Planet's Top Choices

Pianostrada (p124) Urban bistro chic in the *centro storico*.

Panella (p131) The ultimate budget-dine ticket, any time of day.

Sbanco (p138) Hit pizzeria with a buzzy, warehouse-vibe.

Pizzarium (p129) Sliced pizza to go from Rome's master pizza maker.

La Ciambella (p124) Hybrid restaurant-bar by the Pantheon.

⊗ Ancient Rome

Terrazza Caffarelli   Cafe €

(Caffetteria dei Musei Capitolini; ☑06 6919 0564; Piazzale Caffarelli 4; ⊘9.30am-7pm; ☐Piazza Venezia) The Capitoline Museums' stylish terrace cafe is a memorable place to relax over a drink or light lunch (*panini,* salads, pastas) and swoon over magical views of the city's domes and rooftops. Although it is part of the museum complex, you don't need a ticket to come here as it has an independent entrance on Piazzale Caffarelli.

Terre e Domus   Lazio €€

(☑06 6994 0273; Via Foro Traiano 82-4; meals €30-40; ⊘8.30am-midnight Mon & Wed-Sat, 10am-midnight Sun; ☐Via dei Fori Imperiali) This modern white-and-glass restaurant is the best option in the touristy Forum area. With minimal decor and large windows overlooking the Colonna di Traiano, it's a relaxed spot to sit down to traditional local staples, all made with ingredients sourced from the surrounding Lazio region, and a glass or two of regional wine.

Ristorante Roof Garden Circus   Ristorante €€€

(☑06 678 78 16; www.fortysevenhotel.com; Forty Seven Hotel, Via Petroselli 47; meals €65; ⊘noon-10.30pm; ☐Via Petroselli) The rooftop of the Forty Seven hotel sets the romantic stage for chef Giacomo Tasca's seasonal menu of classic Roman dishes and contemporary Mediterranean cuisine. With the Aventino hill rising in the background, you can tuck into stalwarts such as spaghetti *ajo e ojio* (with garlic and olive oil) or opt for something richer like fillet of beef with zucchini, peppermint and roasted peppers.

⊗ Centro Storico

Caffè Sant'Eustachio   Coffee €

(www.santeustachioilcaffe.it; Piazza Sant'Eusta-chio 82; ⊘8.30am-1am Sun-Thu, to 1.30am Fri, to 2am Sat; ☐Corso del Rinascimento) This small, unassuming cafe, generally three deep at the bar, is reckoned by many to serve the best coffee in town. To make it, the bartenders sneakily beat the first drops of an espresso with several teaspoons of sugar to create a

Caffè Sant'Eustachio

frothy paste to which they add the rest of the coffee. It's superbly smooth and guaranteed to put some zing into your sightseeing.

Roscioli Caffè   Cafe €

(☑06 8916 5330; www.rosciolicaffe.com; Piazza Benedetto Cairoli 16; ⊘7am-11pm Mon-Sat, 8am-6pm Sun; 🚇Via Arenula) The Roscioli name is a sure bet for good food and drink in this town: the family runs one of Rome's most celebrated delis (p125) and a hugely popular bakery and this cafe doesn't disappoint either. The coffee is wonderfully luxurious, and the artfully crafted pastries, petits fours and *panini* taste as good as they look.

La Casa del
Caffè Tazza d'Oro   Coffee €

(☑06 678 97 92; www.tazzadorocoffeeshop. com; Via degli Orfani 84-86; ⊘7am-8pm Mon-Sat, 10.30am-7.30pm Sun; 🚇Via del Corso) A busy, stand-up affair with burnished 1940s fittings, this is one of Rome's best coffee houses. Its espresso hits the mark nicely and there's a range of delicious coffee concoctions, including a cooling *granita di caffè,* a crushed-ice coffee drink served with whipped cream. There's also a small shop and, outside, a coffee *bancomat* for those out-of-hours caffeine emergencies.

Forno Roscioli   Pizza, Bakery €

(☑06 686 40 45; www.anticofornoroscioli.it; Via dei Chiavari 34; pizza slices from €2, snacks €2.50; ⊘7am-7.30pm Mon-Sat, 8am-6pm Sun; 🚇Via Arenula) This is one of Rome's top bakeries, much loved by lunching locals who crowd here for luscious sliced pizza, prize pastries and hunger-sating *supplì* (risotto balls). The pizza margherita is superb, if messy to eat, and there's also a counter serving hot pastas and vegetable side dishes.

Tiramisù Zum   Desserts €

(☑06 6830 7836; www.zumroma.it; Piazza del Teatro di Pompeo 20; desserts €2.50-6; ⊘11am-11pm Sun-Thu, to 1am Fri & Sat; 🚇Corso Vittorio Emanuele II) The ideal spot for a mid-afternoon pick-me-up, this fab dessert bar specialises in tiramisu, that magnificent marriage of mascarpone and liqueur-soaked ladyfinger biscuits. Choose between the classic version with its

---

🍴 Neighbourhood Specialities

The Jewish Ghetto is the place to try *cucina ebraico-romanesca* (Roman-Jewish cooking). Developed between the 16th and 19th centuries when the city's Jews were confined to the ghetto, this hybrid cuisine features a lot of deep-fried dishes, including the neighbourhood's signature *carciofo alla giudia* (Jewish-style artichoke).

To the south of the centre, Testaccio is renowned for its nose-to-tail cuisine. In the past, the district was home to Rome's main slaughterhouse and recipes were created to incorporate the cheap off-cuts abattoir workers were given with their wages. Nowadays, dishes such as *coda alla vaccinara* (oxtail) and pasta with *pajata* (veal's intestines) are much-loved local specialities served in trattorias across the neighbourhood.

---

cocoa powdering or one of several tempting variations – with pistachio nuts, blackberries and raspberries, and Amarena cherries.

Gelateria del Teatro   Gelato €

(☑06 4547 4880; www.gelateriadelteatro.it; Via dei Coronari 65; gelato from €2.50; ⊘10.30am-8pm winter, 10am-10.30pm summer; 🚇Via Zanardelli) All the ice cream served at this excellent gelateria is prepared on-site – look through the window and you'll see how. There are about 40 flavours to choose from, all made from thoughtfully sourced ingredients such as hazelnuts from the Langhe region of Piedmont and pistachios from Bronte in Sicily.

Caffetteria Chiostro
del Bramante   Cafe €

(☑06 6880 9036; www.chiostrodelbramante.it; Via Arco della Pace 5; meals €15-25; ⊘10am-8pm Mon-Fri, to 9pm Sat & Sun; 🛜; 🚇Corso del Rinascimento) Many of Rome's galleries and museums have in-house cafes, but few are as beautifully located as the Caffetteria Chiostro del Bramante on the 1st floor of Bramante's elegant Renaissance cloister. With outdoor

works of art. Curated in every detail, they look superb and taste magnificent, from traditional breakfast *cornetti* (croissants) to *cannoli*, mono-portions of cheesecake and a selection of sumptuous burgers.

⫷◯⫸ Vegetarian Rome

Vegetarians eat exceedingly well in Rome, with a wide choice of bountiful antipasti, pasta dishes, *insalate* (salads), *contorni* (side dishes) and pizzas. Some high-end restaurants such as **Imàgo** (p128) even serve a vegetarian menu, and slowly but surely, exclusively vegetarian and/or vegan eateries and cafes are cropping up: try **Babette** (p128) and **Il Margutta** (p127) near the Spanish Steps, or **Vitaminas 24** (p132) in edgy Pigneto.

Babette
LOTTIE DAVIES/LONELY PLANET ©

tables overlooking the central courtyard and an all-day menu offering everything from cakes and coffee to baguettes, risottos and Caesar salads, it's a great spot for a break.

I Dolci di Nonna Vincenza
Pastries, Cafe €

(⫷🕿⫸06 9259 4322; www.dolcinonnavincenza. it; Via Arco del Monte 98a; pastries from €2.50; ⏱7.30am-8.30pm Mon-Sat, from 8am Sun; ⫷🚇⫸Via Arenula) Bringing the flavours of Sicily to Rome, this pastry shop is a real joy. Browse the traditional cakes and tempting *dolci* (sweet pastries) in the old wooden dressers, before adjourning to the adjacent bar to tear into the heavenly selection of creamy, flaky, puffy pastries and ricotta-stuffed *cannoli*.

Pasticceria De Bellis
Pastries €

(⫷🕿⫸06 686 1480; Piazza del Paradiso 56-57; pastries €3.50-6, burgers €6-12; ⏱9am-8pm; ⫷🚇⫸Corso Vittorio Emanuele II) The beautifully crafted cakes, pastries and *dolci* made at this chic *pasticceria* are miniature

Supplizio
Fast Food €

(⫷🕿⫸06 8916 0053; www.supplizioroma.it; Via dei Banchi Vecchi 143; supplì €3-7; ⏱11.30am-4pm & 4.30-10pm Mon-Sat; ⫷🚇⫸Corso Vittorio Emanuele II) Rome's favourite snack, the *supplì* (a fried croquette filled with rice, tomato sauce and mozzarella), gets a gourmet makeover at this elegant street-food joint. Sit back on the vintage leather sofa and dig into a crispy classic or push the boat out and try something different, maybe a little fish number stuffed with fresh anchovies, cheese, bread and raisins.

Pianostrada
Ristorante €€

(⫷🕿⫸06 8957 2296; www.facebook.com/pianostrada; Via delle Zoccolette 22; meals €40; ⏱1-4pm & 7pm-midnight Tue-Fri, 10am-midnight Sat & Sun; ⫷🚇⫸Via Arenula) Hatched in foodie Trastevere but now across the river in a mellow white space with vintage furnishings and glorious summer courtyard, this bistro is a fashionable must. Reserve ahead, or settle for a stool at the bar and enjoy big bold views of the kitchen at work. Cuisine is refreshingly creative, seasonal and veg-packed, including gourmet open sandwiches and sensational homemade focaccia as well as full-blown mains.

Emma Pizzeria
Pizza €€

(⫷🕿⫸06 6476 0475; www.emmapizzeria.com; Via del Monte della Farina 28-29; pizzas €8-18, meals €35; ⏱12.30-3pm & 7-11.30pm; ⫷🚇⫸Via Arenula) Tucked in behind the Chiesa di San Carlo ai Catinari, this smart, modern pizzeria is a top spot for a cracking pizza and smooth craft beer (or a wine from its pretty extensive list). It's a stylish set-up with outdoor seating and a spacious, art-clad interior, and a menu that lists seasonal, wood-fired pizzas alongside classic Roman pastas and mains.

La Ciambella
Italian €€

(⫷🕿⫸06 683 29 30; www.la-ciambella.it; Via dell'Arco della Ciambella 20; meals €35-45; ⏱bar 8am-midnight Tue-Sat, from 10am Sun, wine bar & restaurant noon-11pm Tue-Sun; ⫷🚇⫸Largo di Torre

Argentina) Central but largely undiscovered by the tourist hordes, this friendly wine-bar-cum-restaurant beats much of the neighbourhood competition. Its spacious, light-filled interior is set over the ruins of the Terme di Agrippa, visible through transparent floor panels, and its kitchen sends out some excellent food, from tartares and chickpea pancakes to slow-cooked beef and traditional Roman pastas.

Armando al Pantheon   Roman €€
(✆06 6880 3034; www.armandoalpantheon. it; Salita dei Crescenzi 31; meals €40; ⏱12.30-3pm Mon-Sat & 7-11pm Mon-Fri; 🚇Largo di Torre Argentina) With its cosy wooden interior and unwavering dedication to old-school Roman cuisine, Armando al Pantheon is a regular go-to for local foodies. It has been on the go for more than 50 years and has served its fair share of celebs, but it hasn't let fame go to its head and it remains as popular as ever. Reservations essential.

Retrobottega   Ristorante €€
(✆06 6813 6310; www.retro-bottega.com; Via della Stelletta 4; meals €38-60; ⏱7-11.30pm Mon, from noon Tue-Sun; 🚇Corso del Rinascimento) Something of a departure for Rome, Retro-bottega is an advocate of the casual dining experience. Here you'll be setting your own place and sitting at high bar-style tables or a counter overlooking the open kitchen. The food, in keeping with the young, modern vibe, is creative and artfully presented.

Osteria dell'Ingegno   Italian €€
(✆06 678 06 62; www.osteriadellingegno.com; Piazza di Pietra 45; meals €35-45; ⏱10am-1am; 🚇Via del Corso) An all-day restaurant wine-bar with a colourful, art-filled interior, a casual, inclusive vibe, and a prime location on a charming central piazza. The daily menu hits all the right notes with a selection of seasonal pastas, creative mains and homemade desserts, while the 200-strong wine list boasts some interesting Italian labels.

Renato e Luisa   Roman €€
(✆06 686 96 60; www.renatoeluisa.it; Via dei Barbieri 25; meals €35-45; ⏱8pm-12.30am Tue-Sun; 🚇Largo di Torre Argentina) Highly rated locally, this small backstreet trattoria is often

packed. Chef Renato's menu features updated Roman classics that are modern and seasonal but also undeniably local, such as his signature *cacio e pepe e fiori di zucca* (pasta with pecorino cheese, black pepper and courgette flowers). Bookings recommended.

Ditirambo   Trattoria €€
(✆06 687 16 26; www.ristoranteditirambo. it; Piazza della Cancelleria 74; meals €35-40; ⏱12.45-3.15pm & 7-11pm, closed Mon lunch; 🚇Corso Vittorio Emanuele II) Since opening in 1996, Ditirambo continues to win diners over with its informal trattoria vibe and seasonal, organic cuisine. Dishes cover many bases, ranging from old-school favourites to thoughtful vegetarian offerings and more exotic fare such as a *millefoglie* of sea bream and crunchy artichokes. Book ahead.

Salumeria Roscioli   Deli, Ristorante €€€
(✆06 687 52 87; www.salumeriaroscioli.com; Via dei Giubbonari 21; meals €55; ⏱12.30-4pm & 7pm-midnight Mon-Sat; 🚇Via Arenula) The name Roscioli has long been a byword for foodie excellence in Rome, and this luxurious deli-restaurant is the place to experience it. Tables are set alongside the deli counter, laden with mouth-watering Italian and foreign delicacies, and in a small bottle-lined space behind it. The sophisticated food is top notch and there are some truly outstanding wines to go with it.

Casa Bleve   Ristorante €€€
(✆06 686 59 70; www.casableve.it; Via del Teatro Valle 48-49; meals €55-70; ⏱12.30-3pm & 7.30-11pm Mon-Sat; 🚇Largo di Torre Argentina) Ideal for a special-occasion dinner, this palatial restaurant-wine-bar dazzles with its column-lined dining hall and stained-glass roof. Its wine list, one of the best in town, accompanies a refined menu of creative antipasti, seasonal pastas and classic main courses.

Casa Coppelle   Ristorante €€€
(✆06 6889 1707; www.casacoppelle.com; Piazza delle Coppelle 49; meals €65, tasting menu €90; ⏱noon-3.30pm & 7pm-midnight; 🚇Corso del Rinascimento) Boasting an enviable setting near the Pantheon and a plush, theatrical

Antico Caffè Greco

JULIE MAYFENG/SHUTTERSTOCK ©

look – think velvet drapes, black lacquer tables and bookshelves – Casa Coppelle sets a romantic stage for high-end Roman-French cuisine. Gallic trademarks like snails and onion soup feature alongside updated Roman favourites such as pasta *amatriciana* (with tomato sauce and pancetta) and *cacio e pepe* (pecorino and black pepper), here re-invented as a risotto with prawns. Book ahead.

⊗ Tridente, Trevi & the Quirinale

Bistrot del Quirino   Italian €

(📞06 9887 8090; www.bistrotquirino.com; Via delle Vergini 7; brunch €10, à la carte €25-30; ⊗noon-3.30pm & 4pm-2am; 🚋Via del Corso) For unbeatable value near the Trevi Fountain, reserve a table at this artsy bistro adjoining Teatro Quirino. Theatre posters add bags of colour to the spacious interior, where a banquet of a 'brunch' buffet – fantastic salads, antipasti, hot and cold dishes – is laid out for knowing Romans to feast on.

Antico Caffè Greco   Cafe €

(📞06 679 17 00; Via dei Condotti 86; ⊗9am-9pm; Ⓜ Spagna) Rome's oldest cafe, open since 1760, is still working the look with the utmost elegance: waiters in black tails and bow tie, waitresses in frilly white pinnies, scarlet flock walls and age-spotted gilt mirrors. Prices reflect this amazing heritage: pay €9 for a cappuccino sitting down or join locals for the same (€2.50) standing at the bar.

Pastificio Guerra   Fast Food €

(📞06 679 31 02; Via della Croce 8; pasta, wine & water €4; ⊗1-9.30pm; Ⓜ Spagna) A brilliant budget find, this old-fashioned pasta shop (1918), with a kitchen hatch, serves up two choices of pasta at lunchtime. It's fast food, Italian style – freshly cooked (if you time it right) pasta, with wine and water included. Grab a space to stand and eat between shelves packed with packets of dry pasta, or take it away.

Canova Tadolini   Cafe, Bar €

(📞06 3211 0702; www.canovatadolini.com; Via del Babuino 150a/b; ⊗8am-midnight; Ⓜ Spagna) In 1818 sculptor Canova signed a contract for this studio that agreed it would be forever preserved for sculpture. The place is still stuffed with statues, and it's a unique experience to sit among the great maquettes and sip a cappuccino, beer or wine over snacks, cake or *panino*. Pay first at the till then head left to the bar.

Gelateria Dei Gracchi　Gelato €

(☑06 322 47 27; www.gelateriadeigracchi.it; Via di Ripetta 261; cones & tubs €2.50-4.50; ☺11.45am-8pm Tue-Sun; Ⓜ Flaminio) Handily located just off Piazza del Popolo, this outpost of the venerable Gelataria dei Gracchi, by the Vatican, is known for its superb ice cream made from the best ingredients. Flavours are classic.

Fiaschetteria Beltramme　Trattoria €€

(☑06 6979 7200; Via della Croce 39; meals €35-40; ☺12.15-3pm & 7.30-10.45pm; Ⓜ Spagna) A super spot for authentic Roman dining near the Spanish Steps, Fiaschetteria (meaning 'wine-sellers') is a hole-in-the-wall, stuck-in-time place with a short menu. Fashionistas with appetites dig into traditional Roman dishes made using recipes unchanged since the 1930s when a waiter at the 19th-century wine bar (from 1886 to be precise) started serving food. Seeking the perfect carbonara? This is the address.

Il Margutta　Vegetarian €€

(☑06 3265 0577; www.ilmargutta.bio; Via Margutta 118; lunch buffet weekdays/weekends €15/25, meals €15-60; ☺8.30am-11.30pm; ☑; Ⓜ Spagna, Flaminio) This chic art-gallery-bar-restaurant gets packed at lunchtime with Romans feasting on its good-value, eat-as-much-as-you-can buffet deal. Everything is organic, the evening menu tempting with creative dishes such as tofu with marinated ginger and smoked tubers, or grilled chicory with almond cream and candied tangerine. Among the various tasting menus is a vegan option.

Ginger　Brasserie €€

(☑06 9603 6390; www.ginger.roma.it; Via Borgognona 43; sandwiches €7.50-10, salads €9-14, meals €35-50; ☺10am-midnight; Ⓜ Spagna) ✔ This buzzy white-tiled space is a fantastic all-day dining spot near the Spanish Steps. The

---

🍴 Fine Dining & Michelin Stars

The number of special-occasion, fine-dining restaurants is ever rising in Rome. Five chefs in Rome were awarded their first Michelin star in 2017, while Riccardo di Giacinto at **All'Oro** (☑06 9799 6907; www.ristorantealloro.it; Via Giuseppe Pisanelli 23-25; tasting menus €88-150; ☺7-11pm daily, 1-2.45pm Sat & Sun; Ⓜ Flaminio) raised the gastronomic bar by moving premises and incorporating a gorgeous, 14-room boutique hotel into his new foodie empire. At Palazzo Manfredi, enviably across the street from the Colosseum, Giuseppe Di Iorio continues to create a buzz at Michelin-starred **Aroma** (p139), as does Francesco Apreda at **Imàgo** (p128) – views from both addresses are as sensational as the mind-blowing cuisine. Favouring a modern Roman cuisine, these top chefs look to traditional Roman dishes or ingredients for inspiration, and play with unexpected flavours and combinations to create a highly creative, gastronomic dining experience.

---

focus is on organic 'slow food' dishes using seasonal Appellation d'Origine Protégée (AOP) ingredients, and all appetites are catered for with gourmet, French baguette-style sandwiches, steamed 'baskets', meal-sized salads and healthy mains like salmon with orange mayonnaise.

Hostaria Romana　Trattoria €€

(☑06 474 52 84; www.hostariaromana.it; Via del Boccaccio 1; meals €35-40; ☺12.30-3pm & 7.15-11pm Mon-Sat; Ⓜ Barberini) A highly recommended address for lunch or dinner near the Trevi Fountain, Hostaria Romana cooks up meaty, traditional classics like grilled goat chops, veal cutlets, roast suckling pig and T-bone steaks to a mixed Roman and tourist crowd. Busy, bustling and noisy, this is everything an Italian trattoria should be. Sign your name on the graffiti-covered walls before leaving.

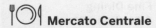

Mercato Centrale

A gourmet food hall for hungry travellers at Stazione Termini, the dazzling three-storey **Mercato Centrale** (www.mercatocentrale.it/roma; Stazione Termini, Via Giolitti 36; snacks/meals from €3/10; ⊗8am-midnight; ⊛; MTermini) is the latest project of Florence's savvy Umberto Montano. You'll find breads, pastries, cakes, veggie burgers, fresh pasta, truffles, pizza and a whole lot more beneath towering vaulted 1930s ceilings, as well as some of the city's most prized producers, including Gabriele Bonci (breads, focaccia and pizza), Roberto Liberati (salami) and Marcella Bianchi (vegetarian).

Vineria II Chianti   Tuscan €€

(🖉06 679 24 70; www.vineriailchianti.com; Via del Lavatore 81-82a; meals €45; ⊗noon-1am; 🚇Via del Tritone) With a name like Il Chianti, this pretty ivy-clad wine bar can only be Tuscan. Cosy up inside its bottle-lined interior or grab a table on the street terrace and dig into superb Tuscan dishes like *stracotto al Brunello* (beef braised in Brunello wine) or handmade pasta laced with *lardo di Colonnata* (aromatic pork fat aged in Carrara marble vats).

Al Gran Sasso   Trattoria €€

(🖉06 321 48 83; www.algransasso.com; Via di Ripetta 32; meals €30-35; ⊗noon-3.30pm & 7-11pm Sun-Fri Sep-Jul; MFlaminio) A top lunchtime spot, this is a classic, dyed-in-the-wool trattoria specialising in old-school country cooking. It's a relaxed place with a welcoming vibe, garish murals on the walls (strangely often a good sign) and tasty, value-for-money food. The fried dishes are excellent, or try one of the daily specials, chalked up on the board outside.

Colline Emiliane   Italian €€

(🖉06 481 75 38; www.collineemiliane.com; Via degli Avignonesi 22; meals €40-45; ⊗12.45-2.45pm & 7.30-10.45pm Tue-Sun, closed Sun dinner & Mon; MBarberini) Sensational regional cuisine from Emilia-Romagna aside, what makes this small white-tablecloth dining address so outstanding is its family vibe and overwhelmingly warm service. It's been a stronghold of the Latini family since the 1930s, and today son Luca runs the show with his mother Paola (dessert queen), aunt Anna (watch her making fresh pasta each morning in the glassed-off lab) and father Massimo.

Imàgo   Italian €€€

(🖉06 6993 4726; www.imagorestaurant.com; Hotel Hassler, Piazza della Trinità dei Monti 6; tasting menus €120-160; ⊗7-10.30pm Feb-Dec; 🖋; MSpagna) Even in a city of great views, the panoramas from the Hassler Hotel's Michelin-starred romantic rooftop restaurant are special, extending over a sea of roofs to the great dome of St Peter's Basilica; request the corner table. Complementing the views are the bold, mod-Italian creations of culinary whizz, chef Francesco Apreda.

Babette   Italian €€€

(🖉06 321 15 59; www.babetteristorante.it; Via Margutta 1d-3; meals €50; ⊗1-3pm & 7.30-11pm Tue-Sun, closed Jan; 🖋; MSpagna, Flaminio) Babette is run by two sisters who used to produce a fashion magazine, hence the effortlessly chic interior of exposed brick walls and vintage painted signs. Cuisine is a feast of Italian dishes with a creative French twist: *tortiglioni* with courgette, saffron and pistachio pesto, for example, followed by rabbit loin in juniper sauce, then *torta Babette* (a light-as-air lemon cheesecake).

Romans flock here at weekends for Babette's good-value lunch buffet (€28), which includes water, bread, dessert and coffee.

Le Tamerici   Seafood €€€

(🖉06 6920 0700; www.letamerici.com; Vicolo Scavolino 79; meals around €50; ⊗12.30-3pm Mon-Fri, 7-11pm Mon-Sat Sep-Jul; 🚇Via del Tritone) Exceptional seafood and wine is a winning epicurean combo at Le Tamerici, a cream-hued, elegant escape from the Trevi Fountain hubbub. Hidden away down an alleyway, it impresses with its wine list, range of *digestivi* and light-as-air homemade pasta dishes laced with seafood – all served in

PINO PACIFICO/REDAGO/UIG VIA GETTY IMAGES ©

Mercato Centrale

two intimate rooms with bleached-wood beamed ceilings.

⊗ Vatican City, Borgo & Prati

Pizzarium Pizza €

(📞06 3974 5416; Via della Meloria 43; pizza slices €5; ⊙11am-10pm Mon-Sat, noon-10pm Sun; Ⓜ Cipro-Musei Vaticani) When a pizza joint is packed at lunchtime on a wet winter's day, you know it's something special. Pizzarium, the takeaway of Gabriele Bonci, Rome's acclaimed pizza king, serves Rome's best sliced pizza, bar none. Scissor-cut squares of soft, springy base are topped with original combinations of seasonal ingredients and served on paper trays for immediate consumption. Also worth trying are the freshly fried *supplì* (risotto balls).

Sciascia Caffè Cafe €

(📞06 321 15 80; Via Fabio Massimo 80/A; ⊙7am-8pm; Ⓜ Ottaviano-San Pietro) There are several contenders for the best coffee in town but, in our opinion, nothing tops the *caffè*

eccellente served at this polished old-school cafe. A velvety smooth espresso served in a delicate cup lined with melted chocolate, it's nothing short of magnificent.

Fatamorgana Gelato €

(📞06 3751 9093; www.gelateriafatamorgana. it; Via Leone IV 52; gelato €2.50-5; ⊙noon-11pm summer, to 9pm winter; Ⓜ Ottaviano-San Pietro) The Prati branch of hit gelateria chain. As well as all the classic flavours, there are some wonderfully left-field creations, including a strange but delicious *basilico, miele e noci* (basil, honey and hazelnuts).

Fa-Bìo Sandwiches €

(📞06 6452 5810; www.fa-bio.com; Via Germanico 43; sandwiches €5; ⊙10.30am-5.30pm Mon-Fri, to 4pm Sat; 🚊Piazza del Risorgimento, Ⓜ Ottaviano-San Pietro) 🍴 Sandwiches, wraps, salads and fresh juices are all prepared with speed, skill and fresh organic ingredients at this friendly takeaway. Locals, Vatican tour guides and in-the-know visitors come here to grab a quick lunchtime bite, and if you can find room in the tiny interior, you'd do well to follow suit.

Cotto Crudo — Sandwiches €

(📞06 6476 0954; www.cottocrudo.it; Borgo Pio
46; panini from €4.50; ⏰10am-9pm Mon-Thu,
to 10pm Fri & Sat, to 8pm Sun; 🚃Piazza del
Risorgimento, Ⓜ️Ottaviano-San Pietro) Among
the tourist traps on Borgo Pio, the main
drag through what's left of the medieval
Borgo neighbourhood, this hole-in-the-
wall sandwich shop is ideal for a Vatican
pit stop. Specialising in produce from
Emilia-Romagna, it serves *panini* laden with
delectable fillings such as aged Parma ham,
mortadella and *culatella* (a type of salami),
as well as cheeses and vegetables.

Il Sorpasso — Italian €€

(📞06 8902 4554; www.sorpasso.info; Via
Properzio 31-33; meals €20-35; ⏰7.30am-1am
Mon-Fri, 9am-1am Sat; 🚃Piazza del Risorgimento)
A bar-restaurant hybrid sporting a vintage
cool look – vaulted stone ceilings, exposed
brick, rustic wooden tables – Il Sorpasso is
a Prati hotspot. Open throughout the day,
it caters to a fashionable crowd, serving
everything from salads and pasta specials
to *trapizzini* (pyramids of stuffed pizza),
cured meats and cocktails.

Velavevodetto Ai Quiriti — Roman €€

(📞06 3600 0009; www.ristorantevelavevo
detto.it; Piazza dei Quiriti 5; meals €30-35;
⏰12.30-3pm & 7.45-11pm; Ⓜ️Lepanto) This
welcoming restaurant wins you over with
its unpretentious, earthy food and honest
prices. The menu reads like a directory
of Roman staples, and while it's all pretty
good, standout choices include *fettuccine
con asparagi, guanciale e pecorino* (pasta
ribbons with asparagus, *guanciale* (cured
pig's cheek) and pecorino cheese) and
polpette di bollito (meatballs).

Hostaria Dino e Toni — Roman €€

(📞06 3973 3284; Via Leone IV 60; meals €25-
30; ⏰12.30-3pm & 7-11pm Mon-Sat, closed
Aug; Ⓜ️Ottaviano-San Pietro) A bustling
old-school trattoria, Dino e Toni offers
simple, no-frills Roman cooking. Kick off
with its house antipasto, a minor meal
of fried *supplì*, olives and pizza, before
plunging into its signature pasta dish,
rigatoni all'amatriciana (pasta tubes with
bacon-like guanciale, chilli and tomato
sauce). No credit cards.

Panella

Del Frate — Ristorante €€

(☑06 323 64 37; www.enotecadelfrate.it; Via degli Scipioni 122; meals €40-45; ☺12.30-3pm & 6.30-11.45pm Mon-Sat; Ⓜ Ottaviano-San Pietro) Locals love this upmarket *enoteca* (wine bar) with its simple wooden tables and high-ceilinged brick-arched rooms. Dishes are designed to complement the extensive wine list, so there's a formidable selection of cheeses (everything from Sicilian ricotta to Piedmontese robiola), alongside a refined menu of tartars, salads, fresh pastas and main courses.

Enoteca La Torre — Ristorante €€€

(☑06 4566 8304; www.enotecalatorreroma.com; Villa Laetitia, Lungotevere delle Armi 22; fixed-price lunch menu €60, tasting menus €95-130; ☺12.30-2.30pm Tue-Sat, 7.30-10.30pm Mon-Sat; ☐ Lungotevere delle Armi) The romantic art nouveau Villa Laetitia provides an aristocratic setting for this refined Michelin-starred restaurant. Since opening in 2013, it has firmly established itself on Rome's fine-dining scene with its sophisticated brand of contemporary creative cuisine and a stellar wine list.

Ristorante L'Arcangelo — Ristorante €€€

(☑06 321 09 92; www.larcangelo.com; Via Giuseppe G Belli 59; meals €50; ☺1-2.30pm Mon-Fri, 8-11pm Mon-Sat; ☐ Piazza Cavour) Styled as an informal bistro with wood panelling, leather banquettes and casual table settings, L'Arcangelo enjoys a stellar local reputation. Dishes are modern and creative yet still undeniably Roman in their use of traditional ingredients such as sweetbreads and *baccalà* (cod). A further plus is the wine list, which boasts some interesting Italian labels.

⊗ Monti, Esquilino & San Lorenzo

Panella — Bakery, Cafe €

(☑06 487 24 35; www.panellaroma.com; Via Merulana 54; meals €7-15; ☺7am-11pm Mon-Thu & Sun, to midnight Fri & Sat; Ⓜ Vittorio Emanuele) Pure heaven for foodies, this enticing bakery is littered with well-used trays of freshly baked pastries loaded with confectioner's custard,

---

★ **Top Five for Traditional Roman Cuisine**

Flavio al Velavevodetto (p139)

Da Felice (p139)

Armando al Pantheon (p125)

Da Enzo (p137)

Da Augusto (p134)

---

wild-cherry fruit tartlets, *pizza al taglio, aranci-ni* (rice balls) and focaccia – the smell alone is heavenly. Grab a bar stool between shelves of gourmet groceries inside or congratulate yourself on scoring a table on the flowery, sun-flooded terrace – one of Rome's loveliest.

Necci dal 1924 — Cafe, Bar €

(☑06 9760 1552; www.necci1924.com; Via Fanfulla da Lodi 68; ☺8am-1am Sun-Thu, to 2am Fri & Sat; 🛜 💷; ☐ Via Prenestina) An all-round hybrid in edgy Pigneto, iconic Necci opened as a gelateria in 1924 and later became a favourite of film director Pier Paolo Pasolini. These days, with English chef and owner Ben Hirst at its helm, Necci caters to a buoyant hipster crowd with its laid-back vibe, retro interior and food served all day. Huge kudos for the fabulous summertime terrace.

La Bottega del Caffè — Cafe €

(☑06 474 15 78; Piazza Madonna dei Monti 5; ☺8am-2am; 🛜; Ⓜ Cavour) On one of Rome's prettiest squares in Monti, La Bottega del Caffè – named after a comedy by Carlo Goldoni – is the hot spot in Monti for lingering over coffee, drinks, snacks and lunch or dinner. Heaters in winter ensure balmy al-fresco action year-round.

Aromaticus — Health Food €

(☑06 488 13 55; www.aromaticus.it; Via Urbana 134; meals €10-15; ☺11.30am-3.30pm Mon, 11am-10pm Tue-Sun; 🛜; Ⓜ Cavour) Few addresses exude such a healthy vibe. Set within a shop selling aromatic plants and edible flowers, this inventive little cafe is the perfect place to satisfy green cravings. Its short but sweet menu features lots of creative salads, soups and gazpacho, tartare

🍽️ Roman Cuisine

Like most Italian cuisines, the *cucina romana* (Roman cooking) was born of careful use of local ingredients – making use of the cheaper cuts of meat, like *guanciale* (pig's cheek), and greens that could be gathered wild from the fields.

There are a few classic Roman dishes that almost every trattoria and restaurant in Rome serves. These carb-laden comfort foods are seemingly simple, yet notoriously difficult to prepare well. Iconic Roman dishes include carbonara (pasta with pig's cheek, egg and salty *pecorino romano;* sheep's milk cheese), *alla gricia* (with pig's cheek and onions), *amatriciana* (invented when a chef from Amatrice added tomatoes to *alla gricia*) and *cacio e pepe* (with *pecorino romano* cheese and black pepper). As wonderful and deeply gratifying as these timeless dishes, are the centuries-old dining traditions that have been meticulously preserved alongside them: many trattorias in Rome, as tradition demands, only cook up gnocchi (dumplings) on Thursdays, *baccalà* with *ceci* (salted cod with chickpeas) on Fridays, and tripe on Saturdays.

and carpaccio, juices and detox smoothies – all to stay or go.

Alle Carette   Pizza €

(📞06 679 27 70; www.facebook.com/allecarette; Via della Madonna dei Monti 95; pizza €5.50-9; ⊗11.30am-4pm & 7pm-midnight; 👶; Ⓜ️Cavour) Honest pizza, super-thin and swiftly cooked in a wood-burning oven, is what this traditional Roman pizzeria on one of Monti's prettiest car-free streets has done well for decades. Tobacco-coloured walls give the place a vintage vibe and Roman families pile in here at weekends. Begin your local feast with some battered and deep-fried zucchini flowers or some *baccalà* (salted cod).

Pasta Chef   Fast Food €

(📞06 488 31 98; www.pastachefroma.it; Via Baccina 42; pasta €5-10; ⊗12.30-9.30pm; Ⓜ️Cavour) 'Gourmet street food' is the strapline of this fast-food pasta joint where chefs Mauro and Leopoldo whip up steaming bowls of perfectly cooked pasta laced with carbonara, *pomodoro e basilico* (tomato and basil), bolognese and other classic sauces for a discerning, budget-conscious crowd. There's a veggie lasagne and other vegetarian options. The dynamic duo also runs pasta-cooking classes.

Vitaminas 24   Vegetarian, Vegan €

(📞331 2045535; http://vitaminas24.com; Via Ascoli Piceno 40-42; meals €15; ⊗noon-midnight; 🛜🖊️; 🚋Circonvallazione Casilina) 🍃 Produce from Rome's agricultural surrounds goes into the delicious smoothies, soups, wraps, salads, burgers and other vegetarian and vegan cuisine cooked up at this stylish bistro. Glass conservation jars filled with beans, seeds and pulses decorate the open kitchen, and the Brazilian heritage of creative owner Giuliana injects an appealing tropical vibe. Her veggie-packed *vellutate* ('velvet' soups) are a local legend.

Ai Tre Scalini   Italian €€

(📞06 4890 7495; www.facebook.com/aitrescalini; Via Panisperna 251; meals €25; ⊗12.30pm-1am; Ⓜ️Cavour) A firm favourite since 1895, the 'Three Steps' is always packed, with crowds spilling out of the funky violet-painted door and into the street. Tuck into a heart-warming array of cheeses, salami and dishes such as *polpette al sugo* (meatballs with sauce), washed down with superb choices of wine or beer.

Da Valentino   Trattoria €€

(📞06 488 06 43; Via del Boschetto 37; meals €30; ⊗12.30-2.45pm & 8-11pm Mon-Sat; 🚋Via Nazionale) The 1930s sign outside says 'Birra Peroni' and its enchanting vintage interior feels little changed. Come to this mythical dining address for delicious bruschetta, grilled meats, the purest of hamburgers and *scamorza,* a type of Italian cheese that is grilled and melted atop myriad different ingredients: tomato and rocket, artichokes, wafer-thin slices of aromatic *lardo di colonnata* (pork fat) from Tuscany and porcini mushrooms. No coffee.

L'Asino d'Oro   Italian €€

(☑06 4891 3832; www.facebook.com/asinodoro; Via del Boschetto 73; weekday lunch menu €16, meals €45; ☺12.30-2.30pm & 7.30-11pm Tue-Sat; MCavour) This fabulous restaurant was transplanted from Orvieto, and its Umbrian origins resonate in Lucio Sforza's exceptional cooking. Unfussy yet innovative dishes feature bags of flavourful contrasts, like lamb meatballs with pear and blue cheese. Save room for the equally amazing desserts. Intimate, informal and classy, this is one of Rome's best deals – its lunch menu is a steal.

Tram Tram   Osteria €€

(☑06 49 04 16; www.tramtram.it; Via dei Reti 44; meals €35-45; ☺12.30-3pm & 7.30-11pm Tue-Sun; ◻Via Tiburtina, ◻Via dei Reti) This wildly popular, old-style trattoria with lace curtains takes its name from the trams that rattle by outside. It's a family-run affair with a kitchen that unusually mixes classical Roman dishes with seafood from Puglia in Italy's hot south. Taste sensation *tiella di riso, patate e cozze*

(baked rice dish with rice, potatoes and mussels) is not to be missed. Book well ahead.

Temakinho   Sushi €€

(☑06 4201 6656; www.temakinho.com; Via dei Serpenti 16; meals €40; ☺12.30-3.30pm & 7pm-midnight; MCavour) In a city where most food is still resolutely (though deliciously) Italian, this Brazilian-Japanese hybrid serving up sushi and ceviche makes for a sensationally refreshing change. As well as delicious, strong caipirinhas, which combine Brazilian *cachaça,* sugar, lime and fresh fruit, there are 'sakehinhas' made with sake. It's very popular; book ahead.

Trattoria Monti   Trattoria €€

(☑06 446 65 73; Via di San Vito 13a; meals €40-45; ☺1-2.45pm & 8-10.45pm Tue-Sat, 1-2.45pm Sun; MVittorio Emanuele) The Camerucci family runs this elegant brick-arched trattoria proffering top-notch traditional cooking from the Marches region. There are wonderful *fritti* (fried things), delicate pastas and ingredients such as *pecorino di fossa* (sheep's milk cheese aged in caves), goose, swordfish and truffles. Try the egg-yolk *tortelli* pasta. Desserts are

Necci dal 1924 (p131)

Da Augusto

delectable, including apple pie with *zabaglione* (egg and marsala custard). Book ahead.

Trattoria Da Danilo   Trattoria €€

(☎06 7720 0111; www.trattoriadadanilo.com; Via Petrarca 13; meals €40; ☺12.45-3pm & 7.45-11pm Tue-Sat, 7.45-11pm Mon; Ⓜ Vittorio Emanuele, Manzoni) Ideal if you're looking for a fine robust meal, this upmarket version of the classic neighbourhood trattoria offers icons of Roman cooking in a rustic, classical trattoria atmosphere. It's renowned for its *pasta cacio e pepe* (pasta with caciocavallo cheese and pepper) and carbonara. Top marks for its roll-down shutter, a street-art lesson in spaghetti-eating etiquette.

Antonello Colonna Open   Italian €€€

(☎06 4782 2641; www.antonellocolonna.it; Via Milano 9a; lunch/brunch €16/30, à la carte meals €80-100; ☺12.30-3.30pm & 8-11pm Tue-Sat, 12.30-3.30pm Sun; ❄; ☐ Via Nazionale) Spectacularly set at the back of Palazzo delle Esposizioni, super-chef Antonello Colonna's Michelin-starred restaurant lounges dramatically under a dazzling all-glass roof. Cuisine is

new Roman – innovative takes on traditional dishes, cooked with wit and flair – and the all-you-can-eat lunch buffet and weekend brunch are unbeatable value. On sunny days, dine al fresco on the rooftop terrace.

Said   Italian €€€

(☎06 446 92 04; www.said.it; Via Tiburtina 135; meals €40-50; ☺10am-12.30am Tue-Thu, to 1.30am Fri, 11am-1.30am Sat, 11am-12.30am Sun; 📶; ☐ Via Tiburtina, ☐ Via dei Reti) Housed in an early-1920s chocolate factory, this hybrid cafe-bar, restaurant and boutique is San Lorenzo's coolest hipster haunt. Its Japanese pink-tea pralines, indulged in with a coffee or bought wrapped to take home, are glorious, and dining here is urban chic, with battered sofas, industrial antiques and creative cuisine. Reservations for lunch and dinner, served from 12.30pm and 8pm, are recommended.

⊗ Trastevere & Gianicolo

Da Augusto   Trattoria €

(☎06 580 37 98; Piazza de' Renzi 15; meals €25; ☺12.30-3pm & 8-11pm; ☐ Viale di Trastevere,

🚇Viale di Trastevere) Bag one of Augusto's rickety tables outside and tuck into some truly fabulous mamma-style cooking on one of Trastevere's prettiest piazza terraces. Hearty portions of all the Roman classics are dished up here as well as lots of rabbit, veal, hare and *pajata* (calf intestines). Winter dining is around vintage Formica tables in a bare-bones interior, unchanged for decades. Be prepared to queue. Cash only.

Prosciutteria – Cantina dei Papi   Tuscan €

(📞06 6456 2839; www.facebook.com/pg/laprosciutteriatrastevere; Via della Scala 71; taglieri per person €5; ⏱11am-11.30pm; 🚇Piazza Trilussa) For a gratifying taste of Tuscany in Rome, consider lunch or a decadent *aperitivo* at this Florentine *prosciutteria* (salami shop). Made-to-measure *taglieri* (wooden chopping boards) come loaded with different cold cuts, cheeses, fruit and veg, and are best devoured over a glass of Brunello di Montalcino or simple Chianti Classico. Bread comes in peppermint-green tin saucepans and dozens of hams and salami dangle overhead.

Forno La Renella   Bakery €

(📞06 581 72 65; www.panificiolarenella.com; Via del Moro 15-16; pizza slices from €2.50, pizza per kg €9-18; ⏱7am-midnight Sun-Thu, to 3am Fri & Sat; 🚇Piazza Trilussa) Watch urban pizza masters at work behind glass at this historic Trastevere bakery, a fantastic space to hang out in with its wood-fired ovens, bar-stool seating and heavenly aromas of pizza, bread and biscuits baking throughout the day. Piled-high toppings (and fillings) vary seasonally, to the joy of everyone from punks with big dogs to old ladies with little dogs. It's been in the biz since 1870.

Fior di Luna   Gelato €

(📞06 6456 1314; http://fiordiluna.com; Via della Lungaretta 96; gelato from €2.50; ⏱11.30am-11.30pm Easter-Oct, to 9pm Tue-Sun Nov-Easter; 🚇Viale di Trastevere, 🚇Viale di Trastevere) For many Romans this busy little hub makes the best handmade gelato and sorbet in the world. It's produced in small batches using natural, seasonal ingredients – a few

flavours are even made from donk[...] Favourites include walnut and hon[...] berry yoghurt, kiwi (complete with seeds) and pistachio (the nuts are ground by hand).

Le Levain   Bakery €

(📞06 6456 2880; www.lelevainroma.it; Via Luigi Santini 22-23; meals €5.50-10; ⏱8am-8.30pm Mon-Sat, 9am-8pm Sun; 🚇Viale di Trastevere, 🚇Viale di Trastevere) Many a foreigner living in Rome swears by this *pâtisserie au beurre fin* for their daily dose of rich and creamy butter, albeit it in the guise of authentic croissants, *pains au chocolat* and other irresistible French pastries. Traditional French cakes – colourful cream-filled macarons, flaky millefeuilles, miniature *tartes aux pommes* (apple tarts) – are equally authentic.

Panattoni   Pizza €

(Ai Marmi; 📞06 580 09 19; Viale di Trastevere 53; pizzas €6.50-9.50; ⏱6.30pm-2am Thu-Tue; 🚇Viale di Trastevere, 🚇Viale di Trastevere) Also called 'ai Marmi' or *l'obitorio* (the morgue) because of its vintage marble-slab tabletops, this is Trastevere's most popular pizzeria. Think super-thin pizzas, a clattering buzz, testy waiters, a street terrace and some fantastic fried starters – the *supplì* (risotto balls), *baccalà* (salted cod) and zucchini flowers are all heavenly.

Da Olindo   Trattoria €

(📞06 581 88 35; Vicolo della Scala 8; meals €25; ⏱noon-2.30pm & 7.30-11pm Mon-Sat; 🚇Piazza Trilussa) This is your classic family affair – the menu is short, the cuisine is robust, the portions are huge, and the atmosphere is lively. Expect *baccalà con patate* (salted cod stewed with potatoes) on Friday and *trippa* (tripe) on Saturday, but other dishes – such as *coniglio all cacciatore* (rabbit, hunter-style) or *polpette al sugo* (meatballs in sauce) – whichever day you like.

Don   Pizza €

(📞06 581 17 96; www.donpizzafritta.com; Via di San Francesco a Ripa 103; pizzas €4-6.50; ⏱noon-3pm & 7-11pm Tue-Thu & Sun, to midnight Fri & Sat; 🚇Viale di Trastevere, 🚇Viale di Trastevere) A small corner of Naples in Trastevere, Don serves authentic fried pizzas. These

Rome on a Plate

As an alternative to spaghetti, *rigatoni* is often served.

Cream is never used in the authentic Roman dish.

Forget parmesan, the correct cheese is *pecorino romano*.

Both *guanciale* (cured pig's cheek) and *pancetta* are fine to use.

For a seafood version, substitute swordfish for the *guanciale*.

Spaghetti alla Carbonara

Bacon & Egg Roman Style

A staple of trattoria menus across the city, Roman carbonara is a far cry from the foreign cream-laden version. The dish you'll eat in Rome is simplicity it-self, just spaghetti (or *rigatoni*) wrapped in a silky egg sauce spiked with crispy cubes of *guanciale* and seasoned with *pecorino romano* and black pepper. Cooked well, it's one of Rome's great dishes.

★ Top Five for Carbonara

Trattoria Da Danilo (p134) Upmarket trattoria famed for its silky carbonara.
Salumeria Roscioli (p125) A celebrated restaurant-deli serving sublime pasta.
Da Felice (p139) A bastion of authentic Roman cuisine.
Metamorfosi (p140) Carbonara is given a contemporary deconstruction.
Fiaschetteria Beltramme (p127) For timeless classics near the Spanish Steps.

golden half-moons of comforting doughi-ness and melted cheese are delicious and joyfully messy to eat – be careful not to burn your mouth on the first bite! Pizzas come in two sizes (*sorriso* and *Napoli d'Oro*) and feature fillers such as San Marzano tomatoes, sausage and *mozzarella di bufala*.

Locanda del Gelato   Gelato €

(www.locandadelgelato.it; Via di San Francesco a Ripa 71; tubs & cones €2-4.50; ⏲noon-midnight, shorter hours winter; 🚋Viale di Trastevere, 🚊Viale di Trastevere) This artisanal gelateria has quickly risen to the top of the ice-cream charts since it opened in April 2016. It serves classic flavours alongside more adventurous creations such as prosecco and pear. The house speciality is *gelato al vino* (wine ice cream). Alternatively, there are crêpes and great creamy smoothies.

Da Enzo   Trattoria €€

(📞06 581 22 60; www.daenzoal29.com; Via dei Vascellari 29; meals €30; ⏲12.30-3pm & 7.30-11pm Mon-Sat; 🚋Viale di Trastevere, 🚊Viale di Trastevere) Vintage buttermilk walls, red-checked table-cloths and a traditional menu featuring all the Roman classics: what makes this staunchly traditional trattoria exceptional is its careful sourcing of local, quality products, many from nearby farms in Lazio. The seasonal, deep-fried Jewish artichokes and the *pasta cacio e pepe* (cheese-and-black-pepper pasta) in particular are among the best in Rome.

Spirito DiVino   Italian €€

(📞06 589 66 89; www.ristorantespiritodivino.com; Via dei Genovesi 31; meals €35; ⏲7-11.30pm Mon-Sat; 🚊Viale di Trastevere) Chef and 'slow food' aficionado Eliana Catalani buys ingredients directly from local producers. The restaurant's trademark dish is *maiale alla mazio,* an ancient pork and red-wine stew said to have been a favourite of Caesar. Between courses diners can visit the wine cellar, which dates to 80 BC.

Da Teo   Trattoria €€

(📞06 581 83 55; Piazza dei Ponziani 7; meals €35; ⏲12.30-3pm & 7.30-11.30pm Mon-Sat; 🚋Viale di Trastevere, 🚊Viale di Trastevere) One of Rome's classic trattorias, Da Teo buzzes with locals

digging into steaming platefuls of Roman standards, such as carbonara, *pasta cacio e pepe* (cheese-and-black-pepper pasta) and the most fabulous seasonal artichokes – both Jewish (deep-fried) and Roman-style (stuffed with parsley and garlic, and boiled). In keeping with hardcore trattoria tradition, Teo's home-made gnocchi is only served on Thursday. Reservations essential.

Litro   Italian €€

(📞06 4544 7639; www.facebook.com/litro vineria; Via Fratelli Bonnet 5, Monteverde; meals €30-35; ⏲12.30-3.30pm & 5.30pm-midnight Mon-Fri, 12.30pm-1am Sat; 🛜; 🚋Via Fratelli Bonnet) Crunchy brown bread comes in a paper bag and the 1950s clocks on the wall – all three dozen them – say a different time at this understated vintage-styled bistro-bar in wonder-fully off-the-beaten-tourist-track Monteverde. The creative Roman kitchen is predominantly organic, with ingredients sourced from small local producers, and the choice of natural and biodynamic wines is among the best in Rome.

Roma Sparita   Trattoria €€

(📞06 580 07 57; www.romasparita.com; Piazza di Santa Cecilia 24; meals €30-35; ⏲12.30-2.30pm & 7.30-11.30pm Tue-Sat, 12.30-2.30pm Sun, closed last 2 weeks Aug; 🚋Viale di Trastevere, 🚊Viale di Trastevere) With its traditional country-style interior – all whitewashed beams, terracotta tiled floor and pretty pastel colour palette – and summertime terrace overlooking one of Trastevere's most peaceful car-free piazzas, Roma Sparita is something of a find. The cuisine is Roman, with house speciality *pasta cacio e pepe* (cheese and black pepper pasta) served in an edible bowl made of crisp, golden Parmesan. Don't hold back.

🍴 San Giovanni & Testaccio

Trapizzino   Fast Food €

(📞06 4341 9624; www.trapizzino.it; Via Branca 88; trapizzini from €3.50; ⏲noon-1am Tue-Sun; 🚋Via Marmorata) The original of what is now a grow-ing countrywide chain, this is the birthplace of the *trapizzino,* a kind of hybrid sandwich made by stuffing a cone of doughy focaccia with fillers like *polpette al sugo* (meatballs in tomato sauce) or *pollo alla cacciatore* (stewed chicken). They're messy to eat but quite delicious.

Mordi e Vai   Street Food €

(www.mordievai.it; Box 15, Nuovo Mercato di Testaccio; panini €3.50-5; ☺8am-3pm Mon-Sat; 🚇Via Galvani) Chef Sergio Esposito's critically acclaimed and much-frequented market stall – 'Bite and Go' in English – is all about the unadulterated joy of traditional Roman street food. That means *panini* such as his signature *allesso di scottona*, filled with tender slow-cooked beef, and plastic plates of no-nonsense meat-and-veg dishes.

Cafè Cafè   Bistro €

(☎06 700 87 43; www.cafecafebistrot.it; Via dei Santi Quattro 44; meals €15-20; ☺9.30am-8.45pm Wed-Mon, to 4.15pm Tue; 🚇Via di San Giovanni in Laterano) Cosy, relaxed and welcoming, this cafe-bistro is a far cry from the usual impersonal eateries in the Colosseum area. With its rustic wooden tables, butternut walls and wine bottles, it's a charming spot in which to charge your batteries over an egg-and-bacon breakfast, a light lunch, or afternoon tea and homemade cake.

Cups   Street Food €

(Box 44, Nuovo Mercato di Testaccio; dishes €5-8; ☺8am-4pm Mon-Sat; 🚇Via Galvini) This gourmet food stall at Testaccio market is the latest venture of local celebrity chef Cristina Bowerman. It takes its name from the carton cups used to serve dishes such as meatballs in tomato sauce and *brodo di pho*, a scorching take on the traditional Vietnamese soup dish. You can also order *panini*, focaccias, pastries and artisanal gelato.

Pizzeria Da Remo   Pizza €

(☎06 574 62 70; Piazza Santa Maria Liberatrice 44; meals €15; ☺7pm-1am Mon-Sat; 🚇Via Marmorata) For an authentic Roman experience, join the noisy crowds here, one of the city's best-known and most popular pizzerias. It's a spartan-looking place, but the fried starters and thin-crust Roman pizzas are the business, and there's a cheerful, boisterous vibe. Expect to queue after 8.30pm.

Casa Manfredi   Cafe €

(☎334 9511911; Viale Aventino 91-93; ☺7am-9pm Mon-Fri, 8am-9pm Sat, 8am-8pm Sun; 🚇Viale Aventino, 🚇Viale Aventino) Very 'in' when we visited, Casa Manfredi is a good-looking cafe in the wealthy Aventine neighbourhood. Join well-dressed locals for a quick coffee in the gleaming glass and chandelier interior, a light alfresco lunch or chic evening *aperitivo*. It also does a tasty line in artisanal gelato.

Linari   Cafe €

(☎06 578 23 58; Via Nicola Zabaglia 9; ☺7am-9.30pm; 🚇Via Marmorata) An authentic local hang-out, this cafe-*pasticceria* has the busy clatter of a good bar, with excellent pastries, splendid coffee and plenty of bar-side banter. There are a few outside tables, ideal for a cheap lunch, but you'll have to outfox the neighbourhood ladies to get one.

Sbanco   Pizza €

(☎06 78 93 18; Via Siria 1; pizzas €7.50-12.50; ☺7.30pm-midnight Mon-Sat, from 12.30pm Sun; 🚇Piazza Zama) With its informal warehouse vibe and buzzing atmosphere, Sbanco is one of the capital's hottest pizzerias. Since opening in 2016, it has quickly made a name for itself with its creative, wood-fired pizzas and sumptuous fried starters – try the carbonara *supplì* (risotto balls). To top things off, it serves some deliciously drinkable craft beer.

Romeo e Giulietta   Ristorante, Pizza €€

(☎Giulietta 06 4522 9022, Romeo 06 3211 0120; https://romeo.roma.it; Piazza dell'Emporio 28; pizzas €6.50-12, meals €40; ☺Romeo 4pm-2am Tue-Sat, noon-2am Sun, Giulietta 7.30pm-11.30pm daily & noon-3pm Sun; 🚇Via Marmorata) Occupying a former car showroom, this contemporary multi-space food hub is the latest offering from top Roman chef, Cristina Bowerman. The centre of operations is Romeo Chef & Baker, a designer deli, cocktail bar and restaurant offering modern Italian and international fare, but there's also Giulietta Pizzeria (https://giuliettapizzeria.it) dishing up sensational wood-fired pizzas, and, a short hop away, Frigo, an artisanal gelateria.

Wheels of Grana Padano cheese, Eataly (p140)

Flavio al
Velavevodetto   Roman €€

(📞06 574 41 94; www.ristorantevelavevodetto.
it; Via di Monte Testaccio 97-99; meals €30-35;
⊙12.30-3pm & 7.45-11pm; 🚌Via Galvani) Housed
in a rustic Pompeian-red villa set into the
side of Monte Testaccio, a man-made hill of
smashed Roman amphorae, this casual eatery is celebrated locally for its earthy, no-nonsense *cucina romana* (Roman cuisine).
Expect *antipasti* of cheeses, cured meats
and fried titbits, huge helpings of homemade
pastas, and uncomplicated meat dishes.

Da Felice   Roman €€

(📞06 574 68 00; www.feliceatestaccio.it; Via
Mastro Giorgio 29; meals €30-40; ⊙12.30-3pm
& 7-11.30pm; 🚌Via Marmorata) Much loved by
local foodies and well-dressed diners, this
historic stalwart is famous for its unwavering
dedication to Roman culinary traditions. In
contrast to the light-touch modern decor, the
menu is pure old school with a classic weekly
timetable: *pasta e fagioli* (pasta and beans)
on Tuesdays, *bollito di manzo* (boiled beef)
on Thursdays, fish on Fridays. Reservations
essential.

Aroma   Ristorante €€€

(📞06 9761 5109; www.aromarestaurant.it; Via
Labicana 125; meals €120-150; ⊙12.30-3pm &
7.30-11.30pm; 🚌Via Labicana) One for a special
occasion, the rooftop restaurant of the Palazzo Manfredi hotel offers once-in-a-lifetime
views of the Colosseum and Michelin-starred
food that truly amazes. Overseeing the kitch-
en is chef Giuseppe Di Iorio, whose seasonal
menus reflect his passion for luxurious,
forward-thinking Mediterranean cuisine.

✖ Villa Borghese &
Northern Rome

Neve di Latte   Gelato €

(📞06 320 84 85; Via Poletti 6; gelato €2.50-5;
⊙noon-11pm Sun-Thu, to midnight Fri & Sat, shorter
hours winter; 🚌Viale Tiziano) Behind the MAXXI
gallery, this out-of-the-way gelateria is one of
Rome's best. There are few exotic flavours,
rather the onus is on the classics, all prepared
with high-quality seasonal ingredients. The
pistachio, made with nuts from the Sicilian
town of Bronte, is excellent, as is the crème
caramel.

L'Archeologia Ristorante

Osteria Flaminio   Ristorante €€

(📞06 323 69 00; www.osteriaflaminio.com; Via Flaminia 297; lunch buffet €8-12, meals €30-35; ⊗12.30-3.30pm & 7.30pm-midnight; 🚇Via Flaminia) This friendly eatery makes for a fine lunch stop after a visit to the MAXXI art museum. The vibe is casual and its interior is a handsome mix of dark-wood floors, large street-facing windows and muted greys and whites. Foodwise, it serves a popular lunch buffet (vegetarian on Mondays, fish on Fridays) and a full menu of modern Italian and international fare.

Pro Loco Pinciano   Lazio, Pizza €€

(📞06 841 41 36; www.prolocopinciano.it; Via Bergamo 18; meals €20-35; ⊗12.30-3pm & 7.30-11.30pm; 🚇Via Salaria) Like a number of Rome's newer eateries – it opened in late 2014 – Pro Loco Pinciano is something of a culinary all-rounder. It serves regional cured meats and cheeses from a well-furnished deli counter, wood-fired pizzas, and a menu of salads, pastas and mains. All this in a good-looking interior of exposed brick walls and trendy mismatched furniture.

Metamorfosi   Ristorante €€€

(📞06 807 68 39; www.metamorfosiroma.it; Via Giovanni Antonelli 30; tasting menus €110-140; ⊗12.30-2.30pm & 8-10.30pm, closed Sat lunch & Sun; 🚇Via Giovanni Antonelli) This Michelin-starred Parioli restaurant is one of Rome's top dining tickets, offering international fusion cuisine and a contemporary look that marries linear clean-cut lines with warm earthy tones. Chef Roy Carceres' cooking is eclectic, often featuring playful updates of traditional Roman dishes, such as his signature Uovo 65° carbonara antipasto, a deconstruction of Rome's classic pasta dish.

⊗ Southern Rome

Eataly   Italian €

(www.eataly.net; Piazzale XII Ottobre 1492; meals €10-50; ⊗shops 9am-midnight, restaurants typically noon-3.30pm & 7-11pm; 🛜; 🚇Piramide) Be prepared for some serious taste-bud titillation in this state-of-the-art food emporium of gargantuan proportions. Four shop floors showcase every conceivable Italian food product (dried and fresh), while multiple themed food stalls and restaurants offer plenty of opportunity to taste or feast on Italian cuisine.

Doppiozeroo   Italian €

(📞06 5730 1961; www.doppiozeroo.com; Via Ostiense 68; meals €15-35; ⏲7am-2am; 🖳Via Ostiense, Ⓜ Piramide) This easygoing bar was once a bakery, hence the name ('double zero' is a type of flour). But today the sleek, modern interior attracts hungry, trendy Romans who pile in here for its cheap canteen-style lunches, famously lavish *aperitivo* (6pm to 9pm) and abundant weekend brunch (12.30pm to 3.30pm).

Verde
Pistacchio   Vegetarian, Vegan €

(📞06 4547 5965; www.facebook.com/verde pistacchioroma; Via Ostiense 181; lunch menu €14; ⏲11am-4pm & 6pm-midnight Mon-Thu, 11am-4pm & 6pm-2am Fri, 5.30pm-2am Sat & Sun; 🛜📝; 🖳Via Ostiense, Ⓜ Garbatella) Camilla, Raffaele and Francesco are the trio of friends behind Green Pistachio, a stylish bistro and cafe with a minimalist, vintage interior and streetside tables in the sun in summer. The kitchen cooks up fantastic vegetarian and vegan cuisine, and the lunchtime deal is a steal. Lunch here before or after visiting Rome's second-largest church, a stone's throw away on the same street.

Andreotti   Pastries €

(📞06 575 07 73; www.andreottiroma.it; Via Ostiense 54; pastries from €1.20; ⏲7.30am-10pm; 🖳Via Ostiense, Ⓜ Piramide) Film director and Ostiense local Ferzan Ozpetek is such a fan of the pastries crafted at this 1934 *pasticceria* that he's known to cast them in his films. They're all stars, from the buttery *crostate* (tarts) to the piles of golden *sfogliatelle romane* (ricotta-filled pastries). Hanging out with a coffee on the sunny pavement terrace is a warm-weather delight.

Andreotti cooks up cheap meals too; pasta dishes ring in at €5.

Pizzeria Ostiense   Pizza €

(📞06 5730 5081; www.pizzeriaostiense.it; Via Ostiense 56; pizzas from €5.50; ⏲6.30pm-1am, closed Tue winter; 🖳Via Ostiense, Ⓜ Piramide) Run by folk formerly of the much-lauded classic

Roman pizzeria Remo in Testaccio, Pizza Ostiense offers similarly paper-thin, crispy bases and delicious fresh toppings and scrumptious *fritti* (fried things) in unfussy surroundings. There's a friendly vibe.

Porto Fluviale   Italian €€

(📞06 574 31 99; www.portofluviale.com; Via del Porto Fluviale 22; meals €25-30; ⏲10.30am-2am Sun-Thu, to 3am Fri & Sat; 🛜; Ⓜ Piramide) A hip, buzzing restaurant-bar in the industrial-chic vein, Porto Fluviale attracts a mixed crowd – lots of families included – with its spacious lounge-style interior and good-value kitchen that turns out everything from pasta, pizza and *cicchetti* (tapas-style appetisers) to burgers and meal-sized salads, all available in half-portions too. Streetside seating is limited to an attractive handful of turquoise bistro tables.

Between meals, relax over a coffee, *aperitivo* or an evening drink to a soundtrack of jazz.

Qui Nun Se More Mai   Italian €€

(📞06 780 39 22; www.facebook.com/qvinun semoremai; Via Appia Antica 198; meals around €40; ⏲noon-3pm & 7.30-11.45pm Tue-Sat, 12.30-3pm Sun; 🖳Via Appia Antica) This small, charismatic restaurant has an open fire for grilling, plus a small terrace for when the weather's good. The menu offers Roman classics such as pasta *amatriciana,* carbonara, *alla gricia* and *cacio e pepe* – just the thing to set you up for the road ahead.

L'Archeologia
Ristorante   Italian €€€

(📞06 788 04 94; www.larcheologia.it; Via Appia Antica 139; meals €50; ⏲12.30-3pm & 8-11pm; 🖳Via Appia Antica) At home in an old horse exchange on the Appian Way, this 19th-century inn exudes vintage charm. Dining is elegant, with white-tablecloth-covered tables beneath age-old beams or in front of the fireplace. In summer, dining is al fresco and fragrant with the blooms of a magnificent 300-year-old wisteria. Cuisine is traditional Roman, and the wine list exemplary. Reservations recommended.

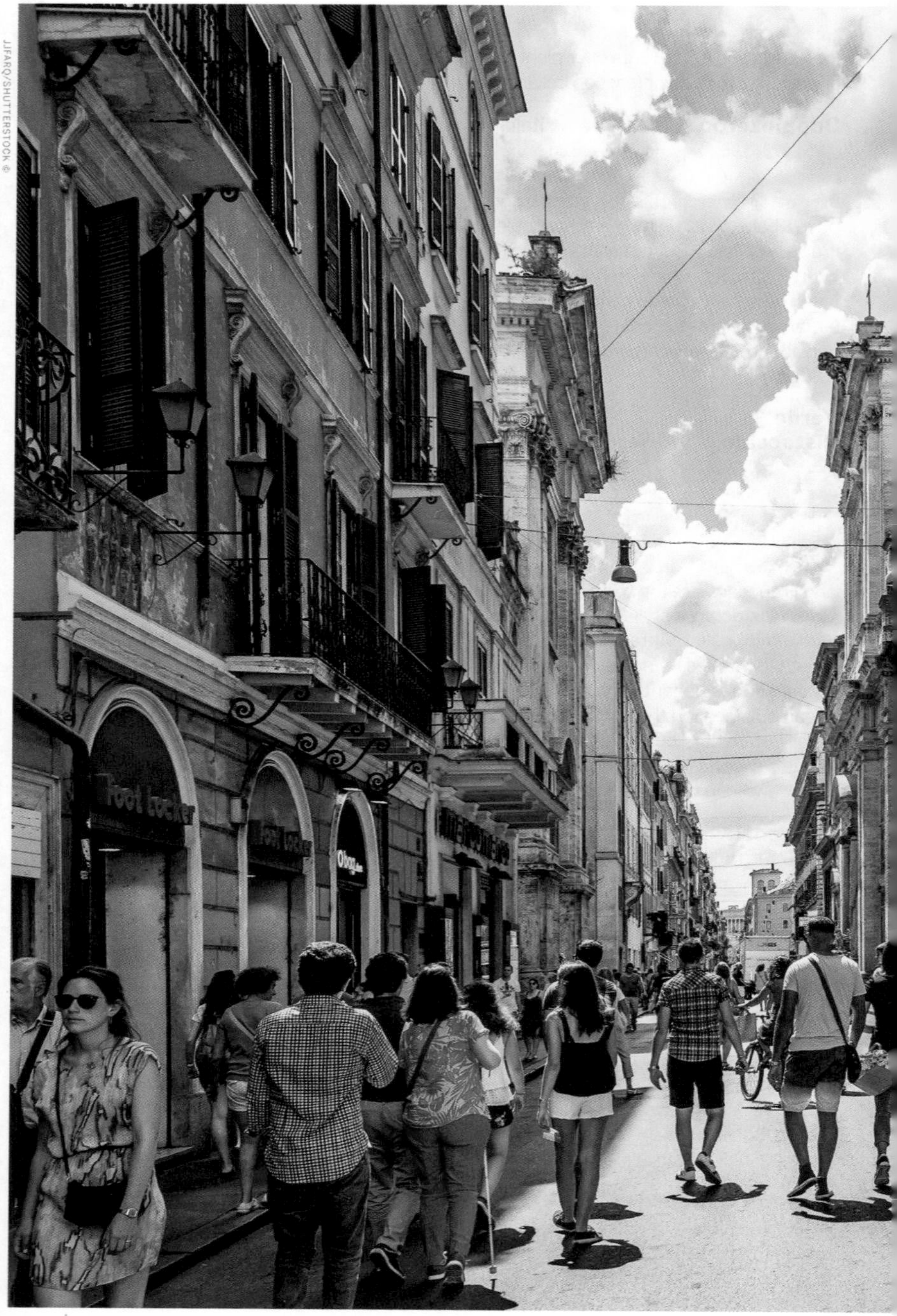
Foot Locker
Foot Locker
Obag

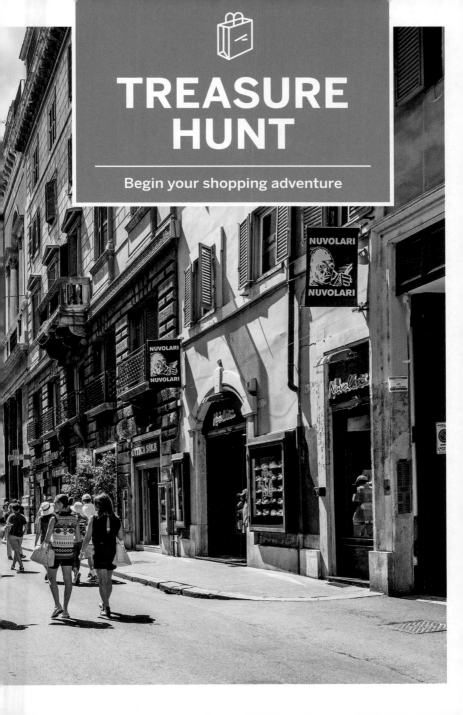

TREASURE HUNT

Begin your shopping adventure

Treasure Hunt

Rome enthrals with a fabulous portfolio of department stores, specialist shops, independent boutiques and artisan workshops. 'Retro' is one of the Roma shopping scene's many unique qualities, with jewel-like boutiques run by third-generation artisans, dusty picture-framing and basket-weaving workshops and historic department stores, all oozing an impossibly chic, old-school glamour.

'Made in Italy' has long been a byword for quality and Rome is a great place to shop for designer fashions, shoes and handcrafted leather goods. Foodies will be spoiled for choice in the city's delis and neighbourhood markets; design fans will enjoy looking for homeware and stylish accessories.

In This Section

Useful Phrases

I'd like to buy... Vorrei comprare (vo.*ray* kom.*pra*.re)

I'm just looking. Sto solo guardando (sto *so*.lo gwar.*dan*.do)

Can I look at it? Posso dare un'occhiata? (*po*.so *da*.re oo.no.*kya*.ta)

How much is this? Quanto costa questo? (*kwan*.to. *kos*.ta. *kwe*.sto)

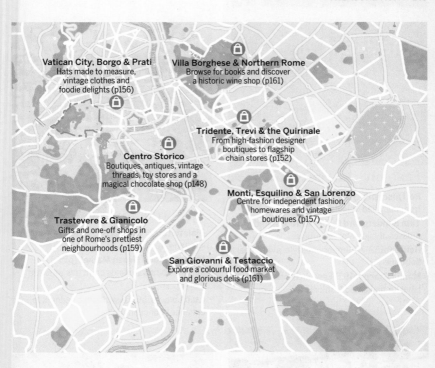

Vatican City, Borgo & Prati
Hats made to measure,
vintage clothes and
foodie delights (p156)

Villa Borghese & Northern Rome
Browse for books and discover
a historic wine shop (p161)

Tridente, Trevi & the Quirinale
From high-fashion designer
boutiques to flagship
chain stores (p152)

Centro Storico
Boutiques, antiques, vintage
threads, toy stores and a
magical chocolate shop (p148)

Monti, Esquilino & San Lorenzo
Centre for independent fashion,
homewares and vintage
boutiques (p157)

Trastevere & Gianicolo
Gifts and one-off shops in
one of Rome's prettiest
neighbourhoods (p159)

San Giovanni & Testaccio
Explore a colourful food market
and glorious delis (p161)

Opening Hours

Most city-centre shops 9am to
7.30pm (or 10am to 8pm) Monday to
Saturday; some close Monday morning

Smaller shops 9am to 1pm and
3.30pm to 7.30pm (or 4pm to 8pm)
Monday to Saturday

Sales

Rome's winter sales (*saldi*) run from
early January, usually the first Saturday
of the month, to mid- or late February.
Summer sales are from the first Saturday of July to late August.

The Best...

Experience Rome's best shopping

Fashion

Re(f)use (p152) Bags and jewellery made from upcycled objects.

Tina Sondergaard (p157) Retro-inspired dresses at bijou Monti boutique.

Gente (p152) An emporium-style, multi-label boutique.

Manila Grace (p152) Essential homegrown label for dedicated fashionistas.

Homewares

Bialetti (p161) The place to go for cool Italian kitchenware.

Mercato Monti Urban Market (p158) Vintage homeware finds cram this weekend market.

c.u.c.i.n.a. (p156) Gastronomic gadgets to enhance your culinary life.

Shoes

Benheart (p159) Fashionable, handmade shoes by one of Italy's most talented young designers.

Marta Ray (p149) Women's ballerina flats in a rainbow of stylish colours.

Fausto Santini (p154) Rome's best-known shoe designer.

Borini (p151) Unfussy shop for women's high-street footwear fashions.

Delis & Gourmet Food

Volpetti (p161) Bulging with delicious delicacies, and notably helpful staff.

Antica Caciara Trasteverina (p159) Century-old deli brimming with goodies.

Salumeria Roscioli (p148) Byword for foodie excellence, with mouth-watering delicacies.

Biscottificio Innocenti (p159) Enchanting, old-world biscuit shop in Trastevere backstreet.

Confetteria Moriondo & Gariglio (p148) A magical chocolate shop.

Handicrafts

Artisanal Cornucopia (p152) Concept store showcasing artisan pieces by Italian designers.

Ibiz – Artigianato in Cuoio (p148) Wallets, bags and sandals in a kaleidoscope of leathers.

Il Sellaio (p156) Beautifully crafted leather bags, belts and accessories.

Flumen Profumi (p153) Fragrances with a 'made in Rome' couture label.

Gifts & Souvenirs

La Bottega del Marmoraro (p153) Commission a marble inscription.

Federico Buccellati (p154) Handcrafted silverware by top silver- and goldsmith.

Flumen Profumi (p153) Unique 'made in Rome' scents.

Aldo Fefè (p149) Artisanal hand-crafted notebooks and photo albums.

Bookshops

Almost Corner Bookshop (p159) Superbly stocked, English-language bookshop.

Feltrinelli International (p157) An excellent range of latest releases in several languages.

★Lonely Planet's Top Choices

Benheart (p159) Street-fashion shoes and jackets by one of Italy's savviest young talents.

Porta Portese Market (p159) Mammoth, Sunday-morning flea market.

Confetteria Moriondo & Gariglio (p148) Historic shop selling chocolates made from 19th-century recipes.

Re(f)use (p152) Ethical fashion accessories by Roman designer Ilaria Venturini Fendi.

La Bottega del Marmoraro (p153) Carve out a message in marble for a loved one.

Salumeria Roscioli (p148) Foodie heaven.

Confetteria Moriondo & Gariglio

🅐 Centro Storico

Confetteria Moriondo & Gariglio
Chocolate

(🕿06 699 08 56; Via del Piè di Marmo 21-22; ⊙9am-7.30pm Mon-Sat; 🚇Via del Corso) Roman poet Trilussa was so smitten with this historic chocolate shop – established by the Torinese confectioners to the royal house of Savoy – that he was moved to mention it in verse. And we agree, it's a gem. Decorated like an elegant tearoom, with crimson walls, tables and glass cabinets, it specialises in delicious handmade chocolates, many prepared according to original 19th-century recipes.

Ibiz – Artigianato in Cuoio
Fashion & Accessories

(🕿06 6830 7297; www.ibizroma.it; Via dei Chiavari 39; ⊙10am-7.30pm Mon-Sat; 🚇Corso Vittorio Emanuele II) In her diminutive family workshop, Elisa Nepi and her team craft exquisite, soft-as-butter leather wallets, bags, belts and sandals, in simple but classy designs and myriad colours. You can pick up a belt for about €35, while for a bag you should bank on at least €110.

Bartolucci
Toys

(🕿06 6919 0894; www.bartolucci.com; Via dei Pastini 98; ⊙10am-10pm; 🚇Via del Corso) It's difficult to resist going into this magical toyshop where everything is carved out of wood. By the main entrance, a Pinocchio pedals his bike robotically, perhaps dreaming of the full-size motorbike parked nearby, while inside there are all manner of ticking clocks, rocking horses, planes and more Pinocchios than you're likely to see in your whole life.

Salumeria Roscioli
Food & Drinks

(🕿06 687 52 87; www.salumeriaroscioli.com; Via dei Giubbonari 21; ⊙8.30am-8.30pm Mon-Sat; 🚇Via Arenula) The rich scents of cured meats, cheeses, conserves, olive oil and balsamic vinegar intermingle at this top-class deli, one of Rome's finest. Alongside iconic Italian products, you'll also find a vast choice of wines and a range of French cheeses, Spanish hams and Scottish salmon.

You can also dine here at the deli's excellent in-house restaurant (p125).

namasTèy
Tea

(✆06 6813 5660; www.namastey.it; Via della Palombella 26; ◷10.30am-7.30pm Mon-Sat, 3.30-7.30pm Sun; ⏹Largo di Torre Argentina) After a visit to this charming shop, you'll be reminded of it every time you have a tea. Set up like an apothecary with ceiling-high shelves and rows of jars, it stocks blends from across the globe, as well as everything you could ever need for your home tea ritual – teapots, cups, infusers and filters. It also sells coffee and bite-size snacks.

Calzoleria Petrocchi
Shoes

(✆06 687 62 89; www.calzoleriapetrocchi. it; Vicolo Sugarelli 2; ◷8am-5.30pm Mon-Fri, 9am-1pm Sat, by appointment Sun; ⏹Corso Vittorio Emanuele II/Tassoni) This boutique has been crafting leather shoes by hand for well-heeled Romans and film icons such as Audrey Hepburn and Robert De Niro since 1946. Choose from the ready-to-wear collection or design a bespoke pair of your own: head artisan Marco Cecchi personally takes clients' measurements and customises shoes based on their selection of leather and style.

Marta Ray
Shoes

(✆06 6880 2641; www.martaray.it; Via dei Coronari 121; ◷10am-8pm; ⏹Via Zanardelli) Women's ballet flats and elegant, everyday bags, in rainbow colours and butter-soft leather, are the hallmarks of the emerging Marta Ray brand. At this store, one of three in town, you'll find a selection of trademark ballerinas and a colourful line in modern, beautifully designed handbags.

Luna & L'Altra
Fashion & Accessories

(✆06 6880 4995; www.lunaelaltra.com; Piazza Pasquino 76; ◷3.30-7.30pm Mon, 10am-7.30pm Tue-Sat; ⏹Corso Vittorio Emanuele II) An address for those with their finger on the pulse, this all-white fashion boutique is one of a number of independent stores on and around Via del Governo Vecchio. In its austere, gallery-like interior, clothes by designers Comme des Garçons, Issey Miyake and Yohji Yamamoto are exhibited in reverential style.

One-off Boutiques & Vintage

For cutting-edge designs and vintage clothes make for Via del Governo Vecchio, an atmospheric street running from near Piazza Navona towards the river. You'll also find boutiques on Via del Pellegrino and around Campo de' Fiori.

In the Monti area, Via del Boschetto, Via Urbana and Via dei Serpenti feature unique clothing boutiques, including a couple where you can get your clothes adjusted to fit, as well as jewellery makers. Monti's also a centre for vintage clothes shops, as well as a weekend vintage market, **Mercato Monti Urban Market** (p158).

Atelier Patrizia Pieroni
Fashion & Accessories

(Arsenale Gallery; ✆06 6880 2424; www.patrizia pieroni.it; Via del Pellegrino 172; ◷3.30-7.30pm Mon, 10.30am-7.30pm Tue-Sat; ⏹Corso Vittorio Emanuele II) The atelier of celebrated Roman designer Patrizia Pieroni is a watchword for original, high-end women's fashion. The virgin white interior creates a clean, contemporary showcase for Patrizia's latest colourful creations, and exhibitions and cultural events are often hosted here.

I Colori di Dentro
Art

(✆06 683 24 94; www.mgluffarelli.com; Via dei Banchi Vecchi 29; ◷11am-6.45pm Mon-Sat; ⏹Corso Vittorio Emanuele II) Take home some Mediterranean sunshine. Artist Maria Grazia Luffarelli's paintings are a riotous celebration of Italian colours, with sunny yellow landscapes, blooming flowers, Roman cityscapes and comfortable-looking cats. You can buy original watercolours or prints, as well as postcards, T-shirts, notebooks and calendars.

Aldo Fefè
Arts & Crafts

(✆06 6880 3585; Via della Stelletta 20b; ◷8am-7.30pm Mon-Sat; ⏹Corso del Rinascimento) In his small workshop, master craftsman Aldo Fefè continues to bind books and produce beautifully hand-painted notebooks, albums,

Big-Name Designer Fashions

Big-name designer boutiques gleam in the grid of streets between Piazza di Spagna and Via del Corso. All the great Italian and international names are here as well as many lesser-known designers, all selling clothes, shoes, accessories and dreams. The immaculately clad designer-fashion spine is Via dei Condotti, but plenty of boutiques pepper Via Borgognona, Via della Borghese, Via della Vite and Via del Babuino too.

For chic, independent boutiques stocking pieces by smaller, lesser-known or young up-and-coming designers, mooch the lengths of Via dell'Oca and Via della Penna near Piazza del Popolo.

boxes and photo albums (from €18). You can also buy Florentine wrapping paper and calligraphic pens here.

SBU   Clothing
(☑06 6880 2547; www.sbu.it; Via di San Pantaleo 68-69; ⊙10am-7.30pm Mon-Sat, noon-7pm Sun; ▣Corso Vittorio Emanuele II) The flagship store of hip jeans label SBU, aka Strategic Business Unit, occupies a 19th-century workshop near Piazza Navona, complete with cast-iron columns and wooden racks. Alongside jeans, superbly cut from top-end Japanese denim, you can also pick up casual shirts, jackets, hats, sweaters and T-shirts.

Alberta Gloves   Fashion & Accessories
(☑06 679 73 18; Corso Vittorio Emanuele II 18; ⊙10am-7pm Mon-Sat; ▣Largo di Torre Argentina) From elbow-length silk evening gloves to tan-coloured driving mitts, this tiny family-run shop has a handmade glove for every conceivable occasion. Silk scarves and woolly hats too. Reckon on about €40 to €45 for a classic pair of leather gloves.

Officina Profumo Farmaceutica di Santa Maria Novella   Cosmetics
(☑06 687 96 08; www.smnovella.com; Corso del Rinascimento 47; ⊙10am-7.30pm Mon-Sat; ▣Corso del Rinascimento) A branch of one of Italy's oldest pharmacies stocks natural perfumes and cosmetics as well as herbal infusions, teas and potpourri, all shelved in wooden, glass-fronted cabinets under a flamboyant Murano chandelier. The original pharmacy was founded in Florence in 1612 by the Dominican monks of Santa Maria Novella, and today many of its cosmetics are still based on 17th-century herbal recipes.

Le Artigiane   Arts & Crafts
(☑06 6830 9347; www.leartigiane.it; Via di Torre Argentina 72; ⊙10am-7.30pm; ▣Largo di Torre Argentina) A space for local artisans to showcase their wares, this eclectic shop is part of an ongoing project to sustain and promote Italy's artisanal traditions. It's a browser's dream with an eclectic range of handmade clothes, costume jewellery, ceramics, design objects and lamps.

Patrizia Corvaglia   Jewellery
(☑06 4555 1441; www.patriziacorvaglia.it; Via dei Banchi Nuovi 45; ⊙11am-7.30pm Mon-Sat; ▣Corso Vittorio Emanuele II) At her boutique in the former workshop of Renaissance goldsmith Benvenuti Cellini, Patrizia Corvaglia designs and handcrafts her own line of jewellery. Her abstract, sometimes baroque, creations feature precious silver and gold set with raw gemstones.

Jerry Thomas Emporium   Drinks
(☑06 8697 0138; Vicolo Cellini 16; ⊙2-8pm Tue-Sat; ▣Corso Vittorio Emanuele II) An offshoot of the cult Jerry Thomas Project (p169) speakeasy, this shop stocks a collector's dream of vermouth, spirits and liqueurs. Among the Italian and international labels, you'll find limited editions and artisanal blends made from historical recipes.

Le Tartarughe   Fashion & Accessories
(☑06 679 22 40; www.letartarughe.eu; Via del Piè di Marmo 17; ⊙10am-7.30pm Tue-Sat, 4-7.30pm Mon; ▣Via del Corso) Fashionable, versatile

SBU

and elegant, Susanna Liso's catchy seasonal designs adorn this relaxed, white-walled boutique. Her clothes, often blended from raw silks, cashmere and fine merrino wool, provide vibrant modern updates on classic styles. You'll also find a fine line in novelty accessories.

Rachele   Children's Clothing
(📞329 6481004; www.facebook.com/racheleart; Vicolo del Bollo 6; ⏱10.30am-2pm & 3.30-7.30pm Tue-Sat; 🚌Corso Vittorio Emanuele II) If your 12-year-old (or younger) needs a wardrobe update, you would do well to look up Rachele in her delightful shop just off Via del Pellegrino. With everything from hats and mitts to romper suits and jackets, all brightly coloured and all handmade, this sort of shop is a dying breed. Most items are around the €40 to €50 mark.

Borini   Shoes
(📞06 687 56 70; Via dei Pettinari 86-87; ⏱10am-7.30pm Mon-Sat; 🚌Via Arenula) Don't be fooled by the workaday look of the store – those in the know head to this shop for the latest footwear fashions. Women's styles,

ranging from ballet flats to heeled sandals, are displayed in functional glass cabinets, alongside a small selection of men's boots and leather lace-ups.

De Sanctis   Ceramics
(📞06 6880 6810; www.desanctis1890.com; Piazza di Pietra 24; ⏱10.30am-1.30pm & 3-7.30pm Mon-Sat, 11am-5.30pm Sun; 🚌Via del Corso) In business since 1890, De Sanctis is full of impressive Sicilian and Tuscan ceramics, with sunbursts of colour decorating crockery, kitchenware, house numbers, *Cave Canem* ('Beware of the dog' in Latin) tiles and objets d'art. Items too heavy for your suitcase can be shipped worldwide.

Nardecchia   Art
(📞06 686 93 18; Via del Monserrato 106; ⏱10am-1pm Tue-Sat, 4-7.30pm Mon-Fri; 🚌Lungotevere dei Tebaldi) Famed for its antique prints, historic Nardecchia sells everything from 18th-century etchings by Giovanni Battista Piranesi to more affordable 19th-century panoramas of Rome. Expect to pay at least €150 for a small framed print.

Local Artisans

Rome's shopping scene has a surprising number of artists and artisans who create their goods on the spot in hidden workshops. There are several places in Tridente where you can get a bag, wallet or belt made to your specifications; in other shops you can commission lamps or embroidery.

TERRY VINE/GETTY IMAGES ©

Enoteca al Parlamento Achilli   Wine

(🖉06 687 34 46; www.enotecalparlamento. com; Via dei Prefetti 15; ☺9.30am-10pm Mon-Sat; 🚇Via del Corso) A temple to the finer pleasures of the bottle, this stately *enoteca* stocks a comprehensive selection of Italian and international wines, liqueurs and champagnes. A delectable mingling of scents – wine, chocolate, fine meats and cheeses – greets you as you enter, whether to buy, sample a glass or two, or dine at its Michelin-starred **restaurant** (🖉06 8676 1422; meals from €90, tasting menus €150-170; ☺12.30-2.30pm & 7.30-10.30pm)

🄐 Tridente, Trevi & the Quirinale

Re(f)use   Design

(🖉06 6813 6975; www.carminacampus.com; Via della Fontanelle di Borghese 40; ☺10am-7.30pm Tue-Sat, 3-7.30pm Mon; 🚇Via del Corso) Fascinating to browse, this clever boutique showcases unique Carmina Campus pieces

– primarily bags and jewellery – made from upcycled objects and recycled fabrics. The brand is the love child of Rome-born designer Ilaria Venturini Fendi (of the Fendi family), a passionate advocate of ethical fashion, who crafts contemporary bracelets from beer and soft-drink cans, and bold bags from recycled materials.

Manila Grace   Fashion & Accessories

(🖉06 679 78 36; www.manilagrace.com; Via Frattina 60; ☺10am-8pm; 🅼Spagna) An essential homegrown label for dedicated followers of fashion, Manila Grace mixes bold prints, patterns and fabrics to create a strikingly unique, assertive style for women who like to stand out in a crowd. Think a pair of red stiletto shoes with a fuchsia-pink pom pom on the toe, a striped jacket or a glittering gold bag with traditional tan-leather trim. Alessia Santi is the talented designer behind the brand.

Artisanal Cornucopia   Design

(🖉342 8714597; www.artisanalcornucopia.com; Via dell'Oca 38a; ☺10.30am-7.30pm Tue-Sat, from 3.30 Mon, from 4.30pm Sun; 🅼Flaminio) One of several stylish independent boutiques on Via dell'Oca, this chic concept store showcases exclusive handmade pieces by Italian designers: think a trunk full of Anthony Peto hats, bold sculpture-like lamps by Roman designer Vincenzo Del Pizzo, and delicate gold necklaces and other jewellery crafted by Giulia Barela. It also sells artisan bags, shoes, candles, homewares and other lovely handmade objects.

Gente   Fashion & Accessories

(🖉06 320 76 71; www.genteroma.com; Via del Babuino 77; ☺10.30am-7.30pm Mon-Fri, to 8pm Sat, 11.30am-7.30pm Sun; 🅼Spagna) This multi-label boutique was the first in Rome to bring all the big-name luxury designers – Italian, French and otherwise – under one roof, and its vast emporium-styled space remains an essential stop for every serious fashionista. Labels include Dolce & Gabbana, Prada, Alexander McQueen, Sergio Rossi and Missoni.

It has a sparkling new store for women at **Via Frattini** (🖉06 678 91 32; www.genteroma.

com; Via Frattina 93; ⊙10.30am-7.30pm Mon-Fri, to 8pm Sat, 11.30am-7.30pm Sun; 🚇Via del Corso).

La Bottega del Marmoraro   Art
(📞06 320 76 60; Via Margutta 53b; ⊙8am-7.30pm Mon-Sat; ⓂFlaminio) Watch *marmoraro* (marble artist) Sandro Fiorentini chip away in this enchanting Aladdin's cave filled, floor to ceiling, with his decorative marble plaques engraved with various inscriptions: la dolce vita, *la vita e bella* (life is beautiful) etc. Plaques start at €10 and Sandro will engrave any inscription you like (from €15). On winter days, warm your hands with Sandro in front of the open log fire.

Galleria Alberto Sordi   Shopping Centre
(📞06 6919 0769; www.galleriaalbertosordi.it; Galleria di Piazza Colonna, Piazza Colonna; ⊙8.30am-9pm Mon-Fri, to 10pm Sat, 9.30am-9pm Sun; 🚇Via del Corso) This elegant stained-glass arcade appeared in Alberto Sordi's 1973 classic, *Polvere di stelle* (Stardust), and has since been renamed for Rome's favourite actor, who died in 2003. It's a serene place to browse stores such as Zara and Feltrinelli, and there's an airy cafe ideal for a quick coffee break.

Flumen Profumi   Perfume
(📞06 6830 7635; www.flumenprofumi.com; Via della Fontanella di Borghese 41; ⊙11am-2pm & 3.30-7.30pm; 🚇Via del Corso) Unique 'made in Rome' scents is what this artisan perfumery on Tridente's smartest shopping strip is all about. Natural perfumes are oil-based, contain four to eight base notes and evoke la dolce vita in Italy. Incantro fuses pomegranate with white flower, while Ritrovarsi Ancora is a nostalgic fragrance evocative of long, lazy, family meals around a shared countryside table (smell the fig!).

Balenciaga   Fashion & Accessories
(📞06 8750 2260; www.balenciaga.com; Via Borgognona 7e; ⊙10am-7pm Mon-Sat; ⓂSpagna) Design lovers will adore this boutique of French fashion label Balenciaga, inside a 19th century *palazzo* with vintage furniture and

...a serene place to browse stores such as Zara and Feltrinelli...

Galleria Alberto Sordi

fabulous 'aristocratic residence' vibe. Bold marquetry mixes rare woods in geometric zigzags, and the theatrical overhead lighting is by Italian architect and lighting designer Gae Aulenti (1927–2012), best known for transforming an abandoned Parisian train station into Paris' Musée d'Orsay.

Federico Buccellati   Jewellery

(☎06 679 03 29; www.federicobuccellati.it; Via dei Condotti 31; ☺3-7pm Mon, 10am-1.30pm & 3-7pm Tue-Fri, 10am-1.30pm & 2-6pm Sat; Ⓜ Spagna) Run today by the third generation of one of Italy's most prestigious silver- and goldsmiths, this historical shop opened in 1926. Everything is handcrafted and often delicately engraved with decorative flowers, leaves and nature-inspired motifs. Don't miss the Silver Salon on the 1st floor showcasing some original silverware and jewellery pieces by grandfather Mario.

Fendi   Fashion & Accessories

(☎06 3345 0890; www.fendi.com; Palazzo Fendi, Largo Carlo Goldoni 420; ☺10am-7.30pm Mon-Sat, from 10.30am Sun; Ⓜ Spagna) With traverstine walls, stunning contemporary art and sweeping red-marble staircase, the flagship store of Rome's iconic fashion house inside 18th-century Palazzo Fendi is dazzling. Born in Rome in 1925 as a leather and fur workshop on Via del Plebiscito, this luxurious temple to Roman fashion is as much concept store as *maison,* selling ready-to-wear clothing for men and women (including its signature leather and fur pieces).

Fausto Santini   Shoes

(☎06 678 41 14; www.faustosantini.com; Via Frattina 120; ☺10am-7.30pm Mon-Sat, 11am-7pm Sun; Ⓜ Spagna) Rome's best-known shoe designer, Fausto Santini is famous for his beguilingly simple, architectural shoe designs, with beautiful boots and shoes made from butter-soft leather. Colours are beautiful, and the quality is impeccable. Seek out the end-of-line **discount shop** (☎06 488 09 34; Via Cavour 106; ☺10am-1pm & 3.30-7.30pm Mon-Fri, 10am-1.30pm & 3-7.30pm Sat; Ⓜ Cavour) if the shoes here are out of your price range.

Anglo American Bookshop   Books

(☎06 679 52 22; www.aab.it; Via della Vite 102; ☺3.30-7.30pm Mon, 10.30am-7.30pm Tue-Sat;

Fendi

Ⓜ Spagna) Particularly good for university reference books, the Anglo American Bookshop is well stocked and well known. It has an excellent range of literature, travel guides, children's books and maps, and if it hasn't got the book you want, staff will order it in.

Salumeria Focacci   Food
(☏ 06 679 12 28; www.salumeriafocacci.it; Via della Croce 43; ☺ 8am-8pm Mon-Sat; Ⓜ Spagna) One of several smashing delis along this pretty street, Salumeria Focacci is the place to buy cheese, cold cuts, smoked fish, caviar, pasta, olive oil and wine.

I Vippini   Children's Clothing
(☏ 06 6880 3754; Via della Fontanella di Borghese 65; ☺ 10am-7pm Tue-Sat, 3-7pm Mon; 🚇 Via del Corso) This pretty little boutique sells exquisite designer fashion for *bambini*, from newborns to teens. It stocks Italian designers in the main, alongside its own exclusive handmade label.

LAR   Homewares
(Lavori Artigiani Romani; ☏ 06 687 66 47; www.paralumi.it; Via del Leoncino 29; ☺ 9am-6.30pm Mon-Fri, to 6pm Sat; 🚇 Via del Corso) Artisanal lamps and lampshades have been produced at this colourful family-run workshop since 1938. Their one-off creations, made from materials such as wood, brass and parchment, come in all shapes and sizes, from minimal free-standing white lights to cubist Mondrian-inspired table lamps.

Fabriano   Arts & Crafts
(☏ 06 3260 0361; www.fabrianoboutique.com; Via del Babuino 173; ☺ 10am-8pm; Ⓜ Flaminio, Spagna) Fabriano makes stationery sexy, with deeply desirable leather-bound diaries, funky notebooks and products embossed with street maps of Rome. It's perfect for picking up a gift, with other items including beautifully made leather key rings and quirky paper jewellery by local designers.

Tod's   Shoes
(☏ 06 6821 0066; www.tods.com; Via della Fontanella di Borghese 56a; ☺ 10.30am-7.30pm Mon-Sat, 10am-2pm & 3-7.30pm Sun; 🚇 Via del Corso) The trademark of this luxury Italian brand, known

Food Shopping

Rome is foodie heaven. As well as a number of historic delis selling all manner of gourmet treasures, you'll also come across wonderful food markets – there's usually one in every district – where you can buy cheese, salami and other delicious stuff. At the weekends, there are also farmers markets laden with local seasonal produce.

For an entirely different experience, head to **Eataly** (p140), a vast mall entirely dedicated to food, with shops showcasing Italy's enviable larder, as well as kitchenware and books.

ALEXANDER MAZURKEVICH/SHUTTERSTOCK

more recently as the generous benefactor behind the much-needed clean-up of the northern and southern facades of the Colosseum facade, is its rubber-studded loafers – perfect weekend footwear for kicking back at your country estate.

Patrizia Pepe   Fashion & Accessories
(☏ 06 9437 7891; www.patriziapepe.com; Via del Corso 141; ☺ 10am-8pm; 🚇 Via del Corso) The most recent Patrizia Pepe boutique to open in Rome, this Florentine brand is known for its 'elegant yet still rock' fashion for men, women and children. Designs are contemporary, functional, glamorous and just a little bit sexy.

Pelletteria Nives   Fashion & Accessories
(☏ 333 3370831; 2nd fl, Via delle Carrozze 16; ☺ 9am-7pm Mon-Sat; Ⓜ Spagna) Take the

Tax-Free Shopping

Non-EU residents who spend over €154.94 on any one given day at shops with a 'Tax Free for Tourists' sticker (www.taxrefund.it) are entitled to a tax refund. Complete a form and get it stamped by customs as you leave Italy.

rickety lift to this workshop, choose from the softest leathers, and you will shortly be the proud owner of a handmade, designer-style bag, wallet, belt or briefcase – take a design with you. Bags cost €150 to €350 and take around a week to make.

Sermoneta Fashion & Accessories

(📞06 679 19 60; www.sermonetagloves.com; Piazza di Spagna 61; ⏱9.30am-8pm Mon-Sat, 10.30am-7pm Sun; Ⓜ Spagna) Buying leather gloves in Rome is a rite of passage for some, and its most famous glove-seller opposite the Spanish Steps is the place to go. Choose from a kaleidoscopic range of quality leather and suede gloves lined with silk and cashmere. An expert assistant will size up your hand in a glance. Just don't expect them to crack a smile.

c.u.c.i.n.a. Homewares

(📞06 679 12 75; www.cucinastore.com; Via Mario de' Fiori 65; ⏱3.30-7.30pm Mon, from 10am Tue-Fri, from 10.30am Sat; Ⓜ Spagna) Make your own *cucina* (kitchen) look the part with the designer goods from this famous kitchenware shop, with everything from classic *caffettiere* (Italian coffee makers) to cutlery and myriad devices you'll decide you simply must have.

ⓖ Vatican City, Borgo & Prati

Il Sellaio Fashion & Accessories

(📞06 321 17 19; www.serafinipelletteria.it; Via Caio Mario 14; ⏱9.30am-7.30pm Mon-Fri, 9.30am-1pm & 3.30-7.30pm Sat; Ⓜ Ottaviano-San Pietro) During the 1960s Ferruccio Serafini was one of Rome's most sought-after artisans, making handmade leather shoes

and bags for the likes of John F Kennedy, Liz Taylor and Marlon Brando. Nowadays, his daughter Francesca runs the family shop where you can pick up beautiful hand-stitched bags, belts and accessories. You can also have your own designs made to order.

Rechicle Vintage

(📞06 3265 2469; www.facebook.com/rechicle roma; Piazza dell' Unità 21; ⏱10.30am-1.30pm & 3-7pm Mon-Sat; 🚇Via Cola di Rienzo) Lovers of vintage fashions should make a beeline for this fab boutique. Furnished with antique family furniture and restored cabinets, it's full of wonderful finds such as Roger Vivier comma heels (with their original box), iconic Chanel jackets, Hermès bags, Balenciaga coats and much more besides.

Antica Manifattura Cappelli Hats

(📞06 3972 5679; www.antica-cappelleria. it; Via degli Scipioni 46; ⏱9am-7pm Mon-Sat; Ⓜ Ottaviano-San Pietro) A throwback to a more elegant age, the atelier-boutique of milliner Patrizia Fabri offers a wide range of beautifully crafted hats. Choose from the off-the-peg line of straw Panamas, vintage cloches, felt berets and tweed deerstalkers, or have one made to measure. Prices range from about €70 to €300 and ordered hats can be delivered within the day.

Enoteca Costantini Wine

(📞06 320 35 75; https://enotecacostantinipiero. it; Piazza Cavour 16; ⏱9am-1pm Tue-Sat, 4.30-8pm Mon-Sat; 🚇Piazza Cavour) If you're after a hard-to-find grappa or something special for your wine collection, this excellent *enoteca* is the place to try. Opened in 1972, Piero Costantini's superbly stocked shop is a point of reference for aficionados with its 800-sq-m basement cellar and a colossal collection of Italian and world wines, champagnes and more than 1000 spirits from across the globe.

Paciotti Salumeria Food & Drinks

(📞06 3973 3646; www.paciottisalumeria. it; Via Marcantonio Bragadin 51; ⏱7.30am-8.30pm Mon-Wed, Fri & Sat, 12.30-8.30pm Thu;

EYE35 STOCK/ALAMY STOCK PHOTO ©

[M]Cipro-Musei Vaticani) This family-run deli a short jaunt from St Peter's Basilica stocks a foodie's wish-list of Italian edibles. Prosciutto, cheeses, olive oil, dried pasta, balsamic vinegar, wine and truffle pâtés crowd the shelves, and can be bubbled-wrapped and vacuum-sealed for travel. Patriarch Antonio Paciotti and his three sons merrily advise customers in both Italian and English.

⊙ Monti, Esquilino & San Lorenzo

Tina Sondergaard   Fashion & Accessories

([☎]334 385 07 99; www.facebook.com/tina.son dergaard.rome; Via del Boschetto 1d; ⊙10.30am-7.30pm Mon-Sat, closed Aug; [M]Cavour) Sublimely cut and whimsically retro-esque, Tina Sondergaard's handmade threads for women are a hit with fashion cognoscenti, including Italian rock star Carmen Consoli and the city's theatre and TV crowd. You can have adjustments made (included in the price); dresses cost around €150.

Feltrinelli International   Books

([☎]06 482 78 78; www.lafeltrinelli.it; Via VE Orlando 84-86; ⊙9am-8pm Mon-Sat, 10.30am-1.30pm & 4-8pm Sun; [M]Repubblica) The international branch of Italy's ubiquitous bookseller has a splendid collection of books in English, Italian, Spanish, French, German and Portuguese. You'll find everything from recent bestsellers to dictionaries, travel guides, DVDs and an excellent assortment of maps.

Roma Liuteria di Mathias Menanteau   Musical Instruments

([☎]339 3517677; www.romaliuteria.it; Via di Santa Maria Maggiore 150; ⊙10am-1pm & 3-7pm Mon-Sat; [M]Cavour) A vintage ceramic-tiled wood burner casts a golden glow on this old-fashioned artisan workshop where French luthier Mathias Menanteau crafts and restores cellos and violins by hand.

Transmission   Music

([☎]06 4470 4370; www.transmissionroma.com; Via Salentini 27; ⊙10am-2pm & 3-8pm Mon-Sat; [🚃]Via Tiburtina) One of a handful of shops serving Rome's record collectors, this San

Lorenzo store is vinyl nirvana. Its eclectic collection of LPs, CDs, 7-inch singles, DVDs and Blu-rays covers the whole musical gamut, ranging from classical music and 1950s oldies to jazz, reggae, punk, new wave and modern dance.

Mercato Monti
Urban Market   Market
(www.mercatomonti.com; Via Leonina 46; ⊘10am-8pm Sat & Sun Sep-Jun; MCavour) Vintage clothes, accessories, one-off pieces by local designers: this market in the hip 'hood of Monti is well worth a rummage.

Podere Vecciano   Food
(✆06 4891 3812; www.poderevecciano.com; Via dei Serpenti 33; ⊘10am-8pm Tue-Sun; MCavour) Selling produce from its Tuscan farm, this shop is a great place to pick up presents, such as different varieties of pesto, honey and marmalade, selected wines, olive-oil-based cosmetics and beautiful olive-wood chopping boards. There's even an olive tree growing in the middle of the shop.

Abito   Fashion & Accessories
(✆06 488 10 17; www.legallinelle.com; Via Panisperna 61; ⊘11am-8pm Mon-Sat, 12.30-8pm Sun; MCavour) Wilma Silvestre, founder of local label Le Gallinelle, designs elegant clothes with a difference. Here at her Monti boutique you can browse her chic, laid-back styles and buy off the rack.

Perlei   Jewellery
(✆06 4891 3862; www.perlei.com; Via del Boschetto 35; ⊘10am-8pm Mon-Sat, 11am-2pm & 3-8pm Sun; MCavour) Contemporary women's jewellery created by Noritamy, a collaboration between Tammar Edelman and Elinor Avni, is showcased in this tiny artisan boutique. Think bright polished stones, organic shapes and architectural structures.

Nuovo Mercato
Esquilino   Market
(Via Filippo Turati 160; ⊘5am-3pm Mon, Wed & Thu, to 5pm Tue, Fri & Sat; MVittorio Emanuele) Lap up the real Rome at this buzzing covered food market where budget-conscious Romans and students shop for fresh fruit, veg, exotic herbs, spices and more.

Nuovo Mercato Esquilino

BALONCICI/SHUTTERSTOCK ©

La Bottega del Cioccolato
Food

(📞06 482 14 73; www.labottegadelcioccolato.it; Via Leonina 82; ⏰9.30am-7.30pm Mon-Sat; MCavour) Run by the younger generation of a long line of *chocolatiers*, this is an exotic world of scarlet walls and old-fashioned glass cabinets set into black wood, with irresistible smells wafting in from the kitchen and rows of lovingly homemade chocolates on display. Hot chocolate and cups of milk chocolate, hazelnut or eggnog mousse to take away too.

Fabio Piccioni
Jewellery

(📞339 4627261; Via del Boschetto 148; ⏰2-8pm Mon, 10.30am-1pm & 2-8pm Tue-Sun; MCavour) A sparkling Aladdin's cave of decadent, one-of-a-kind costume jewellery. Artisan Fabio Piccioni recycles old trinkets to create remarkable art-deco-inspired pieces.

🅐 Trastevere & Gianicolo

Benheart
Fashion & Accessories

(📞06 5832 0801; www.benheart.it; Via del Moro 47; ⏰11am-11pm; 🚊Piazza Triussa) From the colourful resin floor papered with children's drawings to the vintage typewriter, dial-up telephone and old-fashioned tools decorating the interior, everything about this artisanal leather boutique is achingly cool. Benheart, a young Florentine designer, is one of Italy's savviest talents and his fashionable handmade shoes (from €190) and jackets for men and women are glorious.

Antica Caciara Trasteverina
Food & Drinks

(📞06 581 28 15; www.facebook.com/anticacaciara; Via di San Francesco a Ripa 140; ⏰7am-8pm Mon-Sat; 🚊Viale di Trastevere, 🚊Viale di Trastevere) The fresh ricotta is a prized possession at this century-old deli, and it's all usually snapped up by lunchtime. If you're too late, take solace in the to-die-for *ricotta infornata* (oven-baked ricotta), 35kg wheels of famous, black-waxed *pecorino romano* DOP (€16.50 per kilo), and aromatic garlands of *guanciale* (pig's jowl) begging to be chopped up, panfried and thrown into the perfect carbonara.

Top Five for Wine Buying

Les Vignerons (p159)
Enoteca Costantini (p156)
namasTèy (p149)
Jerry Thomas Emporium (p150)
Enoteca al Parlamento Achilli (p152)

Biscottificio Innocenti
Food

(📞06 580 39 26; www.facebook.com/biscottificio Innocenti; Via della Luce 21; ⏰8am-8pm Mon-Sat, 9.30am-2pm Sun; 🚊Viale di Trastevere, 🚊Viale di Trastevere) For homemade biscuits, bite-sized meringues and tiny fruit tarts, there is no finer address in Rome than this vintage *biscottificio* with ceramic-tiled interior, flynet door curtain and a set of old-fashioned scales on the counter to weigh out biscuits (€16 to €24 per kilo). The shop has been run with much love and passion for several decades by the ever-dedicated Stefania.

Les Vignerons
Wine

(📞06 6477 1439; www.lesvignerons.it; Via Mameli 61; ⏰4-9pm Mon, 11am-9pm Tue-Thu, 11am-9.30pm Fri & Sat; 🚊Viale di Trastevere, 🚊Viale di Trastevere) If you're looking for some interesting wines to take home, search out this lovely Trastevere wine shop. It boasts one of the capital's best collections of natural wines, mainly from small Italian and French producers, as well as a comprehensive selection of spirits and international craft beers.

Porta Portese Market
Market

(Piazza Porta Portese; ⏰6am-2pm Sun; 🚊Viale di Trastevere, 🚊Viale di Trastevere) To see another side of Rome, head to this mammoth flea market. With thousands of stalls selling everything from rare books and fell-off-a-lorry bikes to Peruvian shawls and MP3 players, it's crazily busy and a lot of fun. Keep your valuables safe and wear your haggling hat.

Almost Corner Bookshop
Books

(📞06 583 69 42; www.facebook.com/almost cornerbookshop; Via del Moro 45; ⏰10am-7.30pm Mon-Thu, to 8pm Fri & Sat, 11am-8pm Sun; 🚊Piazza

Top Rome Souvenirs

Shoes

Nothing screams glamour more than a pair of Italian shoes. Get the latest fashions at Benheart (p159), Marta Ray (p149) or Fausto Santini (p154).

Jewellery

Rome's romantic streets are tailor-made for jewellery shopping. Search out boutiques like Patrizia Corvaglia (p150) and Re(f)use (p152) for original one-offs.

Leather Bag

For a butter-soft hand-stitched leather bag, head to a workshop such as Ibiz – Artigianato in Cuoio (p148) or Il Sellaio (p156).

Deli Treats

Delis Volpetti (p161) and Salumeria Roscioli (p148) are laden with foodie treasures, from wine and olive oil to pasta, parmesan and balsamic vinegar.

Marble Carving

In Vino Veritas. Carpe Diem. Nulla nuova, buona nuova. Choose your fave Italian saying and set it in stone, literally, at La Bottega del Marmoraro (p153).

Trilussa) This is how a bookshop should look: a crammed haven full of rip-roaring reads, with every millimetre of wall space containing English-language fiction and nonfiction (including children's) and travel guides. Heaven to browse.

Roma-Store   Perfume

(📞06 581 87 89; www.romastoreprofumi.it; Via della Lungaretta 63; ⊙10am-8pm; 🚊Viale di Trastevere, 🚊Viale di Trastevere) An enchanting perfume shop crammed full of deliciously enticing bottles of scent, including lots of small, lesser-known brands that will have perfume-lovers practically fainting with joy.

Artigianino   Fashion & Accessories

(📞06 8917 1689; www.artigianino.com; Vicolo del Cinque 49; ⊙11am-1.30pm & 4-9pm Mon-Fri, to 11pm Sat, 4-9pm Sun; 🚊Piazza Trilussa) For buttery leather Made in Italy bags and accessories at a price that won't break the bank, in-the-know locals head to this Trastevere boutique. Expect everything from slouchy bag styles in punchy colours, to classic wallets and briefcases in neutral hues. Belts, key chains, passport holders and a line dedicated exclusively to men round out the collection.

Scala Quattordici   Clothing

(📞06 588 35 80; Via della Scala 13; ⊙10am-1.30pm & 4-8pm Tue-Sat, 4-8pm Mon; 🚊Piazza Trilussa) Make yourself over à la Audrey Hepburn with these classically tailored clothes in beautiful fabrics – either made-to-measure or off-the-peg. Pricey (a frock will set you back €600 plus) but oh so worth it.

🅞 San Giovanni & Testaccio

Volpetti   Food & Drinks

(📞06 574 23 52; www.volpetti.com; Via Marmorata 47; ⊙8.30am-2pm & 4.30-8.15pm Mon-Fri, 8.30am-8.30pm Sat; 🚊Via Marmorata) This super-stocked deli, considered by many the best in town, is a treasure trove of gourmet delicacies. Helpful staff will guide you through the extensive selection of smelly cheeses, homemade pastas, olive oils, vinegars, cured meats, veggie pies, wines and grappas. It also serves excellent sliced pizza.

Soul Food   Music

(📞06 7045 2025; www.haterecords.com; Via di San Giovanni in Laterano 192; ⊙10.30am-1.30pm & 3.30-7.30pm Tue-Sat; 🚊Via di San Giovanni in Laterano) Run by Hate Records, Soul Food is a laidback record store with an eclectic collection of vinyl that runs the musical gamut, from '60s garage and rockabilly to punk, indie, new wave, folk, funk and soul. You'll also find retro T-shirts, fanzines and other groupie clobber.

Nuovo Mercato di Testaccio   Market

(entrances on Via Galvani, Via Beniamino Franklin, Via Volta, Via Manuzio, Via Ghiberti; ⊙7am-3.30pm Mon-Sat; 🚊Via Marmorata) A trip to Testaccio's neighbourhood market is always fun. Occupying a modern, purpose-built site, it hums with morning activity as locals go about their daily shopping, picking, prodding and sniffing the brightly coloured produce and browsing displays of shoes and clothes. You'll also find several stalls serving fantastic street food.

🅞 Villa Borghese & Northern Rome

Bialetti   Homewares

(📞06 8778 4222; www.bialettistore.it; Via Salaria 52; ⊙10am-8pm Mon-Sat, 10am-1.30pm & 4-8pm Sun; 🚊Via Salaria) In 1933 Alfonso Bialetti revolutionised domestic coffee-making by creating his classic *moka caffettiera*. His design has by now become a household staple, as ubiquitous in Italian kitchens as kettles in British homes. Here at this gleaming shop you'll find a full range as well as all manner of cool kitchenware.

Bulzoni   Wine

(📞06 807 04 94; www.enotecabulzoni.it; Viale dei Parioli 36; ⊙8.30am-2pm & 4.30-8.30pm Mon-Sat; 🚊Viale Parioli) This historic *enoteca* has been supplying Parioli's wine buffs since 1929. It has a formidable collection of Italian regional wines, as well as European and New World labels, and a carefully curated selection of champagnes, liqueurs, craft beers, olive oils and gourmet delicacies.

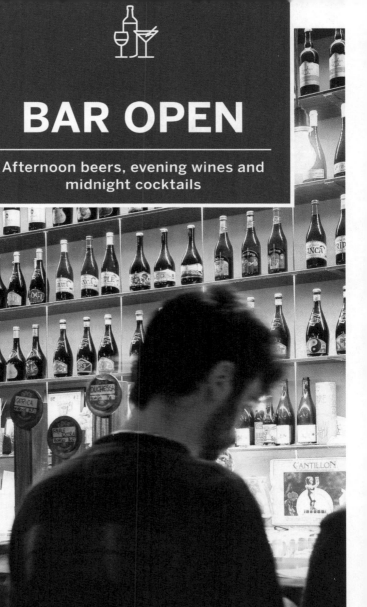

BAR OPEN

Afternoon beers, evening wines and midnight cocktails

Bar Open

Often the best way to enjoy Rome's nightlife is to wander from restaurant to bar, getting happily lost down picturesque cobbled streets. No city has better backdrops for a drink: you can savour a Campari overlooking the Roman Forum or sample artisanal beer while watching the light bounce off baroque fountains. Like most cities, Rome is a collection of neighbourhoods, each with its own character. The centro storico and Trastevere pull in a mixed crowd of well-dressed locals and tourists, Testaccio and Ostiense appeal to clubbers, while students and alternative uptowners make for San Lorenzo and Pigneto.

In This Section

Opening Hours

Most cafes: 7.30am to 8pm

Traditional bars: 7.30am to 1am or 2am

Most bars, pubs and enoteche (wine bars): lunchtime or 6pm to 2am

Nightclubs: 10pm to 4am

Villa Borghese & Northern Rome
From cool bars to hip
alternative venues (p179)

Vatican City, Borgo & Prati
Low-key scene with a sprinkling
of quiet wine bars (p170)

Tridente, Trevi & the Quirinale
Historic haunts and swanky, good-
looking cocktail bars (p170)

Centro Storico
Bars and a few clubs, a mix of
touristy and sophisticated (p168)

Monti, Esquilino & San Lorenzo
Boho bars, attractive enoteche
and grungy underground
clubs (p171)

Trastevere & Gianicolo
Buzzing area riddled with
bars, pubs and cafes (p175)

Ancient Rome
A couple of popular retreats
near the Roman ruins (p168)

San Giovanni & Testaccio
Night owls swarm to Testaccio's
strip of poptastic clubs (p177)

Southern Rome
Serious clubbing territory with
cool venues in Ostiense's ex-
industrial warehouses (p179)

Costs & Tipping

To save, look out for early-evening happy hours and *aperitivo* specials.

Glass of wine From €3

Medium beer About €5

Cocktail From €10

Tipping in bars is not necessary, although many people leave small change (perhaps €0.20) when ordering a coffee at a bar.

Useful Phrases

Aperitivo A food buffet to accompany evening drinks, usually served from around 6pm till 9pm.

Apericena A particularly abundant *aperitivo* spread.

Enoteca A wine bar; can refer to anything from a cosy neighbourhood hang-out to a hip, trendy bar.

Centri sociali Grungy venues that host club nights and gigs.

The Best...

Experience Rome's finest drinking establishments

Clubs

Circolo Illuminati (p179) Wildly popular Ostiense club with an underground vibe and star-topped courtyard garden.

Vinile (p179) Food, music, dancing and party happenings on the southern fringe of Ostiense.

Goa (p179) Rome's serious super-club, at home in a former motorbike repair shop.

For Beer

Bar San Calisto (p176) Linger over cheap beer on Trastevere's loveliest pavement terrace.

Ma Che Siete Venuti a Fà (p177) Pint-sized bar crammed with real-ale choices.

Open Baladin (p168) More than 40 beers on tap and up to 100 bottled brews.

Be.re (p170) Craft beer flows at this modern Vatican newcomer.

Enoteche

Il Sorì (p171) Gourmet wine bar and artisan *bottegha* (shop) with tastings and soirées.

Il Goccetto (p169) An old-school *vino e olio* (wine and oil) shop turned neighbourhood wine bar.

Bibenda Wine Concept (p177) Modern wine bar with a good choice of regional Italian labels.

Litro (p137) A drinking-dining hybrid with a fabulous selection of biodynamic wines.

Alternative

Rivendita Libri, Cioccolata e Vino (p175) Cream-topped shots served in chocolate shot glasses in Trastevere – the place to be after 10pm.

Lanificio 159 (p179) Cool underground venue hosts live gigs and club nights.

Yeah! Pigneto (p174) Pigneto bar with live gigs and DJs in Rome's most boho district.

Terraces & Gardens

Zuma Bar (p170) Possibly Rome's most glamorous rooftop bar .

Stravinskij Bar (p170) Hotel de Russie's elegant bar, with courtyard garden backed by Borghese gardens.

Il Palazzetto (p170) Terrace with five-star views over the Spanish Steps.

Aperitivo

Freni e Frizioni (p175) Perenially cool bar with lavish nightly buffet.

Gatsby Café (p172) Gourmet *aperitivi* in a retro cafe-bar in Esquilino.

Momart (p179) Students and local professionals love the expansive array of snacks.

Pimm's Good (p176) Pimms cocktails, generous nibbles and party-loving staff in Trastevere.

To See & Be Seen

Etablì (p169) Chic bar near Campo de' Fiori, with vintage French furniture and laid-back cool.

Salotto 42 (p169) A lounge bar, offering cocktails facing the ancient Roman Stock Exchange.

Co.So (p172) World-class craft cocktails in Pigneto.

Spirito (p171) Cocktails with the cool set in a Pigneto speakeasy.

★Lonely Planet's Top Choices

Gatsby Café (p172) Fantastic coffee, cocktails and uber-chic retro vibe in an upcycled 1950s hat shop.

Spirito (p171) Fashionable cocktail bar hidden, speakeasy-style, in the back of a Pigneto sandwich shop.

Barnum Cafe (p169) Cool vintage armchairs to sink into by day and dressed-up cocktails by night.

Open Baladin (p168) Craft beer and pub vibe in the *centro storico*.

✪ Ancient Rome

BrewDog Roma — Craft Beer

(📞06 4555 6932; www.brewdog.com/bars/world wide/roma; Via delle Terme di Tito 80; ⊙noon-1am Sun-Thu, to 2am Fri & Sat; Ⓜ Colosseo) This new bar by Scottish brewery BrewDog has proved a hit with Rome's craft-beer lovers since opening in the shadow of the Colosseum in late 2015. With a stripped-down grey-and-brick look, and up to 20 brews on tap, it's a fine spot to kick back after a day on the sights.

Cavour 313 — Wine Bar

(📞06 678 54 96; www.cavour313.it; Via Cavour 313; ⊙12.30-2.45pm daily & 6-11.30pm Mon-Thu, 6pm-midnight Fri & Sat, 7-11pm Sun, closed Aug; Ⓜ Cavour) Close to the Forum, Cavour 313 is a historic wine bar, a snug, wood-panelled retreat frequented by everyone from tourists to actors and politicians. It serves a selection of salads, cold cuts and cheeses (€9 to €12), but the headline act here is the wine. And with more than 1000 labels to choose from, you're sure to find something to please your palate.

0,75 — Bar

(📞06 687 57 06; www.075roma.com; Via dei Cerchi 65; ⊙11am-2am; 🛜; 🚌 Via dei Cerchi) This welcoming bar overlooking the Circo Massimo is good for a lingering evening drink, an *aperitivo* or casual meal (mains €6 to €16.50). It's a friendly place with a laid-back vibe, an international crowd, attractive wood-beam look, and cool tunes.

✪ Centro Storico

Open Baladin — Craft Beer

(📞06 683 89 89; www.openbaladinroma.it; Via degli Specchi 6; ⊙noon-2am; 🛜; 🚌 Via Arenula) For some years, this cool, modern pub near Campo de' Fiori has been a leading light in Rome's craft-beer scene, and with more than 40 beers on tap and up to 100 bottled brews (many from Italian artisanal microbreweries), it's still a top place for a pint. There's also a decent food menu with *panini,* gourmet burgers and daily specials.

Open Baladin

ILPO MUSTO/ALAMY STOCK PHOTO ©

Barnum Cafe
Cafe

(📞06 6476 0483; www.barnumcafe.com; Via del Pellegrino 87; ⏰9am-10pm Mon, to 2am Tue-Sat; 🛜; 🚇Corso Vittorio Emanuele II) A laid-back *Friends*-style cafe, evergreen Barnum is the sort of place you could quickly get used to. With its shabby-chic vintage furniture and white bare-brick walls, it's a relaxed spot for a breakfast cappuccino, a light lunch or a late-afternoon drink. Come evening, a coolly dressed-down crowd sips seriously good cocktails.

Etablì
Wine Bar, Cafe

(📞06 9761 6694; www.etabli.it; Vicolo delle Vacche 9a; ⏰7am-1am Mon-Wed, to 2am Thu-Sat, 9am-1am Sun; 🛜; 🚇Corso del Rinascimento) Housed in a 16th-century *palazzo,* Etablì is a rustic-chic lounge-bar-restaurant where you can drop by for a morning coffee, have a light lunch or chat over an *aperitivo*. It's laid-back and good-looking, with original French-inspired country decor – leather armchairs, rough wooden tables and a crackling fireplace. It also serves full restaurant dinners (€45) and hosts occasional live music.

Gin Corner
Cocktail Bar

(📞06 6880 2452; www.thegincorner.com; Hotel Adriano, Via Pallacorda 2; ⏰6pm-midnight; 🚇Via di Monte Brianzo) Forget fine wines and craft beers, this chic bar in the Hotel Adriano is all about the undistilled enjoyment of gin. Here the making of a simple gin and tonic is raised to an art form – the menu lists more than 10 varieties – and martinis are beautifully executed. You can also get cocktails made from other spirits if gin isn't your thing.

Jerry Thomas Project
Cocktail Bar

(📞370 1146287; www.thejerrythomasproject.it; Vicolo Cellini 30; ⏰10pm-4am Mon-Sat; 🚇Corso Vittorio Emanuele II) A self-styled speakeasy with a 1920s look and a password to get in – check the website and call to book – this hidden bar has led the way in Rome's recent love affair with cocktails. Its master mixologists know their stuff and the retro decor gives the place a real Prohibition-era feel. Note there's a €5 'membership' fee.

 An Evening in the Centro Storico

Nightlife in the *centro storico* is centred on two main areas: the lanes around Piazza Navona, with a number of elegant bars catering to the hip beautiful people; and the rowdier area around Campo de' Fiori, where the crowd is younger and the drinking heavier. This is where people congregate after football games and students head out on the booze.

L'Angolo Divino
Wine Bar

(📞06 686 44 13; www.angolodivino.it; Via dei Balestrari 12; ⏰11am-3pm Tue-Sat, plus 5pm-1am daily; 🚇Corso Vittorio Emanuele II) A hop and a skip from Campo de' Fiori, this warm wine bar is an oasis of genteel calm, with a carefully curated wine list (mostly Italian but a few French and New World labels), a selection of regional Italian cheeses and cured meats, and a small daily menu of hot and cold dishes.

Salotto 42
Bar

(📞06 678 58 04; www.salotto42.it; Piazza di Pietra 42; ⏰10.30am-2am; 🚇Via del Corso) On a picturesque piazza, facing the columns of the Temple of Hadrian, this is a glamorous lounge bar, complete with subdued lighting, vintage 1950s armchairs, Murano lamps and heavyweight design books. Come for the daily lunch buffet or to hang out with the 'see and be seen' crowd over one of its signature cocktails.

Il Goccetto
Wine Bar

(www.facebook.com/Ilgoccetto; Via dei Banchi Vecchi 14; ⏰noon-2.30pm Tue-Sat, plus 6.30pm-midnight Mon-Sat, closed mid-Aug; 🚇Corso Vittorio Emanuele II) This authentic, old-school *vino e olio* (wine and oil) shop has everything you could want in a neighbourhood wine bar: a colourful cast of regulars, a cosy, bottle-lined interior, a selection of cheeses and cold cuts, and a serious, 800-strong wine list.

Dress the Part

Romans tend to dress up to go out, and most people will be looking pretty sharp in the smarter clubs and bars in the *centro storico* (historic centre) and Testaccio. However, over in Pigneto and San Lorenzo or at the *centri sociali* (social centres), the style is much more alternative.

Escosazio
Juice Bar

(📞06 6476 0784; www.escosazio.it; Via dei Banchi Vecchi 135; ⊘8am-8pm Mon-Sat, 10am-6pm Sun; 🚇Corso Vittorio Emanuele II) Rome is discovering juice bars right now and this friendly bolthole is a good bet for a refreshing smoothie or juice extract. Keep it simple with a freshly squeezed OJ, or spice things up with a *digestivo* made from orange, pineapple, fennel and ginger. If you're hungry, stop by at lunch for a tasty risotto or made-to-order *panino*.

Gran Caffè La Caffettiera
Cafe

(📞06 679 81 47; www.grancaffelacaffettiera. com; Piazza di Pietra 65; ⊘7.30am-9pm Mon-Fri, 8.30am-9pm Sat, 9am-9pm Sun; 🚇Via del Corso) This stately art-deco cafe overlooking graceful Piazza di Pietra is a polished performer. Star of the show are its Neapolitan cakes, including that most beloved of pastries, *sfogliatella* (a flaky pastry shell stuffed with ricotta and shards of candied fruit).

🟢 Tridente, Trevi & the Quirinale

Il Palazzetto
Cafe, Cocktail Bar

(📞06 6993 4560; Vicolo del Bottino 8; ⊘noon-6pm winter, 4pm-midnight summer, closed in bad weather; 🚇Spagna) No terrace proffers such a fine view of the comings and goings on the Spanish Steps over an expertly shaken cocktail (€10 to €13). Ride the lift up from the discreet entrance on narrow Via dei Bottino or look for steps leading to the bar from the top of the steps. Given everything is al fresco, the bar is only open in warm, dry weather.

Zuma Bar
Cocktail Bar

(📞06 9926 6622; www.zumarestaurant.com; Palazzo Fendi, Via della Fontanella di Borghese 48; ⊘6pm-1am Sun-Thu, to 2am Fri & Sat; 🤙; 🚇Via del Corso) Dress up for a drink on the rooftop terrace of Palazzo Fendi of fashion-house fame – few cocktail bars in Rome are as sleek, hip or achingly sophisticated as this. City rooftop views are predictably fabulous; cocktails mix exciting flavours like shiso with juniper berries, elderflower and prosecco; and DJ sets spin Zuma playlists at weekends.

Stravinskij Bar
Bar

(📞06 3288 8874; Hotel de Russie, Via del Babuino 9; ⊘9am-1am; 🚇Flaminio) Can't afford to stay at the celeb-magnet **Hotel de Russie** (📞06 32 88 81; www.roccofortehotels.com/it; d from €646; ❄🤙)? Then splash out on a drink at its swish bar. There are sofas inside, but best is a drink in the sunny courtyard, with sun-shaded tables overlooked by terraced gardens. Impossibly romantic in the best dolce vita style, it's perfect for a pricey cocktail or beer accompanied by appropriately posh bar snacks.

Locarno Bar
Bar

(www.hotellocarno.com; Hotel Locarno, Via della Penna 22; ⊘7pm-1am; 🚇Flaminio) Fashionistas and style gurus congregate at this rakish lounge bar for their 7pm *aperitivo*. Part of the art-deco **Hotel Locarno** (📞06 361 08 41; d from €200; 🅿❄🤙;) near Piazza del Popolo, it's an inspiring spot for a sundowner with romantic corners, a shaded outdoor terrace, heavy cast-iron tables and a decadent Agatha Christie–era feel.

🟢 Vatican City, Borgo & Prati

Be.re
Craft Beer

(📞06 9442 1854; www.be-re.eu; Piazza del Risorgimento, cnr Via Vespasiano; ⊘11am-2am; 🚇Piazza del Risorgimento) Rome's craft-beer fans keenly applauded the opening of this contemporary bar in late 2016. With its copper beer taps, exposed-brick decor and

Salotto 42 (p169)

high vaulted ceilings, it's a good-looking spot for an evening of Italian beers and cask ales. And should hunger strike, there's a branch of hit takeaway Trapizzino right next door.

Passaguai · Wine Bar

(☑06 8745 1358; www.passaguai.it; Via Leto 1; ⏱10am-2am Mon-Fri, 6pm-2am Sat & Sun; ⏳; 🚇Piazza del Risorgimento) A basement bar with tables in a cosy stone-clad interior and on a quiet side street, Passaguai feels pleasingly off-the-radar. It's a great spot for a post-sightseeing cocktail or glass of wine – there's an excellent choice of both – accompanied by cheese and cold cuts, or even a full meal from the small menu.

Makasar Bistrot · Wine Bar, Teahouse

(☑06 687 46 02; www.makasar.it; Via Plauto 33; ⏱noon-midnight Mon-Thu, to 2am Fri & Sat, 5pm-midnight Sun; 🚇Piazza del Risorgimento) Recharge your batteries with a quiet drink at this bookish *bistrot*. Pick your tipple from the 250-variety tea menu or opt for an Italian wine, and sit back in the softly lit earthenware-hued interior. For something

to eat, there's a small menu of salads, bruschetta, baguettes and hot dishes.

🍷 Monti, Esquilino & San Lorenzo

Spirito · Cocktail Bar

(☑327 2983900; www.club-spirito.com; Via Fanfulla da Lodi 53; ⏱7.30pm-3.30am Wed-Mon; 🚇Via Prenestina) A fashionable address only for those in the know, Spirito is spirited away behind a simple white door at the back of a sandwich shop in edgy Pigneto. This New Yorker Prohibition–style speakeasy has expertly mixed craft cocktails (around €10), gourmet food, live music and shows, roulette at the bar and a fun-loving crowd.

No mobile phones, no groups, no more drinks for those who've drunk too much. Find it inside La Premiata Panineria Pigneto; table reservations recommended.

Il Sorì · Wine Bar

(☑393 4318681; www.ilsori.it; Via dei Volsci 51; ⏱6pm-2am Mon-Sat; 🚇Via Tiburtina) Every last

Ice Club

salami slice and chunk of cheese has been carefully selected from Italy's finest artisanal and small producers at this gourmet wine bar and *bottega* (shop), an unexpected pearl of a stop for dedicated foodies in student-driven San Lorenzo. Interesting and unusual wine tastings, theme nights, 'meet the producer' soirées and other events cap off what is already a memorable drinking (and dining) experience.

Gatsby Café   Bar, Cafe

(☑06 6933 9626; www.facebook.com/gatsby cafe; Piazza Vittorio Emanuele II 106; cocktails €7-10; ☺8am-midnight Sun-Wed, to 1am Thu, to 2am Fri & Sat; Ⓜ Termini) There's good reason why the friendly bar staff here all wear flat caps, feather-trimmed trilbys and other traditional gents hats: this fabulous 1950s-styled space with salvaged vintage furniture and flashes of funky geometric wallpapering was originally a milliner's shop called Galleria Venturini. Brilliant rhubarb or elderflower *spritz,* craft cocktails, gourmet *panini* (€5) and *taglieri* (salami and cheese platters) make it a top *aperitivo* spot.

Co.So   Cocktail Bar

(☑06 4543 5428; Via Braccio da Montone 80; ☺7pm-3am Mon-Sat; ᴨ Via Prenestina) The chicest bar in Pigneto, tiny Co.So (meaning 'Cocktails & Social') is run by Massimo D'Addezio (a former master mixologist at Hotel de Russie) and is hipster to the hilt. Think Carbonara Sour cocktails (with pork-fat-infused vodka), bubblewrap coasters, and popcorn and M&M's bar snacks. Check its Facebook page for the latest happenings.

Yellow Bar   Bar

(☑06 4470 2868; www.the-yellow.com; Via Palestro 40; ☺24hr; ☎; Ⓜ Castro Pretorio) With its vintage zinc bar, high vaulted ceiling and amusing house rules chalked on the blackboard, this is a definite notch up from your bog-standard pub. Across the street from the hostel of the same name, around-the-clock Yellow is constantly packed with young, fun, international travellers. DJs spin tunes from 10pm until 4am, there are live bands at weekends and themed parties galore. Breakfast and all-day food is also served.

Ice Club
Bar

(☑06 9784 5581; www.iceclubroma.it; Via della Madonna dei Monti 18; ⏰5pm-1am Sun-Thu, to 2am Fri & Sat; MCavour) Novelty value is what the Ice Club is all about. Pay €15 (you get a free vodka cocktail served in a glass made of ice), don a (completely unflattering) hospital-blue thermal cloak and mittens, and enter the bar, in which everything is made of ice (temperature: −5°C). Most people won't chill here for too long.

Streat San Lorenzo
Lounge, Bar

(☑06 6401 3486; www.facebook.com/streatSL; Piazza dei Campani 5; ⏰8.30am-2am Mon-Sat; 📶; 🚌Via dei Reti) The sort of place where you can really kick back and relax, this lounge bar is an enticing all-rounder for meals, late-night cocktails or afternoons lounging over drinks. Vintage curiosities – an old Polaroid camera, printing blocks, copper teapots – add visual interest, and mixed-bag seating covers everything from bar stools and beanbags to saggy leather sofas. Yes, punters can tinkle on the piano.

Cargo
Bar

(☑349 7404620; www.cargopigneto.com; Via del Pigneto 20; ⏰5pm-2am; 📶; 🚌Circonvallazione Casilina, 🚌Via Prenestina) Year-round the steely black street terrace of Cargo is the hottest place for lounging in the sun – or under outdoor heaters in the winter – on Pigneto's main pedestrian drag. The bar rocks during its sacrosanct, *aperitivo*-fuelled 'happy hour' (actually from 5.30pm to 9.30pm). Weekend DJ sets, jazz evenings and party nights too; check its Facebook page for what's on.

Gente di San Lorenzo
Bar

(☑06 445 44 25; Via degli Aurunci 42; ⏰7am-2am; 📶; 🚌Via dei Reti) San Lorenzo's signature neighbourhood bar is a chilled place to hang with students over a drink, snack or meal. The interior is airy, with warm wooden floors, brick arches and a couple of sofas, but the real action happens outside on the pavement terrace where there are prime people-watching views of Piazza dell'Immacolata and its throngs of students lazing beneath orange trees on balmy nights.

Craft Beer & Lazio Wine

In recent years beer drinking has really taken off in Italy, and especially in Rome, with specialised bars and restaurants offering microbrewed beers. Local favourites include Birradamare in Fiumicino, Porto Fluviale in Ostiense, and Birra Del Borgo in Rieti (on the border between Lazio and Abruzzo), which opened local beer haunts **Bir & Fud** (p176) and **Open Baladin** (p168). Local beers reflect the seasonality that's so important in Rome – for example, look for winter beers made from chestnuts.

Other important addresses on the artisanal beer trail include **Ma Che Siete Venuti a Fà** (p177) and **Be.re** (p170).

Lazio wines may not be household names, but it's well worth trying some local wines while you're here. Although whites dominate Lazio's production, there are a few notable reds as well. To sample Lazio wines, **Palatium** (☑06 6920 2132; http://enotecaregionalepalatium.it; Via Frattina 94; meals €45-50; ⏰bar 11am-11pm, restaurant 12.30-3.30pm & 7.30-10.30pm; 🚌Via del Corso) and **Terre e Domus** (p122) are the best places to go. For biodynamic vintages, head for **Litro** (p137) in Monteverdi.

DJs and occasional live music; check its Facebook page for details.

Trimani
Wine Bar

(☑06 446 96 30; www.trimani.com; Via Cernaia 37b; meals €35-45; ⏰11.30am-3pm & 5.30pm-midnight Mon-Sat; MTermini) Part of the Trimani family's wine empire (their vast shop around the corner on Via Goito stocks 4000-odd international labels), this is an unpretentious yet highly professional *enoteca*, with knowledgeable, multilingual staff. It's Rome's biggest wine bar and has a vast selection of Italian regional wines as well as an ever-changing food menu including local salami, cheese, oysters and the like.

Gay & Lesbian Rome

There is only a smattering of dedicated gay and lesbian clubs and bars in Rome, though many nightclubs host regular gay and lesbian nights. For local information, pick up a copy of the monthly magazine *AUT,* published by Circolo Mario Mieli (www.mariomieli.org). There's also info at AZ Gay (www.azgay.it). Lesbians can find out more about the local scene at Coordinamento Lesbiche Italiano (www.clrbp.it).

Most gay venues (bars, clubs and saunas) require you to have an Arcigay (www.arcigayroma.it) membership card. These cost €15/8 per year/three months and are available from any venue that requires one.

Il Tiaso   Bar

(☑349 5891498; www.facebook.com/ilTiasoal Pigneto; Via Ascoli Piceno 25; ◎6pm-2am; 🛜; 🚇Circonvallazione Casilina) Think living room with zebra-print chairs, walls of indie art, Lou Reed biographies wedged between wine bottles, and 30-something owner Gabriele playing his favourite New York Dolls album to neo-beatnik chicks, corduroy-clad professors and the odd neighbourhood dog. Expect well-priced wine, an intimate chilled vibe, regular live music and lovely pavement terrace.

Libreria Caffè Bohemien   Bar, Cafe

(☑339 7224622; www.caffebohemien.it; Via degli Zingari 33-36; ◎5pm-1am Sun, Mon, Wed & Thu, to 2am Fri & Sat; 🅼Cavour) This hybrid wine bar, tearoom and bookshop with fantastic paint-peeling front door lives up to its name; it feels like something you might stumble on in Left Bank Paris. It's small, with mismatched vintage furniture and an eclectic crowd drinking wine by the glass, aperitifs, tea and coffee.

Locanda Atlantide   Club

(☑06 9604 5875; www.facebook.com/locanda. atlantide; Via dei Lucani 22b; cover varies; ◎9pm-late Oct-Jun; 🚇Scalo San Lorenzo) Come and tickle Rome's grungy underbelly. Descend

through a door in a graffiti-covered wall into this cavernous basement dive, packed to the rafters with studenty, alternative crowds and featuring everything from prog-folk to techno and psychedelic trance. It's good to know that punk is not dead.

Al Vino al Vino   Wine Bar

(☑06 48 58 03; Via dei Serpenti 19; ◎10am-2pm & 6pm-midnight; 🅼Cavour) Mixing lovely ceramic-topped bistro tables with bottle-lined walls and the odd contemporary painting, this rustic *enoteca* is an attractive spot in which to linger over a fine collection of wine, including several *passiti* (sweet wines). The other speciality is *distillati* – grappa, whisky and so on.

Bar Celestino   Bar

(☑06 4547 2483; www.facebook.com/bar-celes tino; Via degli Ausoni 62; ◎7.30am-2am Mon-Sat; 🚇Via Tiburtina) Few places evoke the San Lorenzo student vibe quite like this grungy, shabby drinking den near Piazza dei Sanniti. A die-hard icon of this working-class neighbourhood, Celestino first opened its doors in 1904 and is still going strong thanks to its simple, unpretentious vibe. Grab a seat on the pavement terrace or head inside. Find party updates on its Facebook page.

Zest Bar   Bar

(☑06 4448 4384; Via Filippo Turati 171; ◎10.30am-midnight; 🛜; 🅼Vittorio Emanuele) In need of a cocktail in the Termini district? Pop up to the 7th-floor bar at the slinkily designed **Radisson Blu es. hotel** (☑06 44 48 41; www.radissonblu.com/eshotel-rome; d €198-265; 🛏❄@🏊) . Chairs are by Jasper Morrison, views are through plate-glass, and there's a sexy outdoor rooftop pool to gaze at, open May to September.

Yeah! Pigneto   Bar

(☑06 6480 1456; www.yeahpigneto.com; Via Giovanni de Agostini 43; ◎7.30pm-2am; 🚇Via Casilina) We say 'si!' to Yeah! Pigneto, a relaxed boho-feeling bar with a mismatched vintage look, DJs playing jazz and the walls covered in collages and classic album covers. It's a good place for lingering over drinks and food. Regular weekend gigs.

Trastevere & Gianicolo

Rivendita Libri, Cioccolata e Vino — Cocktail Bar

(06 5830 1868; www.facebook.com/ciocco lateriatrastevere; Vicolo del Cinque 11a; shot €3-5; 6.30pm-2am Mon-Fri, 2pm-2am Sat & Sun; Piazza Trilussa) There is no finer or funnier spot in the whole of Rome for a swift French Kiss, Orgasm or One Night Stand than this highly inventive cocktail bar, packed every night from around 10pm with a fun-loving, post-dinner crowd. Cocktails are served in miniature chocolate cups, filled with various types of alcohol and topped with whipped cream.

Each has a sexually suggestive name and guarantees a giggle. Seek advice from the friendly bar staff on how best to down your shot, then sit back and mellow out in the eclectic Aladdin's-cave-style interior with books, piano and glass chandeliers.

Keyhole — Cocktail Bar

(Via dell'Arco di San Calisto 17; midnight-5am; Viale di Trastevere, Viale di Trastevere) The latest in a growing trend of achingly hip, underground speakeasies in Rome, Keyhole ticks all the boxes: no identifiable name or signage outside the bar; a black door smothered in keys; and Prohibition-era decor including leather Chesterfield sofas, dim lighting and an electric *craft* cocktail menu. Not sure what to order? Ask the talented mixologists to create your own bespoke cocktail (around €10).

No password is required to get into Keyhole, but you need to fill in a form to become a member (€5). No phones.

Freni e Frizioni — Bar

(06 4549 7499; www.freniefrizioni.com; Via del Politeama 4-6; 6.30pm-2am; Piazza Trilussa) This perennially cool Trastevere bar is housed in an old mechanic's workshop – hence its name ('brakes and clutches') and tatty facade. It draws a young *spritz*-loving crowd that swells onto the small piazza outside to sip superbly mixed cocktails (€10) and seasonal punches, and fill up on its lavish early-evening *aperitivo* buffet (7pm to 10pm). Table reservations are essential on Friday and Saturday evenings.

Il Tiaso

GARI WYN WILLIAMS/ALAMY LIVE NEWS ©

Coming Out

Bar San Calisto   Cafe

(Piazza San Calisto 3-5; ⊘6am-2am Mon-Sat;
🚊Viale di Trastevere, 🚊Viale di Trastevere) Those
in the know head to 'Sanca' for its basic,
stuck-in-time atmosphere and cheap prices
(beer from €1.50). It attracts everyone from
intellectuals to keeping-it-real Romans,
alcoholics and foreign students. It's famous
for its chocolate – come for hot chocolate
with cream in winter, and chocolate gelato
in summer. Try the *sambuca con la mosca*
('with flies' – raw coffee beans). Expect
occasional late-night jam sessions.

Pimm's Good   Bar

(📞06 9727 7979; www.facebook.com/pimmsgood;
Via di Santa Dorotea 8; ⊘10am-2am; 🛜; 🚊Piazza
Trilussa) 'Anyone for Pimm's?' is the catchline
of this eternally popular bar with part red-
brick ceiling that does indeed serve Pimm's
– the classic way or in a variety of cocktails
(€10). The party-loving guys behind the bar
are serious mixologists and well-crafted
cocktails are their thing. Look for the buzzing street-corner pavement terrace – lit up
in winter with flaming outdoor heaters.

Il Baretto   Bar

(📞06 589 60 55; www.ilbarettoroma.com; Via
Garibaldi 27; ⊘7am-2am Mon-Sat; 🚊Via Garibaldi) Venture a little way up the Gianicolo, up
a steep flight of steps from Trastevere – go
on, it's worth it. Because there you'll discover this good-looking cocktail bar where the
basslines are meaty, the bar staff hip, and
the interior a mix of vintage and pop art.

Bir & Fud   Craft Beer

(📞06 589 40 16; http://birandfud.it; Via Benedetta
23; ⊘noon-2am Mon & Thu-Sun, 6pm-2am Tue &
Wed; 🚊Piazza Trilussa) On a narrow street lined
with raucous drinking holes, this brick-vault-
ed bar-pizzeria wins plaudits for its outstanding collection of craft *bir*, many on tap, and
equally tasty *fud* (food) for when late-night
munchies strike. Its Neapolitan-style wood-
fired pizzas are particularly excellent.

Hýbris   Bar

(📞06 9437 6374; www.hybrisartgallery.com;
Via della Lungaretta 164; ⊘10am-2am; 🛜;
🚊Viale di Trastevere, 🚊Viale di Trastevere) This
modish cafe-bar on pedestrian, shop-
strewn Via della Lungaretta is an artsy spot

for early-evening drinks between marble busts and art works. Vintage typewriters, a piano and armchairs add a generous dose of trendy old-world ambience, and the marble balustrade bar gets top marks for design. Live jazz and blues, DJ sets and art exhibitions too.

Ma Che Siete Venuti a Fà   Pub
(📞06 6456 2046; www.football-pub.com; Via Benedetta 25; ⏱11am-2am; 🚊Piazza Trilussa) Named after a football chant, which translates politely as 'What did you come here for?', this pint-sized Trastevere pub is a beer-buff's paradise, packing in around 15 international craft beers on tap and even more by the bottle. Expect some rowdy drinking.

Mescita Ferrara   Wine Bar
(📞06 5833 3920; www.enotecaferrara.it; Enoteca Ferrara, Piazza Trilussa 41; ⏱6pm-2am; 🚊Piazza Trilussa) This tiny bar inside the entrance to upmarket restaurant Enoteca Ferrara serves delectable *aperitivo* and has a wide range of wines by the glass – perfect for an intimate tête-à-tête.

🚇 San Giovanni & Testaccio

Bibenda Wine Concept   Wine Bar
(📞06 7720 6673; www.wineconcept.it; Via Capo d'Africa 21; ⏱noon-3pm & 6pm-midnight Mon-Thu, noon-3pm & 6pm-1am Fri, 6pm-1am Sat; 🚊Via Labicana) Wine buffs looking to excite their palate should search out this smart modern *enoteca*. Boasting a white, light-filled interior, it has an extensive list of Italian regional labels and European vintages, as well as a small daily food menu. Wines are available to drink by the glass or buy by the bottle.

Rec 23   Bar
(📞06 8746 2147; www.rec23.com; Piazza dell'Emporio 2; ⏱6.30pm-2am daily, 12.30-3.30pm Sat & Sun; 🚊Via Marmorata) All exposed brick and mismatched furniture, this large, New York–inspired venue caters to all moods, serving *aperitivo*, restaurant meals, and a weekend brunch. Arrive thirsty to take on a Bud Spencer, one from the ample list of cocktails, or get to grips with the selection of Scottish whiskies

 Clubbing

Rome has a range of nightclubs, mostly in Ostiense and Testaccio, with music policies ranging from lounge and jazz to dancehall and hip-hop. Clubs tend to get busy after midnight, or even after 2am. Often admission is free, but drinks are expensive. Cocktails can cost from €10 to €20, but you can drink much more cheaply in the studenty clubs of San Lorenzo, Pigneto and the *centri sociali*.

and Latin American rums. Thursday's blues aperitif is a popular weekly appointment.

Coming Out   Bar
(📞06 700 98 71; www.comingout.it; Via di San Giovanni in Laterano 8; ⏱7am-2am; 🚊Via Labicana) On warm evenings, with lively crowds on the street and the Colosseum as a backdrop, there are few finer places to sip a drink at than this friendly gay bar. It's open all day, but is at its best in the evening when the atmosphere hots up, the cocktails kick in and the drag shows and karaoke nights get under way.

L'Oasi della Birra   Bar
(📞06 574 61 22; Piazza Testaccio 41; ⏱4.30pm-1am; 🚊Via Marmorata) Housed in the Palombi Enoteca, a longstanding bottle shop on Piazza Testaccio, this is exactly what it says it is – an Oasis of Beer. With hundreds of labels, from Teutonic heavyweights to British bitters and Belgian brews, as well as wines, cheeses and cold cuts, it's ideally set up for an evening's quaffing, either in the cramped cellar or piazza-side terrace.

Il Pentagrappolo   Wine Bar
(📞06 709 63 01; Via Celimontana 21b; ⏱noon-3pm Mon-Fri, 6pm-2am Tue-Sun; Ⓜ Colosseo) This vaulted, softly lit wine bar is the perfect antidote to sightseeing overload. Join the mellow crowd for an evening of wine, piano music and jazz courtesy of the frequent live gigs. There's also a full menu served at lunch and dinner.

Rome in a Glass

Orange slice to garnish

Ice

3 parts Prosecco

Dash of soda water

2 parts Aperol

Wine glass

Aperol Spritz

MARAZE/SHUTTERSTOCK ©

How to make an Aperol Spritz

○ Fill a wine glass with ice.

○ Pour over the Prosecco, then add a splash of soda water followed by the Aperol.

○ Stir once and garnish with a slice of orange.

Story Behind the Cocktail

The spritz has its roots in the Austro-Hungarian occupation of the Veneto in the 19th century. According, to local legend, Austrian soldiers would dilute the robust local wines with a splash (*spritzen* in German) of sparkling water. Aperol, an orange-red bitter, was invented in Padua in 1919, and when later mixed with white wine and soda gave rise to the hugely popular cocktail.

BY DE.AVU/SHUTTERSTOCK ©

★ Top Bars for Aperol Spritz

Stravinskij Bar (p170)

Co.So (p172)

Gatsby Cafe (p172)

Freni e Frizioni (p175)

Etablì (p169)

⑨ Villa Borghese & Northern Rome

Lanificio 159 — Club

(📞06 4178 0081; www.lanificio.com; Via Pietralata 159a; ⏰club nights 11pm-4.30am Fri & Sat Sep-May; 🚌Via Pietralata) Occupying an ex-wool factory in Rome's northeastern suburbs, this cool underground venue hosts live gigs and hot clubbing action, led by top Roman crews and international DJs. The club is part of a larger complex that stages more reserved events such as Sunday markets, exhibitions and *aperitivi*.

Momart — Cafe

(📞06 8639 1656; www.momartcafe.it; Viale XXI Aprile 19; ⏰noon-2am, to 3am Sat & Sun; 🚌Viale XXI Aprile) A modish restaurant-cafe in the university district near Via Nomentana, Momart serves one of Rome's most bountiful spreads of *apericena* (an informal evening meal involving *aperitivi* and tapas-style food). A mixed crowd of students and local professionals flocks here to fill up on the ample buffet and kick back over cocktails on the pavement terrace.

Lemoncocco — Bar

(Piazza Buenos Aires; ⏰11am-2.30am; 🚌Viale Regina Margherita) This green kiosk-bar has been serving its signature lemoncocco drink for more than 50 years. A zingy blend of velvet-smooth coconut milk and freshly squeezed lemon juice (the precise proportions are a closely guarded secret), it's an ideal thirst quencher on warm summer evenings.

⑨ Southern Rome

Circolo Illuminati — Club, Bar

(📞327 7615286; www.circolodegliilluminati.it; Via Libetta 1a; ⏰10.30pm-late Thu-Sat; Ⓜ Garbatella) Tech house, hip-hop and chill music revs up clubbers at this wildly popular Ostiense club on the international DJ club circuit. The vibe is very much underground, and its courtyard garden with potted plants and olive trees is a gorgeous space in which to kick-start the evening beneath the stars.

Goa — Club

(📞06 574 82 77; www.goaclub.com; Via Libetta 13; ⏰11.30pm-5am Thu-Sat; Ⓜ Garbatella) At home in a former motorbike repair shop down a dead-end alley in industrial-style Ostiense, Goa is Rome's serious super-club with exotic India-inspired decor and international DJs mixing house and techno. Expect a fashion-forward crowd, podium dancers, thumping dance floor, sofas to lounge on and heavies on the door.

Vinile — Club

(📞06 5728 8666; www.vinileroma.it; Via Libetta 19; ⏰8pm-2am Tue & Wed, to 3am Thu, to 4am Fri & Sat, 12.30-3.30pm & 8pm-2am Sun; Ⓜ Garbatella) On weekends a mixed bag of Romans of all ages hits the dance floor at Vinyl, a buzzing bar and club cooking up food, music and party happenings on the southern fringe of Ostiense. Inside its huge cavernous interior – with part-vegetal, part-frescoed ceiling – the night starts with an *aperitivo* banquet from 8pm; DJ sets start at 11.30pm. On Sunday students pile in here for the unbeatable-value brunch.

Neo Club — Club

(📞338 9492526; www.piovra.it; Via degli Argonauti 18; ⏰11pm-late Fri & Sat; Ⓜ Garbatella) This small, dark two-level club has an underground feel and it's one of the funkiest choices in the zone, featuring a dancetastic mish-mash of breakbeat, techno and old-school house.

Gazometro 38 — Cocktail Bar

(📞06 5730 2106; www.gazometro38.com; Via del Gazometro 38; ⏰12.30-3pm & 6.30-11.30pm Tue-Fri, 6.30pm-midnight Sat & Sun; 🚌Via Ostiense, Ⓜ Piramide) It's not so much about the food as the eye-catching industrial design at this contemporary lounge-bar-restaurant in edgy Ostiense. Hobnob over an Elderflower Mule or Raspberry Basil Smash cocktail and a plate of *fritti* (fried courgette flowers) or *supplì* (rice balls) in the lounge area with sofa seating, or at a table in the alley-entrance, plastered with B&W murals of industrial scenes.

SHOWTIME

Opera, jazz, theatre and more

Showtime

Enjoying Rome's colourful street life is often entertainment enough, but there's more to having a good time in the Eternal City than people-watching in its piazzas. The city's music scene runs the gamut, with opera divas, jazz masters, rock icons and underground rappers playing to passionate audiences. Theatres stage everything from Shakespearean drama to avant-garde dance; cinemas screen art-house flicks; and arts festivals turn the city into a stage, particularly in summer, with alfresco performances playing out against backdrops of spectacular Roman ruins.

Whether you're into opera or hip-hop, chamber music or experimental theatre, you're sure to find something to suit your taste.

In This Section

Tickets

Tickets for concerts and theatrical performances are widely available across the city. Hotels can often reserve tickets for guests, or you can contact the venue directly – check listings publications for details. Otherwise you can try:

Vivaticket (www.vivaticket.it)

Orbis (06 482 74 03; www.boxofficelazio. it; Piazza dell'Esquilino 37; 9.30am-1pm & 4-7.30pm Mon-Sat; Via Cavour)

Iana Salenko and Danil Simkin perform at Auditorium Della Conciliazione (p185)

Jazz

Alexanderplatz (p185) Rome's foremost jazz club.

Auditorium Parco della Musica (p188) Stages, among other things, the Roma Jazz Festival.

Charity Café (p186) An intimate space, hosting regular live gigs.

Big Mama (p187) Atmospheric Trastevere venue for jazz, blues, funk, soul and R&B.

Gregory's Jazz Club (p184) Smooth venue popular with local musicians.

Gigs

Nuovo Cinema Palazzo (p185) Exciting creative happenings in San Lorenzo.

Black Market (p186) Bar filled with vintage sofas, great for eclectic, mainly acoustic live music.

Caffè Letterario (p189) Live gigs in a post-industrial former garage. Also gallery, co-working space and lounge bar.

ConteStaccio (p188) Free live music on the Testaccio clubbing strip.

✪ Centro Storico

Isola del Cinema   Outdoor Cinema
(https://isoladelcinema.com; Isola Tiberina;
tickets €6; ⊘mid-Jun–Sep) The Isola Tiberina
sets the stage for a season of outdoor cinema, featuring Italian and international films,
some shown in their original language.

Teatro Argentina   Theatre
(🗂06 684 00 03 11; www.teatrodiroma.net; Largo
di Torre Argentina 52; tickets €12-40; 🚇Largo di
Torre Argentina) Founded in 1732, Rome's top
theatre is one of the two official homes of
the Teatro di Roma – the other is the Teatro
India (p189) in the southern suburbs.
Rossini's *Barber of Seville* premiered here
in 1816, and these days the theatre stages
a wide-ranging program of drama (mostly
in Italian), high-profile dance performances
and classical music concerts.

> *Rome's top theatre is one of
> the two official homes of the
> Teatro di Roma...*

✪ Tridente, Trevi & the Quirinale

Gregory's Jazz Club   Jazz
(🗂327 8263770, 06 679 63 86; www.gregorys
jazz.com; Via Gregoriana 54d; obligatory drink
€15-20; ⊘7.30pm-2am Tue-Sun; 🚇Barberini,
Spagna) If Gregory's were a tone of voice,
it'd be husky: unwind over a whisky in the
downstairs bar, then unwind some more on
squashy sofas upstairs to slinky live jazz
and swing, with quality local performers
who also like to hang out here.

Teatro Quirino   Theatre
(🗂box office 06 679 45 85; www.teatroquirino.
it; Via delle Vergini 7; tickets €13-34; 🚇Via del
Corso) Within splashing distance of the Trevi
Fountain, this grand 19th-century theatre
produces the odd new work and a stream of
well-known classics – expect to see works
(in Italian) by Arthur Miller, Tennessee
Williams, Shakespeare, Seneca and Luigi
Pirandello.

Teatro Argentina

VALESTOCK/SHUTTERSTOCK ©

Teatro Sistina   Theatre

(📞06 420 07 11; www.ilsistina.it; Via Sistina
129; tickets €22-75; MBarberini) Big-budget
theatre spectaculars, musicals, concerts
and comic star turns are the staples of the
Sistina's ever-conservative, ever-popular
repertoire.

✪ Vatican City, Borgo & Prati

Alexanderplatz   Jazz

(📞06 8377 5604; www.alexanderplatzjazzclub.
it; Via Ostia 9; tickets €15-20; ☺8.30pm-
1.30am; MOttaviano-San Pietro) Intimate,
underground and hard to find – look for
the discreet black door – Rome's most
celebrated jazz club draws top Italian and
international performers and a respectful
cosmopolitan crowd. Book a table for the
best stage views or to dine here, although
note that it's the music that's the star act,
not the food.

Fonclea   Live Music

(📞06 689 63 02; www.fonclea.it; Via Crescenzio 82a; ☺6pm-2am Sep-May, concerts
9.30pm; 🚇Piazza del Risorgimento) Fonclea
is a great little pub venue, with nightly
gigs by bands playing everything from
jazz and soul to pop, rock and doo-wop.
Get in the mood with a drink during happy
hour (6pm to 8.30pm daily). In summer,
the pub ups sticks and moves to a site by
the Tiber.

**Auditorium
Conciliazione**   Live Performance

(📞06 6813 4748; www.auditoriumconcilia
zione.it; Via della Conciliazione 4; 🚇Piazza Pia)
On the main approach road to St Peter's
Basilica, this large auditorium plays host
to a wide range of events – classical
and contemporary concerts, cabarets,
dance spectacles, theatre productions,
film screenings, exhibitions and even
conferences.

 Cinema Under the Stars

Rome's historic streets and piazzas set
a fabulous stage for alfresco cinema.
There are various outdoor summer film
festivals and events, including the **Isola
del Cinema** (p184), which screens a
wide range of independent and mainstream films in the romantic setting of
the Isola Tiberina. It runs in conjunction
with the riverside **Lungo il Tevere**
(www.lungoiltevereroma.it; ☺mid-Jun–Aug)
festival.

Isola Tiberina
CALIN STAN/SHUTTERSTOCK ©

✪ Monti, Esquilino & San Lorenzo

**Teatro dell'Opera
di Roma**   Opera, Ballet

(📞06 48 16 01; www.operaroma.it; Piazza
Beniamino Gigli 1; ☺box office 10am-6pm Mon-
Sat, 9am-1.30pm Sun; MRepubblica) Rome's
premier opera house boasts a plush gilt
interior, a Fascist 1920s exterior and an
impressive history: it premiered Puccini's
Tosca, and Maria Callas once sang here.
Opera and ballet performances are staged
between September and June.

**Nuovo
Cinema Palazzo**   Arts Centre

(www.nuovocinemapalazzo.it; Piazza dei Sanniti
9a; ☺hours vary; 🚇Via Tiburtina) Students,
artists and activists are breathing new life
into San Lorenzo's former Palace Cinema
with a bevy of exciting creative happenings:

 Classical Music

Rome's premier orchestra is the world-class Orchestra dell'Accademia Nazionale di Santa Cecilia (www.santacecilia.it), which regularly performs at the **Auditorium Parco della Musica** (p188). In addition, you can catch concerts by the Accademia Filarmonica Romana at the **Teatro Olimpico** (p188). The **Auditorium Conciliazione** (p185), Rome's main classical music venue before the newer auditorium was opened, is still a force to be reckoned with, and the **Istituzione Universitaria dei Concerti** (p186) holds concerts in the Aula Magna of La Sapienza University.

Free classical concerts are held in many of Rome's churches, especially at Easter and around Christmas and New Year; look out for information at Rome's tourist kiosks.

Teatro Olimpico
VITTORIO ZUNINO CELOTTO/GETTY IMAGES ©

think film screenings, theatre performances, DJ sets, concerts, live music, breakdance classes and a host of other artsy events. In warm weather, the action spills outside onto the street terrace, overlooked by a B&W stencil mural by Rome street artists Sten & Lex.

Charity Café   Live Music
(📞06 4782 5881; www.charitycafe.it; Via Panisperna 68; ⏰7pm-2am Tue-Sun; Ⓜ︎Cavour) Think narrow space, spindly tables, dim lighting and laid-back vibe: this is a place to snuggle down and listen to some slinky live jazz and blues. Civilised, relaxed, untouristy

and very Monti. Gigs usually take place from 10pm, with live music and *aperitivo*.

Teatro Ambra Jovinelli   Theatre
(📞06 8308 2884; www.ambrajovinelli.org; Via Pepe 45; Ⓜ︎Vittorio Emanuele) A home away from home for many famous Italian comics, the Ambra Jovinelli is a historic venue for alternative comedians and satirists. Its program is still geared towards comedy today, although it also stages the odd drama, musical and contemporary work.

Wishlist   Live Music
(📞349 7494659; www.facebook.com/wishlist club; Via dei Volsci 126b; €5-10; ⏰hours vary; 🚊Via Tiburtina, 🚊Via dei Reti) A black door marks the entrance to this eternally popular music club, in a low-lying building on one of San Lorenzo's grungiest streets. Gigs cover all sounds, kicking off at 9.30pm or 10pm.

Black Market   Live Music
(www.blackmarketartgallery.it/monti; Via Panisperna 101; ⏰5.30pm-2am; Ⓜ︎Cavour) A bit outside the main Monti hub, this charming living-room-style bar filled with eclectic vintage furniture is a small but rambling place, great for sitting back on mismatched armchairs and having a leisurely, convivial drink. It hosts regular acoustic indie and folk gigs, which feel a bit like having a band in your living room.

Istituzione Universitaria dei Concerti   Live Music
(IUC; 📞06 361 00 51; www.concertiiuc.it; Piazzale Aldo Moro 5; 🚊Via dell'Università) The IUC organises a season of concerts in the Aula Magna of La Sapienza University, including many visiting international artists and orchestras. Performances cover a wide range of musical genres, including baroque, classical, contemporary and jazz.

✪ Trastevere & Gianicolo

Lettere Caffè   Live Music
(📞340 0044154; www.letterecaffe.org; Vicolo di San Francesco a Ripa 100-101; ⏰6pm-2am, closed mid-Aug–mid-Sep; 🚊Viale di Trastevere,

🔲Viale di Trastevere) Like books? Poetry? Blues and jazz? Then you'll love this place, a clutter of bar stools and books, where there are regular live gigs, poetry slams, comedy and gay nights, plus DJ sets playing electronic, indie and new wave. *Aperitivo,* with a tempting vegetarian buffet, is served between 7pm and 9pm.

Big Mama
Blues

(📞06 581 25 51; www.bigmama.it; Vicolo di San Francesco a Ripa 18; ⏰9pm-1.30am, shows 10.30pm, closed Jun-Sep; 🔲Viale di Trastevere, 🔲Viale di Trastevere) Head to this cramped Trastevere basement for a mellow night of Eternal City blues. A long-standing venue, it also stages jazz, funk, soul and R&B acts, as well as popular cover bands.

Teatro Vascello
Theatre

(📞06 588 10 21; www.teatrovascello.it; Via Giacinto Carini 72, Monteverde; 🔲Via Giacinto Carini) Left-field in vibe and location, this independent fringe theatre in off-the-beaten-tourist-track Monteverde stages interesting, cutting-edge new work, including

avant-garde dance, multimedia events and works by emerging playwrights.

Nuovo Sacher
Cinema

(📞06 581 81 16; www.sacherfilm.eu; Largo Ascianghi 1; 🔲Viale di Trastevere, 🔲Viale di Trastevere) Owned by cult Roman film director Nanni Moretti, this small cinema with classic red velvet seats is the place to catch the latest European art-house offering. There are regular screenings of Italian and international films, many in their original language.

✪ San Giovanni & Testaccio

Terme di Caracalla
Opera

(www.operaroma.it; Viale delle Terme di Caracalla 52; tickets from €22; ⏰Jun-Aug; 🔲Viale delle Terme di Caracalla) The hulking ruins of this vast 3rd-century baths complex set the memorable stage for the Teatro dell'Opera's summer

Big-budget theatre spectaculars, musicals, concerts and comic star...

Teatro Sistina (p185)

Auditorium Parco della Musica

season of music, opera and ballet, as well as shows by big-name Italian performers.

ConteStaccio   Live Music

(☎06 5728 9712; www.contestaccio.com; Via di Monte Testaccio 65b; ☻6pm-5am Wed-Sat; 🚇Via Galvani) With an under-the-stars terrace and buzzing vibe, ConteStaccio is one of the top venues on the Testaccio clubbing strip. It's something of a multipurpose outfit with a cocktail bar, pizzeria and restaurant, but is best known for its free live music. Gigs by emerging groups set the tone, spanning indie, rock, acoustic, funk and electronic genres.

✪ Villa Borghese & Northern Rome

Auditorium Parco della Musica   Concert Venue

(☎06 8024 1281; www.auditorium.com; Viale Pietro de Coubertin; 🚇Viale Tiziano) The hub of Rome's thriving cultural scene, the Auditorium is the capital's premier concert venue. Its three concert halls offer superb acoustics and, together with a 3000-seat open-air arena, stage everything from classical music concerts to jazz gigs, public lectures and film screenings.

The Auditorium is also home to Rome's world-class **Orchestra dell'Accademia Nazionale di Santa Cecilia** (www.santa cecilia.it).

Foro Italico   Spectator Sport

(Viale del Foro Italico; 🚇Lungotevere Maresciallo Cadorna) This grand Fascist-era sports complex, built between 1928 and 1938, is centred on Rome's 70,000-seat Stadio Olimpico (p194), home of the capital's two Serie A football teams. It also hosts Italy's premier tennis tournament, the Internazionali BNL d'Italia, in May.

Teatro Olimpico   Theatre

(☎06 326 59 91; www.teatroolimpico.it; Piazza Gentile da Fabriano 17; 🚇Piazza Mancini, 🚌Piazza Mancini) The Teatro Olimpico hosts a varied program of opera, dance, one-man shows, musicals and comedies, as well as

POLIFOTO/SHUTTERSTOCK ©

classical music concerts by the Accademia Filarmonica Romana.

Silvano Toti
Globe Theatre
Theatre

(☑060608; www.globetheatreroma.com; Largo Aqua Felix, Villa Borghese; tickets €10-30; ☑Piazzale Brasile) Like London's Globe Theatre but with better weather, Villa Borghese's open-air Elizabethan theatre serves up Shakespeare (performances mostly in Italian) from July through to early October.

 Southern Rome

Caffè Letterario
Live Music

(☑06 5730 2842; www.caffeletterarioroma.it; Via Ostiense 95; ☑10am-2am Tue-Fri, 4pm-2am Sat & Sun; ☑Via Ostiense, Ⓜ Piramide) Caffè Letterario is an intellectual hang-out housed in the funky converted, post-industrial space of a former garage. It combines designer looks, a bookshop, gallery, co-working space, performance area and lounge bar. There are regular gigs from 10pm to midnight, ranging from soul and jazz to Indian dance.

Teatro Palladium
Theatre

(☑box office 327 2463456; http://teatropalla dium.uniroma3.it; Piazza Bartolomeo Romano; tickets adult/reduced €15/10; Ⓜ Garbatella) Once at risk of being turned into a bingo hall, the historic Teatro Palladium (1926), with a beautifully renovated 1920s interior, stages a rich repertoire of theatre, classical music concerts, cinema and art exhibitions.

Teatro India
Theatre

(☑06 684 00 03 11; www.teatrodiroma.net; Lungotevere Vittorio Gassman 1; Ⓜ Stazione Trastevere) Inaugurated in 1999 in the post-industrial landscape of Rome's southern suburbs, the India is the younger sister of Teatro Argentina. It's a stark modern space in a converted industrial building, a fitting setting for its cutting-edge program, with a calendar of international and Italian works.

 Opera & Dance

Rome's opera house, the **Teatro dell'Opera di Roma** (p185), is a magnificent, grandiose venue, lined in gilt and red, but productions can be a bit hit and miss. It's also home to Rome's official Corps de Ballet and has a ballet season running in tandem with its opera performances. Both ballet and opera move outdoors for the summer season at the ancient Roman baths, **Terme di Caracalla** (p187), which is an even more spectacular setting.

You can also see opera in various other outdoor locations; check listings or at the tourist information kiosks for details.

Rome's **Auditorium Parco della Musica** (p188) hosts classical and contemporary dance performances, as well as the Equilibrio Festival in February. The **Auditorium Conciliazione** (p185) is another good place to catch contemporary dance companies.

Teatro dell'Opera di Roma
CINEBERG/SHUTTERSTOCK ©

La Casa del Jazz
Jazz

(☑06 70 47 31; www.casajazz.it; Viale di Porta Ardeatina 55; ☑hours vary; ☑Viale di Porta Ardeatina) In the middle of a 2500-sq-metre park in the southern suburbs, the Jazz House resides in a three-storey 1920s villa that once belonged to the boss of the *banda del Magliana,* a powerful local mafia outfit. When he was caught, Rome Council converted it into a jazz complex with a 150-seat auditorium, rehearsal rooms, cafe and restaurant.

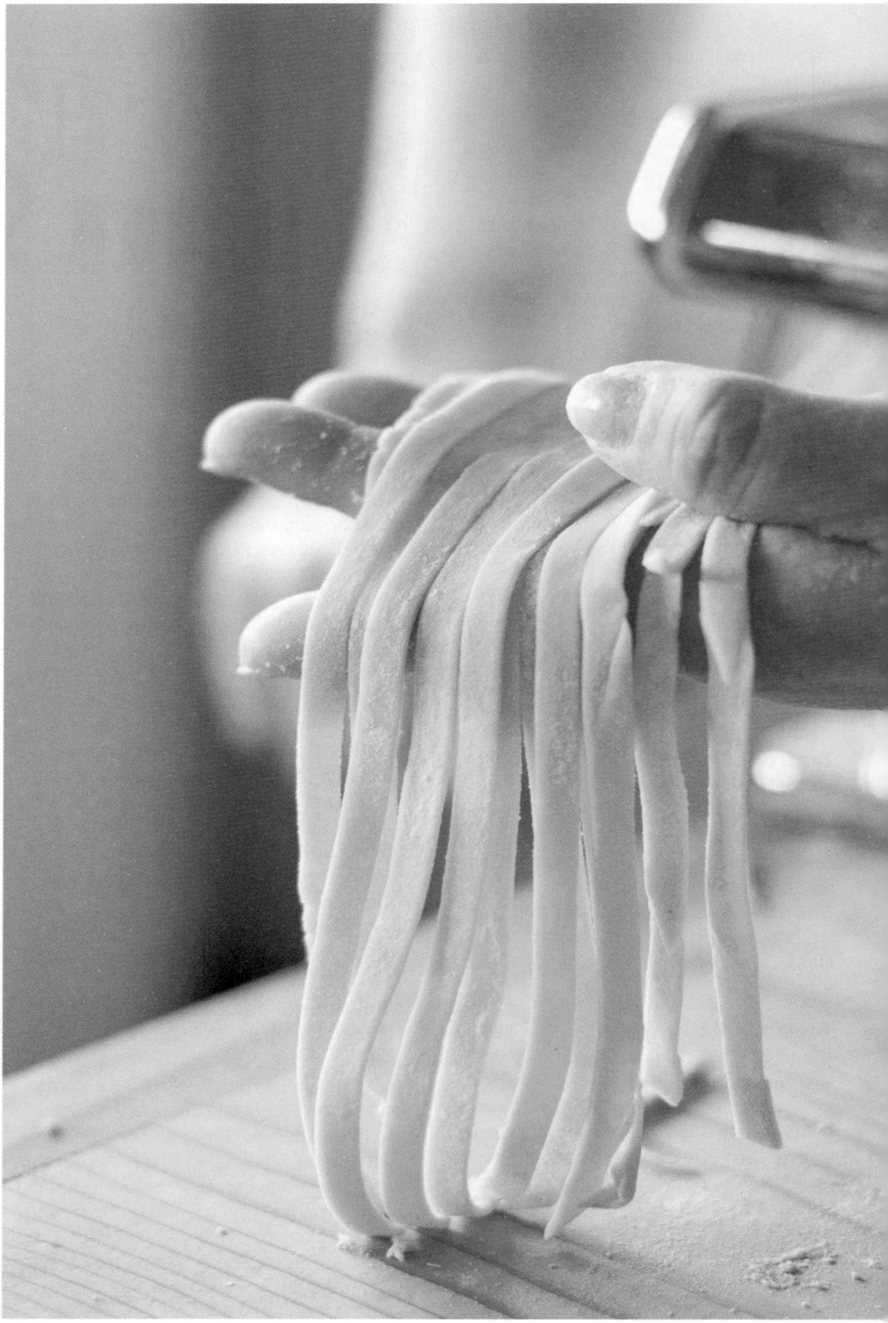

ACTIVE ROME

From football to cooking courses

Active Rome

The Romans have long been passionate about sport. Just as crowds once swarmed to the Colosseum to cheer on gladiators, so modern-day fans flock to the Stadio Olimpico to support the city's two premier football teams. Other regular sports fixtures include international rugby in February and March, and top-flight tennis in May.

If you prefer your pursuits more hands-on, there are plenty of courses you can take, ranging from cooking and wine-tasting primers to language lessons and art classes. Tours – on foot, by bike, even on a Vespa – are also very popular.

In This Section

What to Watch & When to Watch it

Football is the main sport in Rome with the season running from late August to May. Rugby fans can watch international matches on alternate weekends in February and March, and tennis enthusiasts can follow the Internazionale BNL d'Italia in early May.

Cyclists on Via del Fori

Tours

Casa Mia (p194) Food and wine tours with tastings and shop visits.

A Friend in Rome (p194) Tailor-made walking and thematic tours.

Roman Guy (p195) Group and private tours and cocktail-fuelled bar-hops.

The Red Bicycle (p195) See Rome from a saddle with this popular bike outfit.

Arcult (p195) Offers specialist contemporary architecture tours.

Food & Wine Courses

Vino Roma (p197) Wine-tasting classes in a tasting studio.

GT Food & Travel (p195) Cooking classes and in-home dining experiences.

Elizabeth Minchilli (p197) Pasta workshops and olive-oil tasting with a well-known food blogger.

Pasta Chef (p132) Informal, pasta-making classes in Monti.

JON BOWER AT APEXPHOTOS/GETTY IMAGES ©

⊕ Spectator Sports

Stadio Olimpico   Stadium
(📞06 3685 7563; Viale dei Gladiatori 2, Foro Italico; 🚇Lungotevere Maresciallo Cadorna) A trip to Rome's impressive Stadio Olimpico offers an unforgettable insight into Rome's sporting heart. Throughout the football season (September to May) there's a game on most Sundays featuring one of the city's two Serie A teams (Roma or Lazio), and during the Six Nations rugby tournament (February to March) it hosts Italy's home games.

Foro Italico   Spectator Sport
(Viale del Foro Italico; 🚇Lungotevere Maresciallo Cadorna) This grand Fascist-era sports complex, built between 1928 and 1938, is centred on Rome's 70,000-seat Stadio Olimpico home of the capital's two Serie A football teams. It also hosts Italy's premier tennis tournament, the Internazionali BNL d'Italia, in May.

> *Stadio Olimpico offers an unforgettable insight into Rome's sporting heart.*

Piazza di Siena Showjumping Competition   Spectator Sport
(www.piazzadisiena.it; Piazza di Siena, Villa Borghese; ⊙May; 🚇Via Pinciana) Rome's top equestrian and horse-jumping event, held each May in Villa Borghese park.

⊕ Tours

Casa Mia   Tours
(📞346 8001746; www.italyfoodandwinetours. com; 3hr tour with tastings 2/4 people €360/420) Serious food and wine tours, including a Trastevere and Jewish Quarter neighbourhood tour, with tastings and behind-the-scenes meetings with local shopkeepers, producers, chefs and restaurateurs. Bespoke tours, dining itineraries and reservations can also be arranged.

A Friend in Rome   Tours
(📞340 5019201; www.afriendinrome.it) Silvia Prosperi and her team offer a range of private tours covering the Vatican and main

Roma supporters at Stadio Olimpico

historic centre as well as areas outside the capital. They can also organise kid-friendly tours, food and wine itineraries, vintage car drives and horse rides along Via Appia Antica. Rates start at €165 for a basic three-hour tour for up to eight people; add €55 for every additional hour.

Roman Guy   Tours
(✆342 8761859; https://theromanguy.com) A professional setup that organises a wide range of group and private tours. Packages, led by English-speaking experts, include skip-the-queue visits to the Vatican Museums (US$89), foodie tours of Trastevere and the Jewish Ghetto (US$84), and an evening bar hop through the historic centre's cocktail bars (US$225).

GT Food & Travel   Tours
(✆320 7204222; www.gtfoodandtravel.com; 3hr tour with tastings per person around €120) Small-group food-lover tours, including a themed 'Cucina Povera & Roman Cuisine' tour in Monteverde. Gelato tours (with the option of an add-on gelato-making class), half- and full-day custom tours, cooking classes and in-home dining experiences are also on offer.

Red Bicycle   Cycling
(✆327 5387148; www.rideroma.it; Via Ostilia 4b; 🚇Via Labicana) A cycle shop offering bike hire (€10/15 per half/full day) and a range of cycling tours taking in the city's main neighbourhoods and environs. Prices start at €35 for a three-hour sunset tour, rising to €120 for the 80km ride up to Frascati and Castel Gandolfo.

Arcult   Walking
(✆339 6503172; www.arcult.it) Run by architects, Arcult offers excellent customisable group tours focusing on Rome's contemporary architecture. Prices depend on the itinerary but range from €250 to €370 for two to 10 people.

Eating Italy
Food Tours   Food & Drink
(✆06 9480 4492; www.eatingitalyfoodtours.com; tours €59-96) This cheery company offers informative food tours around Testaccio (the heartland of traditional

 Football

In Rome, footballing allegiances are split between the city's two Serie A teams: Roma (www.asroma.it), known as the *giallorossi* (yellow and reds), and Lazio (www.sslazio.it), the *biancazzurri* (white and blues).

Throughout the football season (late August to May) there's a game most Sundays at the Stadio Olimpico, the stadium both sides currently share. However, that's likely to change in a few years time as Roma have recently received the go-ahead to start building a new stadium in the southern Tor de Valle district.

Match tickets cost from €20 depending on the game and can be bought at Lottomatica outlets, the stadium, ticket agencies, www.listicket.it or one of the several Roma or Lazio stores around town. When buying, note that *i romanisti* (Roma fans) flock to the Curva Sud (South Stand) while *i laziali* (Lazio supporters) occupy the Curva Nord (North Stand). Note also that you'll need to keep your wits about you at the stadium as crowd trouble is not unheard of at games. Security measures now dictate that all tickets must bear the holder's name and that a passport or photo ID must be shown when entering the stadium.

To get to the Stadio Olimpico, take metro line A to Ottaviano—San Pietro and then bus 32.

Lazio v Fiorentina, Stadio Olimpico

 Running

Footpaths along the Tiber, sections of which are decorated with fantastic street art like William Kentridge's monumental *Triumphs and Laments* mural, provide the perfect jogging track for many a Roman who enjoys a morning run. Grassy routes, kinder to the knees and greener on the eyes, include Circo Massimo, the landscaped park of Villa Doria Pamphij, and out-of-town Parco della Caffarella in the Parco Regionale Appia Antica.

Serious runners can sign up for the annual Rome Marathon, held each year in March or April. The 42km-long course starts and finishes near the Colosseum, taking in many of the city's big sights.

Runners on a Tiber footpath
BLINDSPOTS/SHUTTERSTOCK ©

Roman cooking) and Trastevere, with chances to taste various delicacies on the way. Prices start at €77 per person and there's a maximum of 12 people per tour.

Through Eternity Cultural Association — Walking

(☑06 700 93 36; www.througheternity.com) A reliable operator offering private and group tours led by English-speaking experts. Popular packages include a twilight tour of Rome's piazzas and fountains (€39, 2½ hours), a night visit to the Vatican Museums (€69, 3½ hours), and a foodie tour of Testaccio (€79, four hours).

TopBike Rental & Tours — Cycling

(☑06 488 28 93; www.topbikerental.com; Via Labicana 49; ☺8.30am-7pm; ☐Via Labicana) Offers a series of bike tours throughout the city, including a four-hour 16km exploration of the city centre (€45) and an all-day 30km ride through Via Appia Antica and environs (€79). Out-of-town tours take in Castel Gandolfo, Civita di Bagnoregio and Orvieto.

Also offers bike hire from €15 per day.

Vespa Style Roma — Tours

(☑06 446 62 68; www.vespastyleroma.it; Via Milazzo 3a; Vespa rental per hour/day €15/69, bikes per day €15; ☺9am-7pm; ⓜTermini) Wannabe Audrey Hepburns can rent a Vespa to scoot around town from Vespa Style Roma, across the road from Stazione Termini. It also rents e-bikes and organises guided Vespa/e-bike tours (from €70/40).

Bici & Baci — Tours

(☑06 482 84 43; www.bicibaci.com; Via del Viminale 5; bike tours from €30, Vespa tours from €145; ☺8am-7pm; ⓜRepubblica) Bici & Baci runs a range of daily bike tours, taking in the main historical sites and Via Appia Antica, as well as tours on vintage Vespas, in classic Fiat 500 cars or in funky three-wheeled Ape Calessinos. Its sparkling flagship branch is near Stazione Termini.

Bici & Baci also rents bicycles/e-bikes (€12.50/25 a day) and a variety of scooters (from €32 a day).

Rome Boat Experience — Boating

(☑06 8956 7745; www.romeboatexperience.com; adult/reduced €18/12; ☺Apr-Oct) From April to October, this outfit runs hop-on, hop-off cruises along the Tiber. From May to October there are also dinner cruises (€65, two hours) every Friday and Saturday, and a daily wine-bar cruise (€30, 1½ hours) from Monday to Thursday. The main embarkation point is Molo Sant'Angelo, over the river from Castel Sant'Angelo.

Open Bus Vatican & Rome — Bus

(☑06 69 89 61; www.operaromanapellegrinaggi.org; single tour €12, 24/48hr ticket €25/28) The

Vatican-sponsored Opera Romana Pellegrinaggi runs a hop-on, hop-off bus departing from Piazza Pia and Termini. Stops are situated near to main sights including St Peter's Basilica, Piazza Navona, the Trevi Fountain and the Colosseum. Tickets are available on board, online, or at the info point just off St Peter's Square.

Courses

Città di Gusto   Cooking
(☎06 5511 2211; www.gamberorosso.it; Via Ottavio Gasparri 13-17; 🚇Viale dei Colli Portuensi) Demonstrations, workshops, lessons and courses are held at the seat of the Italian food organisation, Gambero Rosso, in the Monteverde neighbourhood west of Testaccio. Reckon on around €60 for a three-hour course.

Vino Roma   Wine
(☎328 4874497; www.vinoroma.com; Via in Selci 84g; 2hr tastings per person €50; 🚇Cavour) With beautifully appointed century-old cellars and a chic tasting studio, Vino Roma guides novices and experts in tasting wine under the knowledgeable stewardship of sommelier Hande Leimer and her expert team. Also on offer is a wine-and-cheese dinner (€60) with snacks, cheeses and cold cuts to accompany the wines, and bespoke three-hour food tours. Book online.

Tastings are in English, but German, Japanese, Italian and Turkish sessions are available on special request.

Latteria Studio   Cooking
(☎835 29990; https://latteriastudio.com; Via di Ponziano 29; 🚇Viale di Trastevere, 🚇Viale di Trastevere) Highly personalised market tours and cooking classes in a stylish food-photography studio in backstreet Trastevere. Prices vary, depending on the course. Count on around €75 for a day's fresh pasta-making class with lunch.

Elizabeth Minchilli   Cooking
(www.elizabethminchilliinrome.com; tours/classes per person from €130/220) Small-group cooking classes and food tours, with tastings, led by Rome based, American food blogger Elizabeth Minchilli.

Art Studio Lab   Art
(☎348 6099758, 344 0971721; box@savellireligious.com; Savelli Arte e Tradizione, Via Paolo VI 27-29; ⊗9.30am-7pm; 🚇Lungotevere in Sassia) This mosaic school, operating out of the Savelli Arte e Tradizione shop, offers individually tailored workshops and courses. In a basic three-hour workshop, which includes a bite to eat, you'll learn how to cut marble and enamels and make your own frames, mirrors or tiles. Reckon on €90/80 per adult/child for a group of one to three people.

Torre di Babele Centro di Lingua e Cultura Italiana   Language
(☎06 4425 2578; www.torredibabele.com; Via Cosenza 7; 🚇Via Bari) As well as language lessons, this school offers courses on cooking, art, architecture and several other subjects. Individual language lessons start at €39, with an enrolment fee of €80.

🟢 Spas

Hotel De Russie Spa   Spa
(☎06 3288 8820; www.roccofortehotels.com/it; Via del Babuino 9; ⊗6.30am-10pm; 🚇Flaminio) In one of Rome's top hotels, this glamorous and gorgeous day spa boasts a salt water pool, steam room, Finnish sauna and well-equipped gym. A wide choice of treatments are available (for him and her), including shiatsu and deep-tissue massages; count on at least €100 for a 50-minute massage.

Kami Spa   Spa
(☎06 4201 0039; www.kamispa.com; Via degli Avignonesi 11-12; massage €120-280; ⊗10am-10pm; 🚇Barberini) A luxurious spa not far from the Trevi Fountain, this is a soothing place to recharge your batteries. Think hot stone massages, Balinese palm massages, massages with Moroccan rose petal oil, turmeric and sandalwood body wraps, and green-tea body cocoons.

REST YOUR HEAD

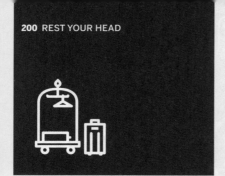

Rest Your Head

Accommodation is plentiful in Rome, so whether you want to splurge like royalty or bunk down in a hostel, you'll find somewhere to suit your style. At the top end of the market, opulent five-star hotels occupy stately palazzi (mansions) and chic boutique guesthouses boast discreet luxury. Family-run B&Bs and pensioni offer character and a warm welcome, while religious houses cater to pilgrims and cost-conscious travellers. Hostel-goers can choose between party-loving hang-outs or quieter, more restrained digs.

In This Section

Taxes

Everyone overnighting in Rome must pay a room-occupancy tax on top of their bill: €3 per person per night in one- and two-star hotels, €3.50 in B&Bs and room rentals, and €4/6/7 in three-/four-/five-star hotels.

Tipping

Tipping is not necessary, but leaving up to €5 for porter, maid or room service in a top-end hotel is fine.

Bernini Bristol Hotel

Reservations

○ Always try to book ahead, especially in high season (Easter to September) and during major religious festivals.

○ Ask for a *camera matrimoniale* for a room with a double bed; a *camera doppia* has twin beds.

Checking In & Out

○ When you check in you'll need to present your passport or ID card.

○ Checkout is usually between 10am and noon. In hostels it's around 9am.

○ Most guesthouses and B&Bs require you to arrange, in advance, a time to check in.

🔵 Accommodation Types

Pensioni & Hotels

The bulk of Rome's accommodation consists of *pensioni* (pensions) and *alberghi* (hotels).

A *pensione* is a small family-run hotel, often in a converted apartment. Rooms are usually fairly simple, though most come with a private bathroom.

Hotels are rated from one to five stars, though this relates to facilities only and gives no indication of value, comfort, atmosphere or friendliness. Most hotels in Rome's *centro storico* (historic centre) tend to be three-star and above. As a rule, a three-star room will come with a hairdryer, a minibar (or fridge), a safe, air-con and wi-fi. Some may also have satellite TV.

A common complaint in Rome is that hotel rooms are small. This is especially true in the *centro storico* and Trastevere, where many hotels are housed in centuries-old *palazzi*. Similarly, a spacious lift is a rare find, particularly in older *palazzi,* and you'll seldom find one that can accommodate more than one average-sized person with luggage.

Breakfast in cheaper hotels is rarely worth setting the alarm for, so if you have the option, pop into a bar for a coffee and *cornetto* (croissant) instead.

B&Bs & Guesthouses

Alongside traditional B&Bs, Rome has many boutique-style guesthouses offering chic, upmarket accommodation at mid to top-end prices.

Breakfast in a Roman B&B usually consists of bread rolls, croissants, yoghurt, ham and cheese. Some places offer breakfast in a nearby cafe; check when you make your booking.

Hostels

Rome's hostels cater to everyone from backpackers to budget-minded families.

> *Most hotels in Rome's centro storico (historic centre) tend to be three-star and above.*

Waldorf Astoria Cavalieri

LOU ARMOR/SHUTTERSTOCK ©

Many offer hotel-style rooms alongside traditional dorms.

Some hostels don't accept reservations for dorm beds, so it's first come, first served.

The city's new breed of hostels are chic, designer pads with trendy bar-restaurants, bike rental, the occasional stunning rooftop garden and a fantastic array of organised tours and activities on offer.

Religious Accommodation

Unsurprisingly Rome is well furnished with religious institutions, a number of which offer cheap(ish) guest rooms. Bear in mind, though, that many have strict curfews and that the accommodation, while spotlessly clean, tends to be short on frills.

There are a number of centrally located options, but most places are situated out of the centre, typically in the districts north and west of the Vatican. Book well in advance.

Rental Accommodation

For longer stays, renting an apartment will generally work out cheaper than an extended hotel sojourn. Bank on about €900 per month for a studio apartment or one-bedroom flat. For longer stays, you'll probably have to pay bills plus a building maintenance charge.

🖴 Seasons & Rates

Rome doesn't have a low season as such, but rates are at their lowest from November to March (excluding Christmas and New Year) and from mid-July to the end of August. Expect to pay top rates in spring (April to June) and autumn (September and October) and over the main holiday periods (Christmas, New Year and Easter).

 Online Rentals

Websites such as Airbnb and VRBO offer the chance to select and book accommodation online.

These sites have a vast range of options, from single rooms in private houses to fully equipped apartments. Listings are often good value and many will save you money, especially in expensive areas such as the *centro storico* or Trastevere. They'll also give you the chance to get away from touristy hotspots and see another side to the city – characterful neighbourhoods include Testaccio and Garbatella. Just be sure to research the location when you book and, if necessary, work out how to get there (eg public transport, a pick-up from the property owner etc).

Always check the property's reviews for things such as noise (an issue in central locations) and privacy. You'll also need to check whether Rome's obligatory accommodation tax is included in the rate or has to be paid separately.

Payment

Most midrange and top-end hotels accept credit cards. Budget places might, but it's always best to check in advance.

Minerva Hotel

🚌 Getting There

Most tourist areas are a bus ride or metro journey from Stazione Termini. If you come by car, be warned that much of the city centre is a ZTL (limited traffic zone) and is off-limits to unauthorised traffic. Note also that there is a terrible lack of on-site parking facilities in the city centre, although your hotel should be able to direct you to a private garage. Street parking is not recommended.

🌐 Useful Websites

• **Lonely Planet** (lonelyplanet.com/italy/rome/hotels) Consult a list of author-reviewed accommodation options and book online.

• **Cross Pollinate** (www.cross-pollinate.com) Personally vetted rooms and apartments by the team behind Rome's super-efficient and stylish Beehive hostel.

• **060608** (www.060608.it/en/accoglienza/dormire) Official Comune di Roma site with accommodation lists.

• **Bed & Breakfast Association of Rome** (www.b-b.rm.it) Lists B&Bs and short-term apartment rentals.

• **Bed & Breakfast Italia** (www.bbitalia.it) Rome's longest-established B&B network.

• **Rome As You Feel** (www.romeasyoufeel.com) Apartment rentals, from cheap studio flats to luxury apartments.

Where to Stay

Accommodation in Rome is expensive, and with the city busy year-round, it pays to book as far ahead as possible.

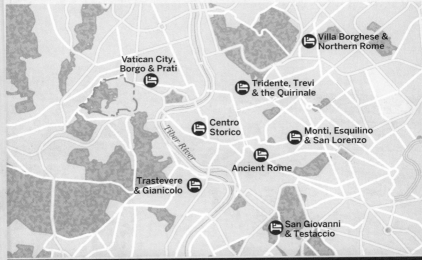

Neighbourhood	Atmosphere
Ancient Rome	Close to major sights such as Colosseum, Roman Forum and Capitoline Museums; quiet at night; not cheap; restaurants are touristy.
Centro Storico	Atmospheric area with everything on your doorstep – Pantheon, Piazza Navona, restaurants, bars, shops; most expensive part of town; can be noisy.
Tridente, Trevi & the Quirinale	Good for Spanish Steps, Trevi Fountain and designer shopping; excellent midrange to top-end options; good transport links; subdued after dark.
Vatican City, Borgo & Prati	Near St Peter's Basilica; decent range of accommodation; some excellent shops and restaurants; on the metro; not much nightlife; sells out quickly for religious holidays.
Monti, Esquilino & San Lorenzo	Lots of budget accommodation around Stazione Termini; top eating in Monti and good nightlife in San Lorenzo and Pigneto; good transport links; some dodgy streets near Termini.
Trastevere & Gianicolo	Gorgeous, atmospheric area; party vibe with hundreds of bars, cafes and restaurants; some interesting sights; expensive; noisy, particularly on summer nights.
San Giovanni & Testaccio	Authentic atmosphere with good eating and drinking options; Aventino is a quiet, romantic area; Testaccio is a top food and nightlife district; not many big sights.
Villa Borghese & Northern Rome	Largely residential area good for the Auditorium and Stadio Olimpico; some top museums; generally quiet after dark.

View from St Peter's Basilica

In Focus

Rome City Hall

Rome Today

Rome's position as Italy's number-one tourist destination seems assured as visitor numbers continue to rise. The city's museums have never been busier and many high-profile monuments are sparkling after recent restorations. A rash of new Michelin stars has also invigorated the city's restaurant scene. But away from the bright lights, the city has struggled with controversy in City Hall, rubbish on the streets and in-fighting in the Vatican.

Controversy in City Hall

In summer 2016 Rome elected its first-ever woman mayor. Virginia Raggi, a 37-year-old city councillor swept to victory, taking 67% of the vote as candidate for the populist *Movimento 5 Stelle* (5 Star Movement). Promising to take on corruption and improve the city's dire public services, her message hit a real chord with a Roman public weary of cutbacks and political scandal.

However, her first year in office proved a disappointment to many. She got off to a rocky start after several key appointees resigned, and then, in early 2017, she was placed under investigation for abuse of office. Later in the year, she was heavily criticised for failing to deal with a breakdown in rubbish collection. She was even blamed for the state of the city's Christmas tree, a threadbare spruce nicknamed *lo Spelacchio* or 'Mangy One'.

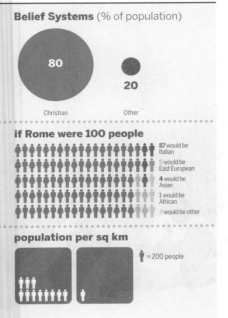

Belief Systems (% of population)

80 Christian

20 Other

if Rome were 100 people

87 would be Italian
5 would be East European
4 would be Asian
1 would be African
3 would be other

population per sq km

≈ 200 people

In the midst of all this, she did, however, manage to make some big decisions. She withdrew Rome's bid for the 2024 Olympic Games and gave the go-ahead for a new football stadium in the city's southern reaches. She also passed a €5.3-billion budget, earmarking €430 million for upgrading the city's public transport network, including buying new buses and funding ongoing construction on the metro.

Jubilee & Vatican Intrigue

Over on the west bank of the Tiber at the Vatican, Pope Francis declared 2016 a Jubilee, or Holy Year, and millions made the pilgrimage to Rome. According to Vatican estimates, some 21 million people passed through the Holy Door at St Peter's Basilica during the year.

Later, in May 2017, the pope welcomed US President Donald Trump to the Vatican. In the visit, described by the Holy See as 'cordial', the two exchanged views on global issues including climate change and migration.

Behind the scenes, however, the atmosphere within the Vatican has become increasingly toxic as internal opposition to Pope Francis' progressive politics grows. With his easygoing manner and popular charm, the Argentinean pontiff has won worldwide acclaim, but his liberal line has enraged conservatives within the Church. Central to this dispute are the pope's efforts to reform teachings on family, marriage and divorce.

Monumental Makeovers

For several years now, Rome's cultural administrators have been courting private money to shore up municipal budgets and help cover the cost of maintaining the city's historic sites and monuments. This policy has often sparked heated debate, but it is now showing signs of fruition. Most notably, the Colosseum is looking better than it has in centuries after the completion of a three-year clean-up. The scrub-down came as the first part of an ongoing €25-million restoration project sponsored by Italian shoemaker Tod's. Similarly, the Spanish Steps are gleaming after a €1.5-million make-over financed by luxury jeweller Bulgari. Nearby, work is scheduled to get underway at the Mausoleo di Augusto with the help of a €6-million donation from Italian telecoms giant TIM.

As well as these high-profile projects, the city has also managed some quieter successes. At the Roman Forum, the Chiesa di Santa Maria Antiqua was reopened after a lengthy restoration, while at the Circo Massimo a renovated section of the original stadium was recently opened to guided tours.

Statue of Romulus and Remus being nursed by a wolf

ANGELIKA STERN/GETTY IMAGES ©

History

Rome's history spans three millennia, from the classical myths of vengeful gods to the follies of Roman emperors, from Renaissance excess to swaggering 20th-century fascism. Everywhere you go in this remarkable city, you're surrounded by the past. Martial ruins, Renaissance palazzi and flamboyant baroque basilicas all have tales to tell of family feuding, historic upheavals, artistic rivalries, dark intrigues and violent passions.

753 BC
According to legend, Romulus kills his twin brother Remus and founds Rome on the Palatino.

509 BC
The Roman Republic is founded, paving the way for Rome's rise to European domination.

15 March 44 BC
On the Ides of March, Julius Caesar is stabbed to death in the Teatro di Pompeo (on modern-day Largo di Torre Argentina).

Colosseum (p36)

EVAN REINHEIMER/GETTY IMAGES ©

The Myth of Ancient Rome

As much a mythical construct as a historical reality, ancient Rome's image has been carefully nurtured throughout history.

Rome's original myth makers were the first emperors. Eager to reinforce the city's status as *caput mundi* (capital of the world), they turned to writers such as Virgil, Ovid and Livy to create an official Roman history. These authors, while adept at weaving epic narratives, were less interested in the rigours of historical research and frequently presented myth as reality. In the *Aeneid,* Virgil brazenly draws on Greek legends and stories to tell the tale of Aeneas, a Trojan prince who arrives in Italy and establishes Rome's founding dynasty.

Ancient Rome's rulers were sophisticated masters of spin; under their tutelage, art, architecture and elaborate public ceremony were employed to perpetuate the image of Rome as an invincible and divinely sanctioned power.

AD 67	80	285
St Peter and St Paul become martyrs as Nero massacres Rome's Christians in a ploy to win popularity after the great fire of AD 64.	The 50,000-seat Flavian Amphitheatre, better known as the Colosseum, is inaugurated by the emperor Titus.	Diocletian splits the Roman Empire in two. The eastern half later joins the Byzantine Empire; the western half falls to the barbarians.

Ostia Antica (p92)

Legacy of an Empire

Rising out of the bloodstained remnants of the Roman Republic, the Roman Empire was the Western world's first great superpower. At its zenith under Emperor Trajan (r AD 98–117), it extended from Britannia in the north to North Africa in the south, from Hispania (Spain) in the west to Palestina (Palestine) and Syria in the east. Rome itself had more than 1.5 million inhabitants. Decline eventually set in during the 3rd century and by the latter half of the 5th century Rome was in barbarian hands.

In AD 285 the emperor Diocletian, prompted by widespread disquiet across the empire, split the Empire into eastern and western halves – the west centred on Rome and the east on Byzantium (later called Constantinople) – in a move that was to have far-reaching consequences for centuries. In the west, the fall of the Western Roman Empire in AD 476 paved the way for the emergence of the Holy Roman Empire and the Papal States, while in the east, Roman (later Byzantine) rule continued until 1453 when the empire was finally conquered by Ottoman armies.

Christianity & Papal Power

For much of its history Rome has been ruled by the pope, and still today the Vatican wields immense influence over the city.

The ancient Romans were remarkably tolerant of foreign religions. They themselves worshipped a cosmopolitan pantheon of gods, ranging from household spirits and former emperors to deities appropriated from Greek mythology such as Jupiter, Juno, Neptune and Minerva. Religious cults were also popular – the Egyptian gods Isis and Serapis enjoyed a mass following, as did Mithras, a heroic saviour-god of vaguely Persian origin, who was worshipped by male-only devotees in underground temples.

476
The fall of Romulus Augustulus marks the end of the Western Empire.

754
Pope Stephen II and Pepin, king of the Franks, cut a deal resulting in the creation of the Papal States.

1084
Rome is sacked by a Norman army after Pope Gregory VII invites them in to help him against the besieging forces of Henry IV.

Emergence of Christianity

Christianity swept in from the Roman province of Judaea in the 1st century AD. Its early days were marred by persecution, most notably under Nero (r 54–68), but it slowly caught on, thanks to its popular message of heavenly reward.

However, it was the conversion of Emperor Constantine (r 306–37) that really set Christianity on the path to European domination. In 313 Constantine issued the Edict of Milan, officially legalising Christianity, and in 378, Theodosius (r 379–95) made Christianity Rome's state religion. By this time, the Church had developed a sophisticated organisational structure based on five major sees: Rome, Constantinople, Alexandria, Antioch and Jerusalem. At the outset, each bishopric carried equal weight, but in subsequent years Rome emerged as the senior party. The reasons for this were partly political – Rome was the wealthy capital of the Roman Empire – and partly religious – early Christian doctrine held that St Peter, founder of the Roman Church, had been sanctioned by Christ to lead the universal Church.

Romulus & Remus

The most famous of Rome's legends is the story of Romulus and Remus and the foundation of the city on 21 April 753 BC.

According to myth, Romulus and Remus were the children of the vestal virgin Rhea Silva and the god of war, Mars. While babies they were set adrift on the Tiber to escape a death penalty imposed by their great-uncle who was battling their grandfather for control of Alba Longa. However, they were discovered by a she-wolf, who suckled them until a shepherd, Faustulus, found and raised them.

Years later they decided to found a city on the site where they'd originally been saved. Not knowing where this was, they consulted the omens. Remus, on the Aventino, saw six vultures; his brother, on the Palatino, saw 12. The meaning was clear, but the two argued and Romulus ended up killing Remus before going on to found his city.

Papal Control

But while Rome had control of Christianity, the Church had yet to conquer Rome. This it did in the dark days that followed the fall of the Roman Empire by skilfully stepping into the power vacuum created by the demise of imperial power. And although no one person can take credit for this, Pope Gregory the Great (r 590–604) did more than most to lay the groundwork. A leader of considerable foresight, he won many friends by supplying free bread to Rome's starving citizens and restoring the city's water supply. He also stood up to the menacing Lombards, who presented a very real threat to the city.

It was this threat that pushed the papacy into an alliance with the Frankish kings, resulting in the creation of the two great powers of medieval Europe: the Papal States and the Holy Roman Empire. In Rome, the battle between these two superpowers translated into endless feuding between the city's baronial families and frequent attempts by the French to claim the papacy for their own. This political and military fighting eventually culminated in the papacy transferring to

1300
Pope Boniface VIII proclaims Rome's first-ever Jubilee, offering a full pardon to anyone who makes the pilgrimage to the city.

1378–1417
Squabbling between factions in the Catholic Church leads to the Great Schism.

1527
Pope Clement VII hides in Castel Sant'Angelo as Rome is sacked by troops loyal to Charles V, King of Spain and Holy Roman Emperor.

Roman Forum (p78)

MARTIN M303/SHUTTERSTOCK ©

the French city of Avignon between 1309 and 1377, and the Great Schism (1378–1417), a period in which the Catholic world was headed by two popes, one in Rome and one in Avignon.

As both religious and temporal leaders, Rome's popes wielded influence well beyond their military capacity. For much of the medieval period, the Church held a virtual monopoly on Europe's reading material (mostly religious scripts written in Latin) and was the authority on virtually every aspect of human knowledge.

Modern Influence

Almost 1000 years on and the Church is still a major influence on modern Italian life. In recent years, Vatican intervention in political and social debate has provoked fierce divisions within Italy. This relationship between the Church and Italy's modern political establishment is a fact of life that dates to the establishment of the Italian Republic in 1946. For much of the First Republic (1946–94), the Vatican was closely associated with Democrazia Cristiana (DC; Christian Democrat Party), Italy's most powerful party and an ardent opponent of communism. At the same time, the Church, keen to weed communism out of the political landscape, played its part by threatening to excommunicate anyone who voted for Italy's Partito Comunista Italiano (PCI; Communist Party). Today, no one political party has a monopoly on Church favour, and politicians across the spectrum tread warily around Catholic sensibilities.

Renaissance, a New Beginning

Bridging the gap between the Middle Ages and the modern age, the Renaissance (*Rinascimento* in Italian) was a far-reaching intellectual, artistic and cultural movement. It emerged in 14th-century Florence but quickly spread to Rome, where it gave rise to one of the greatest makeovers the city had ever seen.

Humanism & Rebuilding

The movement's intellectual cornerstone was humanism, a philosophy that focused on the central role of humanity within the universe, a major break from the medieval world view,

---

1626
St Peter's Basilica is completed on 18 November after 150 years of construction.

1798
Napoleon marches into Rome. A republic is announced, but it doesn't last long and in 1801 Pope Pius VII returns to Rome.

1870
Nine years after Italian unification, Rome's city walls are breached at Porta Pia and Pope Pius IX cedes the city to Italy.

which had placed God at the centre of everything. It was not anti-religious though. One of the most celebrated humanist scholars of the 15th century was Pope Nicholas V (r 1447–84), who is considered the harbinger of the Roman Renaissance.

When Nicholas became pope in 1447, Rome was not in a good state. Centuries of medieval feuding had reduced the city to a semideserted battleground. In political terms, the papacy was recovering from the trauma of the Great Schism and attempting to face down Muslim encroachment in the east.

Against this background, Nicholas decided to rebuild Rome as a showcase of Church power, setting off an enormous program that would see the building of the Sistine Chapel and St Peter's Basilica.

Roman Roads

The ancient Romans were the expert engineers of their day, and the ability to travel quickly was an important factor in their power to rule. The queen of all ancient roads was Via Appia Antica, which connected Rome with the southern Adriatic port of Brindisi, named after Appius Claudius Caecus, the Roman censor who initiated its construction in 312 BC. Via Appia survives to this day, as do many of the other consular roads, Via Aurelia, Via Cassia, Via Flaminia and Via Salaria among them.

Sack of Rome & Protestant Protest

But outside Rome an ill wind was blowing. The main source of trouble was the long-standing conflict between the Holy Roman Empire, led by the Spanish Charles V, and the Italian city-states. This simmering tension came to a head in 1527 when Rome was invaded by Charles' marauding army and ransacked as Pope Clement VII (r 1523–34) hid in Castel Sant'Angelo. The sack of Rome, regarded by most historians as the nail in the coffin of the Roman Renaissance, was a hugely traumatic event. It left the papacy reeling and gave rise to the view that the Church had been greatly weakened by its own moral shortcomings. That the Church was corrupt was well known, and it was with considerable public support that Martin Luther pinned his famous *95 Theses* to a church door in Wittenberg in 1517, thus sparking off the Protestant Reformation.

Counter-Reformation

The Catholic reaction to the Reformation was strong. The Counter-Reformation was marked by a second wave of artistic and architectural activity, as the Church once again turned to bricks and mortar to restore its authority. But in contrast to the Renaissance, the Counter-Reformation was a period of persecution and official intolerance. With the full blessing of Pope Paul III, Ignatius Loyola founded the Jesuits in 1540, and two years later the Holy Office was set up as the Church's final appeals court for trials prosecuted by the Inquisition. In 1559 the Church published the *Index Librorum Prohibitorum* (Index of Prohibited Books) and began to persecute intellectuals and freethinkers.

1922
Some 40,000 fascists march on Rome. King Vittorio Emanuele III invites the 39-year-old Mussolini to form a government.

1929
The Lateran Treaty is signed, creating the state of Vatican City. To celebrate, Via della Conciliazione is bulldozed through the medieval Borgo.

1946
The Italian republic is born after a vote to abolish the monarchy.

Natale di Roma (p9)

★ **Best Historical Celebrations**

Carnevale Romano (p7)

Natale di Roma (p9)

Festa de' Noantri (p12)

Festa della Liberazione (p9)

Festa della Repubblica (p11)

Despite, or perhaps because of, the Church's policy of zero tolerance, the Counter-Reformation was largely successful in re-establishing papal prestige. From being a rural backwater with a population of around 20,000 in the mid-15th century, Rome had grown to become one of Europe's great 17th-century cities, home to Christendom's most spectacular churches and a population of 100,000 people.

The First Tourists

While Rome has a long past as a pilgrimage site, its history as a modern tourist destination can be traced back to the late 1700s and the fashion for the Grand Tour. The 18th-century version of a gap year, the Tour was considered an educational rite of passage for wealthy young men from northern Europe, and Britain in particular.

Rome, enjoying a rare period of peace, was perfectly set up for this English invasion. The city was basking in the aftermath of the 17th-century baroque building boom, and a craze for all things classical was sweeping Europe. Rome's papal authorities were also crying out for money after their excesses had left the city coffers bare, reducing much of the population to abject poverty.

Thousands came, including German writer Goethe, who stopped off to write his travelogue *Italian Journey* (1817), and English poets Byron, Shelley and Keats, who all fuelled their Romantic sensibilities in the city's vibrant streets.

Artistically, rococo was all the rage. The Spanish Steps, built between 1723 and 1726, proved a major hit with tourists, as did the exuberant Trevi Fountain.

Ghosts of Fascism

Rome's fascist history is a deeply sensitive subject, and in recent years historians on both sides of the political spectrum have accused each other of recasting the past to suit their views.

1957
The Treaty of Rome is signed in the Capitoline Museums and establishes the European Economic Community.

1978
Former prime minister Aldo Moro is kidnapped and shot by a cell of the extreme left-wing *Brigate Rosse* (Red Brigades).

2005
Pope John Paul II dies after 27 years on the papal throne. He is replaced by his long-standing ally Josef Ratzinger (Benedict XVI).

Mussolini

Benito Mussolini was born in 1883 in Forlì, a small town in Emilia-Romagna. As a young man he was an active member of the Italian Socialist Party, rising through the ranks to become editor of the party's official newspaper. However, service in WWI and Italy's subsequent descent into chaos led to a change of heart and in 1919 he founded the Italian Fascist Party.

In 1921 Mussolini was elected to the Chamber of Deputies. His parliamentary support was limited, but on 28 October 1922 he marched on Rome with 40,000 black-shirted followers. The march was largely symbolic but it had the desired effect: King Vittorio Emanuele III, fearful of a civil war between the fascists and socialists, invited Mussolini to form a government. By the end of 1925, the king had seized complete control of Italy. In order to silence the Church, Mussolini signed the Lateran Treaty in 1929, which made Catholicism the state religion and recognised the sovereignty of the Vatican State.

Abroad, Mussolini invaded Abyssinia (now Ethiopia) in 1935 and sided with Hitler in 1936. In 1940, from the balcony of Palazzo Venezia, he announced Italy's entry into WWII to a vast, cheering crowd. The good humour didn't last: Rome suffered, first at the hands of its own Fascist regime, then, after Mussolini was ousted in 1943, at the hands of the Nazis. Rome was finally liberated from German occupation on 4 June 1944.

Mafia Capitale

Rome's recent history has seen its fair share of scandal and controversy, most notably in the form of the Mafia Capitale case. This broke in 2014 when allegations surfaced that the city's municipal council had been colluding with a criminal gang to cream off public funds. The subsequent investigation, the largest anti-corruption operation since the Mani Pulite campaign of the 1990s, resulted in hundreds of arrests and convictions for more than 40 people, including former politicians and city officials. The man held to be the ring-leader, a one-eyed gangster and former member of a right-wing terrorist group, received a 20-year prison sentence.

Postwar Period

Defeat in WWII didn't kill off Italian fascism, and in 1946 hard-line Mussolini supporters founded the Movimento Sociale Italiano (MSI; Italian Social Movement). For close on 50 years, this overtly fascist party participated in mainstream Italian politics, while on the other side of the spectrum the PCI grew into Western Europe's largest communist party. The MSI was finally dissolved in 1994, when Gianfranco Fini rebranded it as the post-fascist Alleanza Nazionale (AN; National Alliance). AN remained an important political player until it was incorporated into Silvio Berlusconi's Popolo della Libertà party in 2009.

Outside the political mainstream, fascism (along with communism) was a driving force of the domestic terrorism that rocked Rome and Italy during the *anni di piombo* (years of lead), between the late 1960s and the early '80s.

2013	2014	2016
Pope Benedict XVI becomes the first pope to resign since 1415. Argentinian cardinal Jorge Mario Bergoglio is elected as Pope Francis.	Ex-mayor Gianni Alemanno and up to 100 other public officials are investigated as the Mafia Capitale scandal rocks Rome.	Onlookers applaud the Colosseum's polished new look after an extensive three-year clean-up, the first in its 2000-year history.

Basilica di Santa Maria in Trastevere (p104)

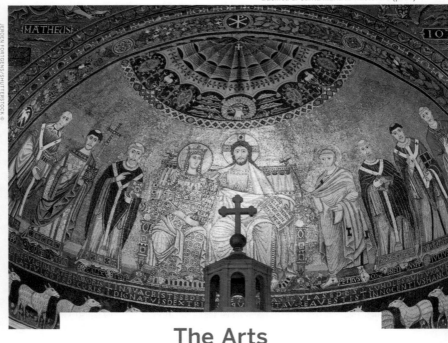

The Arts

Rome has long provided inspiration for painters, sculptors, film-makers, writers and musicians. The great works of Roman antiquity fuelled the imagination of Renaissance artists; Counter-Reformation persecution led to baroque art; the trauma of Mussolini and WWII found expression in neorealist cinema. More recently, urban art has flourished and film-making has returned to the streets of Rome.

Painting & Sculpture

Home to some of the Western world's most recognisable art, Rome is a visual feast. Its churches alone contain more masterpieces than many small countries, and the city's galleries are laden with works by world-famous artists.

Etruscan Groundwork

Laying the groundwork for much later Roman art, the Etruscans placed great importance on their funerary rites and they developed sepulchral decoration into a highly sophisticated art form. Elaborate stone sarcophagi were often embellished with a reclining figure or a couple, typically depicted with a haunting, enigmatic smile. An important example is the *Sarcofago degli sposi* (Sarcophagus of the Betrothed) in the Museo Nazionale Etrusco di Villa Giulia. The Etruscans were also noted for their bronze work and filigree jewellery. One of Rome's most iconic sculptures, the 5th-century-BC *Lupa capitolina* (Capitoline Wolf), held in the Capitoline Museums, is an Etruscan bronze.

Roman Developments

In terms of decorative art, the Roman use of mosaics and wall paintings was derived from Etruscan funerary decoration. By the 1st century BC, floor mosaics were a popular form of home decor. Typical themes included landscapes, still lifes, geometric patterns and depictions of gods. In the Museo Nazionale Romano: Palazzo Massimo alle Terme, you'll find some spectacular wall mosaics and 1st-century-BC frescoes.

Neoclassicism

Emerging in the late 18th and early 19th centuries, neoclassicism signalled a departure from the emotional abandon of the baroque and a return to the clean, sober lines of classical art. Its major exponent was the sculptor Antonio Canova (1757–1822), whose study of Paolina Bonaparte Borghese as *Venere Vincitrice* (Venus Victrix) in the Museo e Galleria Borghese is typical of the mildly erotic style for which he became known.

Sculpture was an important element of Roman art, and was largely influenced by Greek styles. Indeed, early Roman sculptures were often made by Greek artists or were copies of Greek works. They were largely concerned with the male physique and generally depicted visions of male beauty – the *Apollo Belvedere* and the *Laocoön* in the Vatican Museums are classic examples.

In terms of function, Roman art was highly propagandistic and from the time of Augustus (r 27 BC–AD 14), art was increasingly used to serve the state. This new narrative art often took the form of relief decoration – the *Ara Pacis* is a stunning example.

Early Christian Art

The earliest Christian art in Rome are the traces of biblical frescoes in the Catacombe di Priscilla and the Catacombe di San Sebastiano.

With the legalisation of Christianity in the 4th century, these images began to move into the public arena, appearing in mosaics across the city and in churches such as the Basilica di Santa Maria Maggiore.

Eastern influences became much more pronounced between the 7th and 9th centuries, when Byzantine styles swept in from the east, leading to a brighter, golden look. Typical of the style are the mosaics in the Basilica di Santa Maria in Trastevere.

The Renaissance

The Renaissance arrived in Rome in the latter half of the 15th century, and was to have a profound impact on the city, as the top artists of the day were summoned to decorate the many new buildings going up around town.

Rome's most celebrated works of Renaissance art are Michelangelo's paintings in the Sistine Chapel – his cinematic ceiling frescoes, painted between 1508 and 1512, and the *Giudizio Universale* (Last Judgment), which he worked on between 1536 and 1541.

Renaissance art, inspired by humanism, focused heavily on the human form. This, in turn, led artists to develop a far greater appreciation of perspective . But while early Renaissance painters made great strides in formulating rules of perspective, they still struggled to paint harmonious arrangements of figures. And it was this that Raffaello Sanzio (Raphael; 1483–1520) tackled in his great masterpiece *La Scuola di Atene* (The School of Athens; 1510–11) in the Vatican Museums.

San Luigi dei Francesi (p65)

PHOTOGOLFER/SHUTTERSTOCK ©

★ Art Churches

St Peter's Basilica (p46)

Chiesa di San Luigi dei Francesi (p65)

Basilica di Santa Maria del Popolo (p86)

Basilica di Santa Maria in Trastevere (p104)

Basilica di Santa Maria Maggiore (p102)

Counter-Reformation & the Baroque

The baroque burst onto Rome's art scene in the early 17th century. Combining a dramatic sense of dynamism with highly charged emotion, it was enthusiastically appropriated by the Catholic Church, which used it as a propaganda tool in its persecution of Counter-Reformation heretics. The powerful popes of the day eagerly championed the likes of Caravaggio, Gian Lorenzo Bernini, Domenichino, Pietro da Cortona and Alessandro Algardi.

Unsurprisingly, much baroque art has a religious theme and you'll often find depictions of martyrdoms, ecstasies and miracles.

One of the key painters of the period was Caravaggio (1573–1610), whose realistic interpretations of religious subjects often outraged his patrons. In contrast, the exquisite sculptural works of Gian Lorenzo Bernini (1598–1680) proved an instant hit.

Street Art

Increasingly you don't have to go to a gallery to see thought-provoking art in Rome. A recent trend for street painting has taken Rome by storm and many suburbs boast colourful wall displays. These range from a William Kentridge frieze on the Tiber embankment to a rainbow mural of faces by Bolognese artist Blu in Ostiense.

Literature

Rome has a rich literary tradition, encompassing everything from ancient satires to dialect poetry, anti-fascist prose and contemporary thrillers.

Classics

Famous for his blistering oratory, Marcus Tullius Cicero (106–43 BC) was the Roman Republic's pre-eminent author of philosophical works and speeches. His contemporary, Catullus (c 84–54 BC), cut a very different figure with his epigrams and erotic verse.

On becoming emperor in 27 BC, Augustus encouraged the arts, and Virgil (70–19 BC), Ovid, Horace and Tibullus all enjoyed freedom to write.

Rome as Inspiration

Rome has provided inspiration for legions of foreign authors.

In the 18th century the city was a hotbed of literary activity as historians and Grand Tourists poured into Rome from northern Europe. The German author Goethe captures the elation of discovering ancient Rome in his travelogue *Italian Journey* (1817). The city was also a magnet for English Romantic poets: John Keats, Lord Byron, Percy Bysshe Shelley, Mary Shelley and other writers all spent time here.

More recently, Rome has provided settings for many a literary blockbuster, including Dan Brown's thriller *Angels and Demons* (2001).

Writing Today

Rome-born Niccolò Ammaniti is one of Italy's best-selling authors. In 2007 he won the Premio Strega, Italy's top literary prize, for his novel, *Come Dio comanda* (As God Commands), although he's best known internationally for *Io non ho paura* (I'm Not Scared; 2001), the book on which the 2003 film of the same name is based.

Cinema

Rome has a long cinematic tradition, spanning the works of the postwar neorealists and film-makers as diverse as Federico Fellini, Sergio Leone, Nanni Moretti and Paolo Sorrentino, the Oscar-winning director of *La grande bellezza* (The Great Beauty).

The golden age of Roman cinema was the late 1940s, when Roberto Rossellini (1906–77) produced a trio of neorealist masterpieces, most notably *Roma città aperta* (Rome Open City; 1945). Also important was Vittorio de Sica's 1948 *Ladri di biciclette* (Bicycle Thieves).

Sergio Leone

Best known for almost single-handedly creating the spaghetti western, Roman-born Sergio Leone (1929–89) is a hero to many. The son of a silent-movie director, Leone cut his teeth as a screen-writer, before working as assistant director on *Quo Vadis?* (1951) and *Ben-Hur* (1959). He made his directorial debut three years later on *Il colosso di rodi* (The Colossus of Rhodes; 1961).

But it was with his famous dollar trilogy – *Per un pugno di dollari* (A Fistful of Dollars; 1964), *Per qualche dollari in piu* (For a Few Dollars More; 1965) and *Il buono, il brutto, il cattivo* (The Good, the Bad and the Ugly; 1966) – that he really hit the big time.

Stylistically, he introduced a series of innovations that were later to become trademarks. Chief among these was his use of musical themes to identify his characters. In this he was brilliantly supported by his old schoolmate, the composer Ennio Morricone.

Federico Fellini (1920–94) took the creative baton from the neorealists, producing his era-defining hit *La dolce vita* in 1960. The films of Pier Paolo Pasolini (1922–75) are similarly demanding, if very different, in their depiction of Rome's gritty postwar underbelly.

Idiosyncratic and whimsical, Nanni Moretti continues to make films that fall outside of mainstream tradition, including *Habemus papam*, his 2011 portrayal of a pope having a crisis of faith.

Rome itself has featured in a number of recent productions. Villa Borghese and the Terme di Caracalla were among the locations for Ben Stiller's *Zoolander 2*, while the Tiber riverside and Via della Conciliazione both appeared in the James Bond outing, *Spectre*. In the city's southern reaches, a remake of *Ben-Hur* was filmed at the Cinecittà studios, the very same place where the original was shot in 1959.

Music

Despite austerity-led cut-backs, Rome's music scene is bearing up well. International orchestras perform to sell-out audiences, jazz greats jam in steamy clubs, and rappers rage in underground venues.

Jazz has long been a mainstay of Rome's music scene, while recent decades have seen the emergence of a vibrant rap and hip-hop culture. Opera is served up at the Teatro dell'Opera and, in summer, at the spectacular Terme di Caracalla.

Aqua Appia Aqueduct

LUIS PADILLA FOTOGRAFIA/SHUTTERSTOCK ©

Architecture

*From ancient ruins and Renaissance basilicas
to baroque churches and hulking fascist* palazzi
*(mansions), Rome's architectural legacy is unparalleled.
Michelangelo, Bramante, Borromini and Bernini are
among the architects who have stamped their genius
on the city's urban landscape. More recently, a number
of contemporary starchitects have left an imprint,
including Renzo Piano and Zaha Hadid.*

The Ancients

Architecture was central to the success of the ancient Romans. In building their great capital, they were pioneers in using architecture to tackle problems of infrastructure, urban management and communication. For the first time, architects and engineers designed houses, roads, aqueducts and shopping centres alongside temples, tombs and imperial palaces. To do this, the Romans advanced methods devised by the Etruscans and Greeks, developing construction techniques and building materials that allowed them to build on a massive and hitherto unseen scale.

Etruscan Roots

By the 7th century BC, the Etruscans were the dominant force on the Italian peninsula, with important centres at Tarquinia, Caere (Cerveteri) and Veii (Veio). Little remains of their city-states – they built with wood and brick, which didn't age well – and much of what we now know about them derives from findings unearthed in their impressive cemeteries. These were constructed outside the city walls and harboured richly decorated stone tombs covered by mounds of earth.

Roman Developments

When Rome was founded sometime around the 8th century BC, the Etruscans were at the height of their power and Greek colonists were establishing control over southern Italy. In subsequent centuries a three-way battle for domination ensued. Against this background, Roman architects borrowed heavily from Greek and Etruscan traditions, gradually developing their own styles and techniques.

Ancient Roman architecture was monumental in form and often propagandistic in nature. Huge amphitheatres, aqueducts and temples joined muscular and awe-inspiring basilicas, arches and thermal baths in trumpeting the skill and vision of the city's early rulers and the nameless architects who worked for them.

Temples

Early Republican-era temples were based on Etruscan designs, but over time the Romans turned to the Greeks for their inspiration. Whereas Greek temples had steps and colonnades on all sides, the classic Roman temple had a high podium with steps leading up to a deep porch.

The Roman use of columns was also Greek in origin, even if the Romans favoured the more slender Ionic and Corinthian columns over the plain Doric pillars. To see how these differ, study the exterior of the Colosseum, which incorporates all three styles.

Aqueducts & Sewers

One of the Romans' crowning architectural achievements was the development of a water supply infrastructure.

To meet the city's water demand, the Romans constructed a complex system of aqueducts to bring water in from the hills of central Italy and distribute it around town. The first aqueduct to serve Rome was the 16.5km Aqua Appia, which became fully operational in 312 BC. Over the next 700 years or so, up to 800km of aqueducts were built in the city, a network capable of supplying up to one million cubic metres of water per day.

At the other end of the water cycle, waste water was drained away via an underground sewerage system known as the Cloaca Maxima (Great Sewer) and emptied downstream into the Tiber.

Residential Housing

While Rome's emperors and aristocrats lived in luxury on the Palatino (Palatine Hill), the city's poor huddled together in large residential blocks called *insulae*. These poorly built structures were sometimes up to six or seven storeys high, accommodating hundreds of people in dark, unhealthy conditions. Near the foot of the staircase leading up to the Chiesa di Santa Maria in Aracoeli, you can still see a section of what was once a typical city-centre *insula*.

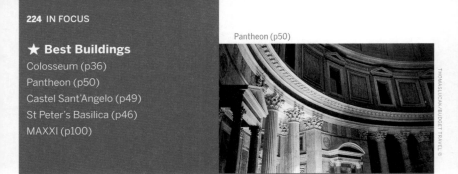

Pantheon (p50)

Concrete & Monumental Architecture

Most of the ruins that litter Rome are the remains of the city's big, show-stopping monuments. The Colosseum, Pantheon and the Forums are not only reminders of the sophistication and scale of ancient Rome – just as they were originally designed to be – but also monuments to the vision and bravura of the city's ancient architects.

One of the key breakthroughs the Romans made was the invention of concrete in the 1st century BC. Made by mixing volcanic ash with lime and an aggregate, often tufa rock or brick rubble, concrete was quick to make, easy to use and cheap. It allowed the Romans to develop vaulted roofing, which they used to span the Pantheon's ceiling and the huge vaults at the Terme di Caracalla.

Early Christian

The most startling reminders of early Christian activity are the catacombs, a series of underground burial grounds built under Rome's ancient roads. Christian belief in the resurrection meant that they could not cremate their dead, as was the custom in Roman times, and with burial forbidden inside the city walls they were forced to go outside the city.

The Christians began to abandon the catacombs in the 4th century and increasingly opted to be buried in the churches the emperor Constantine was building in the city. The most notable of the many churches he commissioned is the Basilica di San Giovanni in Laterano, the model on which many subsequent basilicas were based. Other period show-stoppers include the Basilica di Santa Maria in Trastevere and the Basilica di Santa Maria Maggiore.

A second wave of church-building hit Rome in the period between the 8th and 12th centuries. As the early papacy battled for survival against the threatening Lombards, its leaders took to construction to leave some sort of historical imprint, resulting in churches such as the Chiesa di Santa Maria in Cosmedin, home of the Bocca della Verità (Mouth of Truth).

The Renaissance

Many claim it was the election of Pope Nicholas V in 1447 that sparked the Renaissance in Rome. Nicholas believed that as head of the Christian world Rome had a duty to impress, a theory that was endorsed by his successors, and it was at the behest of the great papal dynasties – the Barberini, Farnese and Pamphilj – that the leading artists of the day were summoned to Rome.

Bramante & the High Renaissance

It was under Pope Julius II that the Roman Renaissance reached its peak, thanks largely to a classically minded architect from Milan, Donato Bramante.

Considered the high priest of Renaissance architecture, Bramante arrived in Rome in 1499 and developed a hugely influential, refined classical style. His 1502 Tempietto, for example, perfectly illustrates his innate understanding of proportion. In 1506 Julius commissioned him to start work on his greatest project – the rebuilding of St Peter's Basilica. The fall of Constantinople's Aya Sofya (Church of the Hagia Sofia) to Islam in the mid-14th century had pricked Nicholas V into ordering an earlier revamp, but the work had never been completed and it wasn't until Julius took over the project that progress was made. Bramante died in 1514, however, and he never got to see how his original Greek-cross design was developed.

St Peter's Basilica occupied most of the other notable architects of the High Renaissance, including Giuliano da Sangallo, Baldassarre Peruzzi and Antonio da Sangallo the Younger. Michelangelo eventually took over in 1547, modifying the layout and creating the basilica's crowning dome. Modelled on Brunelleschi's cupola for the Duomo in Florence, this is considered the artist's finest architectural achievement and one of the most important works of the Roman Renaissance.

Rococo Frills

In the early days of the 18th century, as baroque fashions began to fade and neoclassicism waited to make its 19th century entrance, the rococo burst into life. Drawing on the excesses of the baroque, it was a short-lived, theatrical fad, but one that left several iconic monuments.

The Spanish Steps, built between 1723 and 1726 by Francesco de Sanctis, provided a focal point for the many Grand Tourists who were busy discovering Rome's classical past. A short walk to the southwest, Piazza Sant'Ignazio was designed by Filippo Raguzzini to provide a suitably melodramatic setting for the Chiesa di Sant'Ignazio di Loyola, Rome's second most important Jesuit church. Most spectacular of all was the Trevi Fountain, one of the city's most exuberant and enduringly popular monuments. It was designed in 1732 by Nicola Salvi and completed three decades later.

The Baroque

As the principal motor of the Roman Renaissance, the Catholic Church became increasingly powerful in the 16th century. But with power came corruption and calls for reform. These culminated in the far-reaching Protestant Reformation, which prompted the Counter-Reformation, a vicious campaign to get people back into the Catholic fold. In the midst of this great offensive, baroque art and architecture emerged as a highly effective form of propaganda. Stylistically, baroque architecture aims for a dramatic sense of dynamism, an effect it often achieves by combining spatial complexity with clever lighting and a flamboyant use of painting and sculpture.

One of the first great Counter-Reformation churches was the Jesuit Chiesa del Gesù, designed by the leading architect of the day, Giacomo della Porta. In a move away from the style of earlier Renaissance churches, the facade has pronounced architectural elements that create a contrast between surfaces and a play of light and shade.

The late 16th-century papacy of Sixtus V marked the beginning of major urban-planning schemes. Domenico Fontana and other architects created a network of major thoroughfares to connect previously disparate parts of the sprawling medieval city. Fontana also

St Peter's Square (p49)

designed the main facade of Palazzo del Quirinale, the immense palace that served as the pope's summer residence for almost three centuries.

Bernini Versus Borromini

No two people did more to fashion the face of Rome than Gian Lorenzo Bernini and Francesco Borromini, the great figures of the Roman baroque. Naples-born Bernini, confident and suave, is best known for his work in the Vatican, where he designed St Peter's Square and was chief architect at St Peter's Basilica from 1629.

Under the patronage of the Barberini pope Urban VIII, Bernini was given free rein to transform the city, and his churches, *palazzi*, piazzas and fountains remain landmarks to this day. His fortunes nose-dived, however, when the pope died in 1644. Urban's successor, Innocent X, wanted as little contact as possible with the favourites of his hated predecessor, and instead turned to Borromini.

Borromini, a solitary, peculiar man from Lombardy, created buildings involving complex shapes and exotic geometry, including the Chiesa di Sant'Agnese in Agone on Piazza Navona.

Rationalism & Fascism

Rome entered the 20th century in good shape. During the late 19th century it had been treated to one of its periodic makeovers – this time after being made capital of the Kingdom of Italy in 1870. Piazzas such as Piazza Vittorio Emanuele II and Piazza della Repubblica were built, and roads were laid. To celebrate unification and pander to the ruling Savoy family, the ostentatious Vittoriano monument was built.

The 1920s saw the emergence of architectural rationalism. Its main Italian proponents, the Gruppo Sette, combined classicism with modernism, which tied in perfectly with Mussolini's vision of fascism as the modern bearer of ancient Rome's imperialist ambitions. Mussolini's most famous architectural legacy is Rome's southern EUR district, an Orwellian quarter of wide boulevards and huge linear buildings, built for the Esposizione Universale di Roma in 1942.

Modern Rome

The 21st century has witnessed a flurry of architectural activity in Rome as a clutch of starchitects have made their mark. Italian Renzo Piano worked on the acclaimed Auditorium Parco della Musica; American Richard Meier built a controversial new pavilion for the 1st-century-AD Ara Pacis; Anglo-Iraqi Zaha Hadid won plaudits for the Museo Nazionale delle Arti del XXI Secolo (MAXXI); and Roman-born Massimiliano Fuksas recently completed a striking conference centre in EUR, known as the Nuvola (Cloud).

The Roman Way of Life

As a visitor, it's often difficult to see beyond Rome's spectacular veneer to the large, modern city that lies beneath: a living, breathing capital that's home to almost three million people. So how do the Romans live in their city? Where do they work? Who do they live with? How do they let their hair down?

Work

Employment in the capital is largely based on Italy's bloated state bureaucracy. Every morning armies of suited civil servants pour into town and disappear into vast ministerial buildings to keep the machinery of government ticking over. Other important employers include the tourist sector, finance, media and culture.

But as Italy's economy continues to stagnate, it's tough for young people to get a foot on the career ladder. To land it lucky, it helps to know someone. Official figures are impossible to come by, but it's a widely held belief that personal or political connections are the best way of landing a job.

Like everywhere in Italy, Rome's workplace remains predominantly male. Female unemployment is an ongoing issue and Italian women continue to earn less than their male

Porta Portese Market (p159)

BALONCICI/SHUTTERSTOCK ©

counterparts. That said, recent signs have been positive. Half of Prime Minister Matteo Renzi's 2014 cabinet were women, and in June 2016 Rome elected its first-ever female mayor.

Home Life & Family

Romans, like most Italians, live in apartments, which are often small and expensive. House prices in central Rome are among the highest in the country and many first-time buyers are forced to move out of town or to distant suburbs. Rates of home ownership are relatively high in Rome and properties are commonly kept in the family, handed down from generation to generation. People do rent, but the rental market is largely targeted at Rome's huge student population.

It's still the rule rather than the exception for Romans to stay at home until they marry, which they typically do at around 30. But while faith in the family remains, the family unit is shrinking – Italian women are giving birth later than ever and having fewer children.

Play

Despite the high cost of living in Rome, few Romans would swap their city for anywhere else, and they enjoy it with gusto. You only have to look at the city's pizzerias and trattorias to see that eating out is a much-loved local pastime. Drinking, in contrast, is not a traditional Roman activity and an evening out in Rome is as much about flirting and looking gorgeous as it is about consuming alcohol.

Clothes shopping is a popular Roman pastime, alongside cinema-going and football; a trip to the Stadio Olimpico to watch the Sunday game is considered an afternoon well spent. Romans are inveterate car-lovers and on hot summer weekends they will often drive out to the coast or surrounding countryside.

Religion

Rome is packed with churches. And with the Vatican in the centre of town, the Church is a constant presence in Roman life. Yet the role of religion in modern Roman society is an ambiguous one. On the one hand, most people consider themselves Catholic, but on the other, church attendance is in freefall, particularly among the young.

Catholicism's hold on the Roman psyche is strong, but an increase in the city's immigrant population has led to a noticeable Muslim presence. This has largely been a pain-free process, but friction has flared on occasion and there were violent scenes in summer 2015 when far-right anti-immigration protestors clashed with police in the Casale San Nicola neighbourhood in north Rome.

Fontana di Piazza della Rotonda at the Pantheon (p112)

DAVID SOANES PHOTOGRAPHY/GETTY IMAGES ©

Survival Guide

Directory A–Z

Type L
220V/50Hz

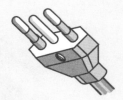

Customs Regulations

If arriving from a non-EU country, the limits are 1L spirits (or 2L fortified wine), 4L still wine, 60mL perfume, 16L beer, 200 cigarettes and other goods up to a value of €300/430 (travelling by land/sea); anything over this must be declared on arrival and the duty paid. On leaving the EU, non-EU residents can reclaim value-added tax (VAT) on expensive purchases.

Electricity

Type F
230V/50Hz

Emergency & Important Numbers

Ambulance	☎ 118
Fire	☎ 115
Police	☎ 112, 113

Gay & Lesbian Travellers

Homosexuality is legal (over the age of 16) and even widely accepted, but Rome is fairly conservative in its attitudes and discretion is still wise.

The city has a thriving, if low-key, gay scene. There are relatively few queer-only venues, but the Colosseum end of Via di San Giovanni in Laterano is a favourite hang out and many clubs host regular gay and lesbian nights.

Internet Access

○ Free wi-fi is widely available in hostels, B&Bs and hotels, though with signals of varying quality. Many bars and cafes also offer wi-fi.

○ There are many public wi-fi hotspots across town run by **Roma Wireless** (https://captivik.uni.it/romawireless) and **WiFimetropolitano** (www.cittametropolitana roma.gov.it/wifimetropo litano). To use these you'll need to register online using a credit card or an Italian mobile phone.

Legal Matters

The most likely reason for a brush with the law is to report a theft. If you have something stolen and you want to claim it on insurance, you must make a statement to the police. Insurance companies won't pay up without official proof of a crime.

Medical Services

Italy has a public health system that is legally bound to provide emergency care to everyone. EU nationals are entitled to reduced-cost, sometimes free, medical care with a European Health Insurance Card (EHIC), available from your home health authority; non-EU citizens should take out medical insurance.

For emergency treatment, you can go to the *pronto soccorso* (casualty) section of an *ospedale* (public hospital). For less serious ailments call the **Guardia Medica Turistica** (📞06 7730 6650; Via Emilio Morosini 30; 🕐24hr; 🚋Viale di Trastevere, 🚋Viale di Trastevere).

To arrange a (paid) home visit by a private doctor, call the **International Medical Centre** (📞06 488 23 71; www. imc84.com/roma; Via Firenze 47; GP call-out & treatment fee €140, 8pm-9am & weekends €200; 🕐24hr; Ⓜ Repubblica).

Pharmacies

Marked by a green cross, *farmacie* (pharmacies) open from 8.30am to 1pm and 4pm to 7.30pm Monday to Friday and on Saturday mornings. Outside these hours they open on a rotational basis, and all are legally required to post a list of places open in the vicinity.

Money

● Italy uses the euro. The seven euro notes come in denominations of €500, €200, €100, €50, €20, €10 and €5. Euro coins are in denominations of €2 and €1, and 50, 20, 10, five, two and one cents.

● You can change your money in banks, at post offices or at a *cambio* (exchange office). There are exchange booths at Stazione Termini and at Fiumicino and Ciampino airports.

ATMs

● ATMs (known in Italy as *bancomat*) are widely available in Rome and most will accept cards tied into the Visa, MasterCard, Cirrus and Maestro systems.

● The daily limit for cash withdrawal is €250.

Credit Cards

● Virtually all midrange and top-end hotels accept credit cards, as do most restaurants and large shops. Some cheaper *pensioni* (pensions), trattorias and pizzerias only accept cash. Don't rely on credit cards at museums or galleries.

● Major cards such as Visa, MasterCard, Eurocard,

Cirrus and Eurocheques are widely accepted. Amex is also recognised, although it's less common.

Opening Hours

Banks 8.30am–1.30pm and 2.45–4.30pm Monday to Friday

Bars and cafes 7.30am–8pm, sometimes until 1am or 2am

Shops 9am–7.30pm or 10am–8pm Monday to Saturday, some 11am–7pm Sunday; smaller shops 9am–1pm and 3.30–7.30pm (or 4-8pm) Monday to Saturday; some shops are closed Monday morning

Clubs 10pm–4am or 5am

Restaurants noon–3pm and 7.30–11pm (later in summer)

Public Holidays

Most Romans take their annual holiday in August. Many businesses and shops close for at least part of the month, particularly around 15 August.

Public holidays include the following:

Capodanno (New Year's Day) 1 January

Epifania (Epiphany) 6 January

Pasquetta (Easter Monday) March/April

Giorno della Liberazione (Liberation Day) 25 April

Festa del Lavoro (Labour Day) 1 May

Festa della Repubblica (Republic Day) 2 June

Festa dei Santi Pietro e Paolo (Feast of Sts Peter & Paul) 29 June

Ferragosto (Feast of the Assumption) 15 August

Festa di Ognisanti (All Saints' Day) 1 November

Festa dell'Immacolata Concezione (Feast of the Immaculate Conception) 8 December

Natale (Christmas Day) 25 December

Festa di Santo Stefano (Boxing Day) 26 December

Safe Travel

Rome is a safe city but petty theft can be a problem. Use common sense and watch your valuables.

○ Pickpockets are active in touristy areas such as the Colosseum, Piazza di Spagna and St Peter's Square.

○ Be extra alert around Stazione Termini and on crowded public transport – the 64 Vatican bus is notorious.

Telephone

○ Rome's area code is 06, which must be dialled even when calling locally.

○ Mobile-phone numbers begin with a three-digit prefix starting with a 3.

○ To call abroad from Italy dial 00, then the country and area codes, followed by the full number.

Mobile Phones

○ Italian mobile phones operate on the GSM 900/1800 network, which is compatible with the rest of Europe and Australia but not always with the North American GSM or CDMA systems – check with your service provider.

○ The cheapest way of using your mobile is to buy a prepaid (*prepagato*) SIM card. TIM (www.tim.it), Wind (www.wind.it), Vodafone (www.vodafone.it) and Tre (www.tre.it) all offer SIM cards and have retail outlets across town.

○ Under Italian law all SIM cards must be registered, so take your passport or ID card when you buy one.

Time

Italy is in a single time zone, one hour ahead of GMT. Daylight-saving time,

when clocks move forward one hour, starts on the last Sunday in March. Clocks are put back an hour on the last Sunday in October.

Italy operates on a 24-hour clock, so 6pm is written as 18:00.

Toilets

Public toilets are not widespread but you'll find them at St Peter's Square and Stazione Termini (€1). If you're caught short, the best thing to do is to nip into a cafe or bar.

Tourist Information

There are tourist information points at **Fiumicino** (International Arrivals, Terminal 3; ☺8am-8.45pm) and **Ciampino** (Arrivals Hall; ☺8.30am-6pm) airports, and locations across the city:

Piazza delle Cinque Lune (☺9.30am-7pm; ▣Corso del Rinascimento) Near Piazza Navona.

Stazione Termini (☏06 06 08; www.turismoroma.it; Via Giovanni Giolitti 34; ☺8am-6.45pm; Ⓜ Termini) In the hall adjacent to platform 24.

Imperial Forums (Via dei Fori Imperiali; ☺9.30am-7pm; ▣Via dei Fori Imperiali)

Via Marco Minghetti (☏06 06 08; www.turismoroma.it; ☺9.30am-7pm; ▣Via del Corso)

Between Via del Corso and the Trevi Fountain.

Via Nazionale (☏06 06 08; www.turismoroma.it; Via Nazionale 184; ◷9.30am-7pm; ▣Via Nazionale) In front of the Palazzo delle Esposizioni.

Castel Sant'Angelo (Piazza Pia; ◷9.30am-7pm summer, 8.30am-6pm winter; ▣Piazza Pia)

For information about the Vatican, contact the **Ufficio Pellegrini e Turisti** (☏06 6988 1662; St Peter's Square; ◷8.30am-6.30pm Mon-Sat; ▣Piazza del Risorgimento, ▣Ottaviano-San Pietro).

The **Comune di Roma** (☏06 06 08; www.060608.it; ◷9am-7pm) runs a free multilingual tourist information telephone line providing info on culture, shows, hotels, transport etc. Its website is also an excellent source of information.

Turismo Roma (www.turismo roma.it), Rome's official tourist website, is another good online resource.

Travellers with Disabilities

◦ Cobbled streets, paving stones, blocked pavements and tiny lifts are difficult for anyone using a wheelchair, while the relentless traffic can be disorienting for partially sighted travellers or those with hearing difficulties.

◦ All stations on metro line B have wheelchair access and lifts except for Circo Massimo, Colosseo and Cavour. On line A, Cipro and Termini are equipped with lifts.

◦ Bus 590 covers the same route as metro line A and is one of 19 bus and tram services with wheelchair access. Routes with disabled access are indicated on bus stops.

◦ Contact ADR Assistance (www.adrassistance.it) for help at Fiumicino or Ciampino airports.

◦ Some taxis are equipped to carry passengers in wheelchairs; ask for a taxi for a *sedia a rotelle* (wheelchair).

◦ Download Lonely Planet's free *Accessible Travel* guide from http://lptravel.to/AccessibleTravel.

Visas

◦ Italy is one of the 26 European countries to make up the Schengen area. There are no customs controls when travelling between Schengen countries, so the visa rules that apply to Italy apply to all Schengen countries.

◦ EU citizens do not need a visa to enter Italy.

◦ Nationals of some other countries, including Australia, Canada, Israel, Japan, New Zealand, Switzerland and the USA, do not need a visa for stays of up to 90 days.

Women Travellers

Sexual harrassment can be an issue in Rome. If you feel

Practicalities

Newspapers Key national dailies include centre-left *la Repubblica* (www.repubblica.it) and its right-wing rival *Corriere della Sera* (www.corriere.it). For the Vatican's take on affairs, *L'Osservatore Romano* (www.osservat oreromano.va) is the Holy See's official paper.

Television The main terrestrial channels are RAI 1, 2 and 3 run by Rai (www.rai.it), Italy's state-owned national broadcaster, and Canale 5, Italia 1 and Rete 4 run by Mediaset (www.mediaset.it), the commercial TV company founded and still partly owned by Silvio Berlusconi.

Smoking Banned in enclosed public spaces, which includes restaurants, bars, shops, and public transport. It's also banned in Villa Borghese and other public parks over the summer, from June to September.

Weights and Measures Italy uses the metric system.

yourself being groped on a crowded bus or metro, a loud *'che schifo!'* (how disgusting!) will draw attention to the incident. Otherwise, take all the usual precautions you would in any large city and, as in most places, avoid wandering around alone late at night, especially in the area around Termini station.

Transport

Arriving in Rome

Most people arrive in Rome by plane, landing at one of its two airports: Leonardo da Vinci, better known as Fiumicino; or Ciampino, hub for European low-cost carrier Ryanair. Flights from New York take around nine hours, from London 2¾ hours, from Sydney at least 22 hours.

As an alternative to short-haul flights, trains serve Rome's main station, Stazione Termini, from a number of European destinations, including Paris (about 15 hours), as well as cities across Italy.

Ferries serve Civitavecchia, some 80km north of the city, from a number of Mediterranean ports.

Flights, cars and tours can be booked online at lonelyplanet.com/bookings.

Leonardo da Vinci Airport

Rome's main international airport, **Leonardo da Vinci** (Fiumicino; ✈06 6 59 51; www.adr.it/fiumicino), aka Fiumicino, is 30km west of the city.

The easiest way to get into town is by train, but there are also buses and private shuttle services.

Train

Leonardo Express (www.trenitalia.com; one way €14) Runs to/from Stazione Termini. Departures from the airport every 30 minutes between 6.23am and 11.23pm, and from Termini between 5.35am and 10.35pm. Journey time is 30 minutes.

FL1 (www.trenitalia.com; one way €8) Connects to Trastevere, Ostiense and Tiburtina stations, but not Termini. Departures from the airport every 15 minutes (half-hourly on Sundays and public holidays) between 5.57am and 10.42pm, from Tiburtina every 15 minutes between 5.01am and 7.31pm, then half-hourly to 10.01pm.

Bus

SIT Bus (✆06 591 68 26; www.sitbusshuttle.com; one way/return €6/11) Regular departures to Stazione Termini (Via Marsala) from 7.15am to 12.40am; from Termini between 4.45am and 8.30pm. All buses stop near the Vatican (Via Crescenzio 2) en route. Tickets are available on the bus. Journey time is approximately one hour.

Cotral (✆800 174471; www.cotralspa.it; one way €5, purchased on bus €7) Runs between Fiumicino and Stazione Tiburtina via Termini. Three to six daily departures including night services from the airport at 1.45am, 3.45am and 5.45am, and from Tiburtina at 12.30am, 2.30am and 4.30am. Journey time is one hour.

Schiaffini Rome Airport Bus (✆06 713 05 31; www.romeairportbus.com; Via Giolitti; one

---

Climate Change & Travel

Every form of transport that relies on carbon-based fuel generates CO_2, the main cause of human-induced climate change. Modern travel is dependent on aeroplanes, which might use less fuel per kilometre per person than most cars but travel much greater distances. The altitude at which aircraft emit gases (including CO_2) and particles also contributes to their climate change impact. Many websites offer 'carbon calculators' that allow people to estimate the carbon emissions generated by their journey and, for those who wish to do so, to offset the impact of the greenhouse gases emitted with contributions to portfolios of climate-friendly initiatives throughout the world. Lonely Planet offsets the carbon footprint of all staff and author travel.

way/return €5.90/8.90) Regular services from the airport to Stazione Termini between 6.05am and 8.30pm; from Termini between 5.10am and 9.30pm. Allow about an hour for the journey.

Private Shuttle

Airport Connection Services (☏ 338 9876465, 06 2111 6248; www.airportconnection. it) Transfers to/from the city centre start at €22 per person.

Airport Shuttle (☏ 06 4201 3469; www.airportshuttle. it) Transfers to/from your hotel for €25 for one person, then €6 for each additional passenger up to a maximum of eight.

Taxi

The set fare to/from the city centre is €48, which is valid for up to four passengers including luggage. Journey time is approximately 45 to 60 minutes depending on traffic.

Ciampino Airport

Ciampino (☏ 06 6 59 51; www.adr.it/ciampino), 15km southeast of the city centre, is used by Ryanair for European and Italian destinations. It's not a big airport but there's a steady flow of traffic and at peak times it can get extremely busy.

To get into town, the best option is to take one of the dedicated bus services. You can also take a bus to Ciampino station and then pick up a train to Termini.

Public Transport Tickets

Public-transport tickets are valid on all of Rome's bus, tram and metro lines, except for routes to Fiumicino airport. They come in various forms:

BIT (*biglietto integrato a tempo,* a single ticket valid for 100 minutes; in that time it can be used on all forms of transport, but only once on the metro) €1.50

Roma 24h (valid for 24 hours) €7

Roma 48h (valid for 48 hours) €12.50

Roma 72h (valid for 72 hours) €18

CIS (*carta integrata settimanale,* a weekly ticket) €24

Children under 10 years travel free.

Buy tickets at *tabacchi* (tobacconist's shops), newsstands and from vending machines at main bus stops and metro stations. They must be purchased before you start your journey and validated in the machines on buses, at the entrance gates to the metro, or at train stations. Ticketless riders risk a fine of at least €50.

Bus

Schiaffini Rome Airport Bus (☏ 06 713 05 31; www.romeairportbus.com; Via Giolitti; one way/return €4.90/8.90) Regular departures to/from Via Giolitti outside Stazione Termini. From the airport, services are between 4am and 10.50pm; from Via Giolitti, buses run from 4.50am to midnight. Buy tickets on board, online, at the airport, or at the bus stop. Journey time is approximately 40 minutes.

SIT Bus (☏ 06 591 68 26; www.sitbusshuttle.com; to/from airport €6/5, return €9) Regular departures from the airport to Via Marsala outside Stazione Termini between 7.45am and 11.59pm, and from Termini between 4.30am and 9.30pm. Get tickets on the bus. Journey time is 45 minutes.

Atral (www.atral-lazio.com) Runs buses between Ciampino Airport and Anagnina metro

station (€1.20) and Ciampino train station (€1.20), where you can get a train to Termini (€1.50).

Taxi

The set rate to/from the airport is €30. Journey time is approximately 30 minutes depending on traffic.

Termini Train Station

Rome's main station and principal transport hub is **Stazione Termini** (www.romatermini.com; Piazza dei Cinquecento; Ⓜ Termini). It has regular connections to other European countries, all major Italian cities and many smaller towns.

From Termini, you can connect with the metro or take a bus from Piazza dei Cinquecento out front. Taxis are outside the main entrance/exit.

Civitavecchia Port

The nearest port to Rome is at Civitavecchia, about 80km north of town. Ferries sail here from Barcelona and Tunis, as well as Sicily and Sardinia. Check www.traghettiweb. it for route details, prices, and to book.

Bookings can also be made at the Termini-based **Agenzie 365** (📞06 4782 5179; www.agenzie365.it; Stazione Termini, Via Giolitti 34; ⊘8am-9pm; Ⓜ Termini), at travel agents or directly at the port.

From Civitavecchia there are half-hourly trains to Stazione Termini (€5 to €16, 45 minutes to 1½ hours). Civitavecchia's station is about 700m from the entrance to the port.

Getting Around

Rome is a sprawling city, but the historic centre is relatively compact. Distances are not great and walking is often the best way of getting around.

Public transport includes buses, trams, metro and a suburban train network. The main hub is Stazione Termini.

Metro

○ Rome has two main metro lines, A (orange) and B (blue), which cross at Termini. A branch line, 'B1', serves the northern

suburbs, and line C runs through the southeastern outskirts, but you're unlikely to need those.

○ Trains run between 5.30am and 11.30pm (to 1.30am on Fridays and Saturdays).

○ Take line A for the Trevi Fountain (Barberini), Spanish Steps (Spagna) and St Peter's (Ottaviano–San Pietro).

○ Take line B for the Colosseum (Colosseo).

Bus

○ The **main bus station** (Piazza dei Cinquecento) is in front of Stazione Termini on Piazza dei Cinquecento, where there's an **information booth** (Piazza dei Cinquecento; ⊘8am-8pm; Ⓜ Termini).

○ Other important hubs are at Largo di Torre Argentina and Piazza Venezia.

○ Buses generally run from about 5.30am until midnight, with limited services throughout the night.

○ Rome's night bus service comprises more than 25 lines, many of which pass Termini and/or Piazza Venezia. Buses are marked with an 'n' before the number, and bus stops have a blue owl symbol. Departures are usually every 15 to 30 minutes, but can be much slower.
The most useful routes:

○ **n1** Follows the route of metro line A.

○ **n2** Follows the route of metro line B.

○ **n7** Piazzale Clodio, Piazza Cavour, Via Zanardelli, Corso del Rinascimento, Corso Vittorio Emanuele II, Largo di Torre Argentina, Piazza Venezia, Via Nazionale and Stazione Termini.

Car & Motorcycle

○ Driving around Rome is not recommended. Riding a scooter or motorbike is faster and makes parking easier, but Rome is no place for learners, so if you're not an experienced rider, give it a miss. Hiring a car for a day trip out of town is worth considering.

○ Most of Rome's historic centre is closed to unauthorised traffic from 6.30am to 6pm Monday to Friday, from 2pm to 6pm (10am to 7pm in some places) Saturday, and from 11pm to 3am Friday and Saturday. Evening restrictions also apply in Trastevere, San Lorenzo, Monti and Testaccio, typically from 9.30pm or 11pm to 3am on Fridays and Saturdays (also Wednesdays and Thursdays in summer).

○ All streets accessing the Limited Traffic Zone (ZTL) are monitored by electronic-access detection devices. If you're staying in this zone, contact your hotel. For further information, check www.agenziamobilita.roma.it.

Driving Licence & Road Rules

● All EU driving licences are recognised in Italy. Holders of non-EU licences should get an International Driving Permit (IDP) to accompany their national licence. Apply to your national motoring association.

● A licence is required to ride a scooter – a car licence will do for bikes up to 125cc; for anything over 125cc you'll need a motorcycle licence.

● A good source of information is the **Automobile Club d'Italia** (ACI; 🚗roadside assistance from Italian phone 803 116, roadside assistance from foreign mobile 800 116800; www.aci.it), Italy's national motoring organisation.

Hire

To hire a car you'll require a driving licence (plus IDP if necessary) and credit card. Age restrictions vary but generally you'll need to be 21 or over.

Car hire is available at both Rome's airports and Stazione Termini. Reckon on at least €40 per day for a small car. Note also that most Italian hire cars have manual gear transmission.
Avis (🚗06 45210 8391; www. avisautonoleggio.it)

Europcar (🚗199 307030; www. europcar.it)

Hertz (🚗Stazione Termini office 06 488 39 67; www.hertz.it)

Maggiore National (🚗Termini office 06 488 00 49, central reservations 199 151120; www. maggiore.it; Stazione Termini, Via Giolitti 34; ⊙7am-9pm; Ⓜ Termini)

To hire a scooter, prices range from about €30 to €120 depending on the size of the vehicle. Reliable operators:
Eco Move Rent (🚗06 4470 4518; www.ecomoverent. com; Via Varese 48-50; bike/ scooter/Vespa hire per day from €11/40/45; ⊙8.30am-7.30pm; Ⓜ Termini)

Treno e Scooter (🚗06 4890 5823; www.trenoescooter.com; Piazza dei Cinquecento; per day from €28; ⊙9am-2pm & 4-7pm)

On Road (🚗06 481 56 69; www. scooterhire.it; Via Cavour 80a; scooter rental per day from €27; ⊙9am-7pm; Ⓜ Termini)

Parking

● Blue lines denote pay-and-display parking – get tickets from meters (coins only) and *tabacchi*.

● Expect to pay up to €1.20 per hour between 8am and 8pm (11pm in some places). After 8pm (or 11pm) parking is free until 8am the next morning.

● Traffic wardens are vigilant and fines are not uncommon. If your car gets towed away, call the **traffic police** (🚗06 6 76 91).

● Useful car parks:
Piazzale dei Partigiani (per hour €0.77; ⊙6am-11pm; Ⓜ Piramide)

Stazione Termini (Piazza dei Cinquecento; per hour/day €2.20/18; ⊙6am-1am; 🚌Piazza dei Cinquecento)

Villa Borghese (🚗06 322 59 34; www.sabait.it; Viale del Galoppatoio 33; per hour/ day €2.30/22; ⊙24hr; 🚌Via Pinciana)

Train

Apart from connections to Fiumicino airport, you'll probably only need the overground rail network if you head out of town.

● Train information is available from the Customer Service area on the main concourse in Stazione Termini. Alternatively, check www.trenitalia.com or phone 89 20 21.

● Buy tickets on the main station concourse, from automated ticket machines, or from an authorised travel agency – look for an FS or *biglietti treni* sign in the window.

● Rome's second train station is **Stazione Tiburtina**, four stops from Termini on metro line B. Of the capital's eight other train stations, the most important are **Stazione Roma-Ostiense** and **Stazione Trastevere**.

Language

Italian pronunciation isn't difficult as most sounds are also found in English. The pronunciation of some consonants depends on which vowel follows, but if you read our pronunciation guides below as if they were English, you'll be understood just fine. Just remember to pronounce double consonants as a longer, more forceful sound than single ones. The stressed syllables in words are in italics in our pronunciation guides.

To enhance your trip with a phrasebook, visit **lonelyplanet.com**. Find Lonely Planet iPhone phrasebooks in the Apple App store.

Basics

Hello.
Buongiorno./Ciao. (pol/inf)   bwon·*jor*·no/chow
How are you?
Come sta?   *ko*·me sta
I'm fine, thanks.
Bene, grazie.   be·ne *gra*·tsye
Excuse me.
Mi scusi.   mee skoo·zee
Yes./No.
Sì./No.   see/no
Please. (when asking)
Per favore.   per fa·*vo*·re
Thank you.
Grazie.   *gra*·tsye
Goodbye.
Arrivederci./Ciao. (pol/inf)   a·ree·ve·*der*·chee/chow
Do you speak English?
Parla inglese?   *par*·la een·*gle*·ze
I don't understand.
Non capisco.   non ka·*pee*·sko
How much is this?
Quanto costa?   kwan·to *ko*·sta

Accommodation

I'd like to book a room.
Vorrei prenotare   vo·*ray* pre·no·*ta*·re
una camera.   *oo*·na *ka*·me·ra
How much is it per night?
Quanto costa per   kwan·to kos·ta per
una notte?   *oo*·na *no*·te

Eating & Drinking

I'd like ..., please.
Vorrei ..., per favore.   vo·*ray* ... per fa·*vo*·re
What would you recommend?
Cosa mi consiglia?   *ko*·za mee kon·*see*·lya
That was delicious!
Era squisito!   *e*·ra skwee·*zee*·to
Bring the bill/check, please.
Mi porta il conto,   mee *por*·ta eel *kon*·to
per favore.   per fa·*vo*·re

I'm allergic (to peanuts).
Sono allergico/a   *so*·no a·*ler*·jee·ko/a
(alle arachidi). (m/f)   (a·le a·*ra*·kee·dee)
I don't eat ...
Non mangio ...   non *man*·jo ...
    fish   pesce   *pe*·she
    meat   carne   *kar*·ne
    poultry   pollame   po·*la*·me

Emergencies

I'm ill.
Mi sento male.   mee *sen*·to *ma*·le
Help!
Aiuto!   a·*yoo*·to
Call a doctor!
Chiami un medico!   *kya*·mee oon *me*·dee·ko
Call the police!
Chiami la polizia!   *kya*·mee la po·lee·*tsee*·a

Directions

I'm looking for (a/the) ...
Cerco ...   *cher*·ko ...
    bank
    la banca   la *ban*·ka
    ... embassy
    la ambasciata de ...   la am·ba·*sha*·ta de ...
    market
    il mercato   eel mer·*ka*·to
    museum
    il museo   eel moo·*ze*·o
    restaurant
    un ristorante   oon rees·to·*ran*·te
    toilet
    un gabinetto   oon ga·bee·*ne*·to
    tourist office
    l'ufficio del turismo   loo·*fee*·cho del too·*reez*·mo

Behind the Scenes

Acknowledgements

Climate map data adapted from Peel MC, Finlayson BL & McMahon TA (2007) 'Updated World Map of the Köppen-Geiger Climate Classification', Hydrology and Earth System Sciences, 11, 163344.

Illustration pp82–83 Javier Zarracina.

This Book

This 3rd edition of Lonely Planet's *Best of Rome* guidebook was researched and written by Duncan Garwood and Nicola Williams and curated by Duncan. The previous two editions were written by Duncan Garwood. This guidebook was produced by the following:

Destination Editor Anna Tyler

Senior Product Editor Elizabeth Jones

Product Editor Genna Patterson

Senior Cartographers Anthony Phelan, Mark Griffiths

Book Designer Gwen Cotter

Assisting Editors Michelle Bennett, Alexander Knights

Assisting Cartographer James Leversha

Cover Researcher Brendan Dempsey-Spencer

Thanks to Ronan Abayawickrema, Alexandra Bruzzese, Sandie Kestell, Kate Kiely, Jessica Ryan, Gabrielle Stefanos, Margaret Thomson, Angela Tinson, Sam Wheeler, Tony Wheeler

Send Us Your Feedback

We love to hear from travellers – your comments keep us on our toes and help make our books better. Our well-travelled team reads every word on what you loved or loathed about this book. Although we cannot reply individually to postal submissions, we always guarantee that your feedback goes straight to the appropriate authors, in time for the next edition. Each person who sends us information is thanked in the next edition, the most useful submissions are rewarded with a selection of digital PDF chapters.

Visit lonelyplanet.com/contact to submit your updates and suggestions or to ask for help. Our award-winning website also features inspirational travel stories, news and discussions.

Note: We may edit, reproduce and incorporate your comments in Lonely Planet products such as guidebooks, websites and digital products, so let us know if you don't want your comments reproduced or your name acknowledged. For a copy of our privacy policy visit lonelyplanet.com/privacy.

Index

A

B

C

D

Villa Borghese park (p56)

Rome Maps

Ancient Rome

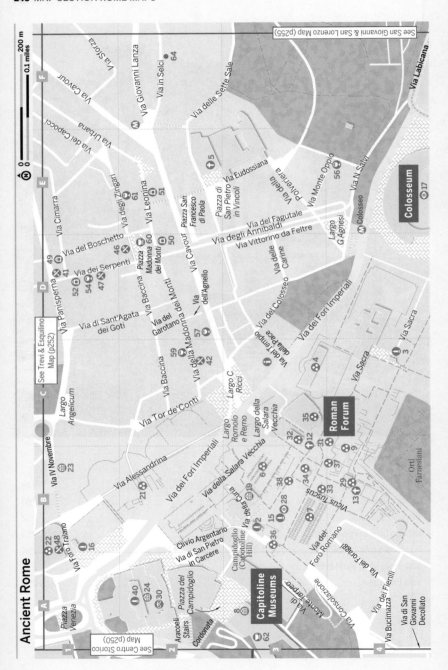

See Centro Storico Map (p250)

See Trevi & Esquilino Map (p252)

See San Giovanni & San Lorenzo Map (p255)

Colosseum

Roman Forum

Capitoline Museums

Orti Farnesiani

0   200 m
0   0.1 miles

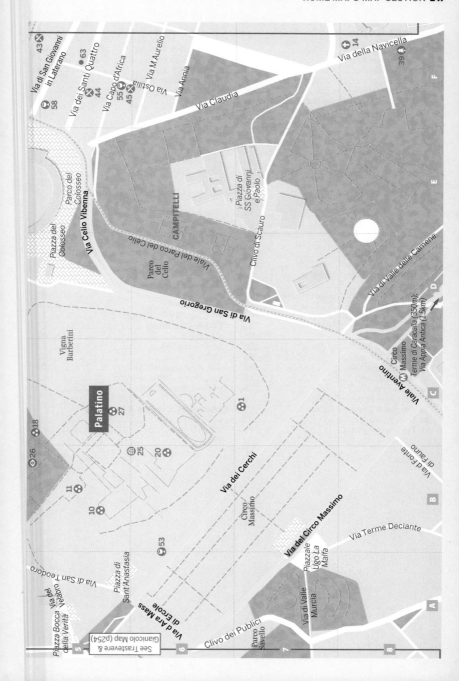

43 ✖
Via di San Giovanni
in Laterano

63 ●
Via dei Santi Quattro
44 ✖

Via Capo d'Africa
55 ➊
45 ✖

Via M Aurelio

Via Ostilia

Via Annia

14 ➕
Via della Navicella

39 ✖

58 ⊗

Via Claudia

Piazza del
Colosseo

Parco del
Colosseo

Piazza del
Colosseo

Via Celio Vibenna

CAMPITELLI

Piazza di
SS Giovanni
e Paolo

Viale del Parco del Celio

Clivo di Scauro

Parco
del
Celio

Via di Valle delle Camene

Via di San Gregorio

Vigna
Barberini

Palatino
27 ✖

1 ✖

Circo
M Massimo
Terme di Caracalla (350m);
Via Appia Antica (1.5km)

Viale Aventino

26 ⊗

18 ➕

25 🏛

20 ✖

11

10 ✖

Via dei Cerchi

Circo
Massimo

Via d Fonte
di Fauno

53 ⊗

Via del Circo Massimo

Piazzale
Ugo La
Malfa

Via Terme Deciante

Via di San Teodoro

Piazza di
Sant'Anastasia

**Via d Ara Mass
di Ercole**

Via del
Velabro

Via di Valle
Murcia

Clivo dei Publici

Parco
Savello

Piazza Bocca
della Verità

See Trastevere &
Gianicolo Map (p254)

Ancient Rome

Centro Storico

Centro Storico

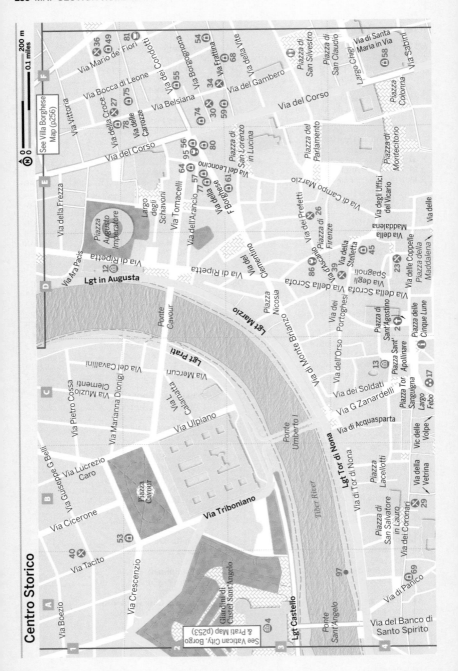

200 m
0.1 miles

See Villa Borghese Map (p256)

See Vatican City, Borgo & Prati Map (p253)

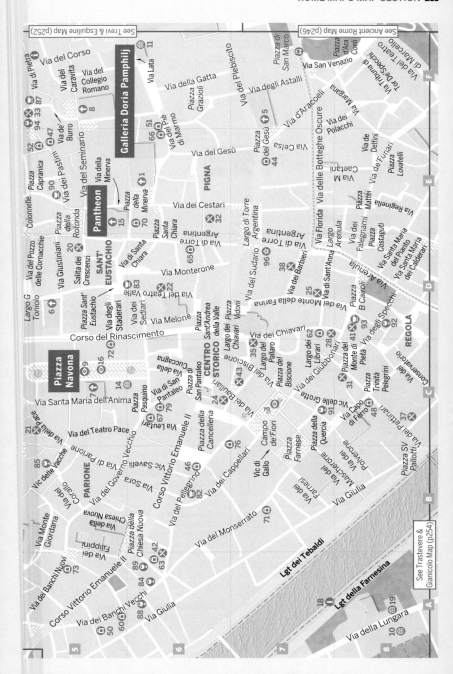

See Trevi & Esquiline Map (p252)

See Ancient Rome Map (p246)

Via del Corso

Via di Pietra

Via del Caravita

Via del Collegio Romano

Via Lata

11

Piazza di San Marco

Via San Venazio

Via del Teatro di Marcello

Piazza d'Ara Coeli

Via della Gatta

Via degli Astalli

Via del Plebiscito

Via del Pié di Marmo

Via del Gesù

Via d'Aracoeli

Via dei Polacchi

Via de Delfini

Via de' Funari

Via del Seminario

Via della Minerva

Galleria Doria Pamphilj

Pantheon

PIGNA

Piazza della Rotonda

Piazza della Minerva

Via dei Cestari

Via di Torre Argentina

Largo di Torre Argentina

Via di Torre Argentina

Via Florida

Via delle Botteghe Oscure

Piazza del Gesù

Piazza Mattei

Via Reginella

SANT'EUSTACHIO

Via di Santa Chiara

Piazza Santa Chiara

Via Monterone

Via del Teatro Valle

Via dei Sediari

Corso del Rinascimento

Piazza Navona

Via di Santa Maria dell'Anima

Piazza Pasquino

Via del Teatro Pace

Via della Pace

PARIONE

Via di Parione

Vic delle Vacche

Via del Corallo

Via Monte Giordana

Via della Chiesa Nuova

Via dei Filippini

Piazza della Chiesa Nuova

Corso Vittorio Emanuele II

Via dei Banchi Vecchi

Via Giulia

Lgt dei Tebaldi

Lgt della Farnesina

See Trastevere & Gianicolo Map (p254)

Lgt della Lungara

Via della Lungara

Trevi & Esquilino

N
0 — 500 m
0 — 0.25 miles

See Villa Borghese Map (p256)

See Centro Storico Map (p250)

See Ancient Rome Map (p246)

See San Giovanni & San Lorenzo Map (p255)

Vatican City, Borgo & Prati

◎ Sights
1 Museo Storico Artistico	B3
2 St Peter's Basilica	B3
3 St Peter's Basilica Dome	B3
4 St Peter's Square	C3
5 Tomb of St Peter	B3
6 Vatican Grottoes	B3
7 Vatican Museums	B2

✈ Activities, Courses & Tours
8 Art Studio Lab	C3

◎ Shopping
9 Antica Manifattura Cappelli	C1
10 Il Sellaio	C1
11 Rechicle	C1

✖ Eating
12 Cotto Crudo	C2
13 Del Frate	C1
14 Fa-Bìo	C1
15 Fatamorgana	B1
16 Il Sorpasso	D2
17 Pizzarium	A2
18 Velavevodetto Ai Quiriti	D1

🍷 Drinking & Nightlife
19 Be.re	C2
20 Makasar Bistrot	C2
21 Passaguai	C2
22 Sciascia Caffè	D1

✪ Entertainment
23 Alexanderplatz	B1
24 Auditorium Conciliazione	D3
25 Fonclea	C2

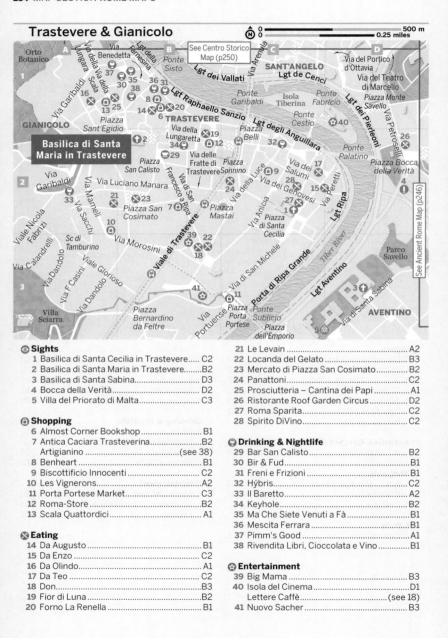

Trastevere & Gianicolo

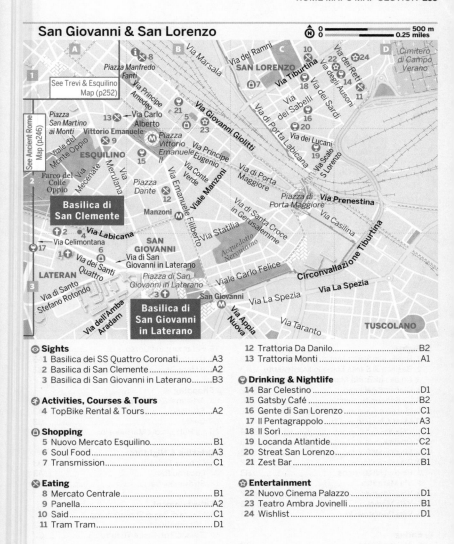

San Giovanni & San Lorenzo

⊙ Sights
1	Basilica dei SS Quattro Coronati	A3
2	Basilica di San Clemente	A2
3	Basilica di San Giovanni in Laterano	B3

⊕ Activities, Courses & Tours
| 4 | TopBike Rental & Tours | A2 |

🛍 Shopping
5	Nuovo Mercato Esquilino	B1
6	Soul Food	A3
7	Transmission	C1

⊗ Eating
8	Mercato Centrale	B1
9	Panella	A2
10	Said	C1
11	Tram Tram	D1
12	Trattoria Da Danilo	B2
13	Trattoria Monti	A1

⊙ Drinking & Nightlife
14	Bar Celestino	D1
15	Gatsby Café	B2
16	Gente di San Lorenzo	C1
17	Il Pentagrappolo	A3
18	Il Sorì	C1
19	Locanda Atlantide	C2
20	Streat San Lorenzo	C1
21	Zest Bar	B1

⊙ Entertainment
22	Nuovo Cinema Palazzo	D1
23	Teatro Ambra Jovinelli	B1
24	Wishlist	D1

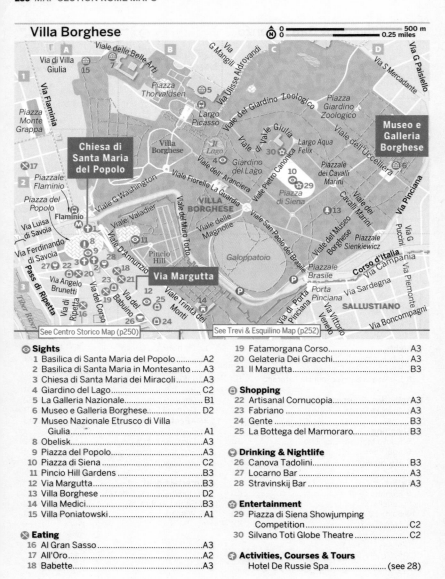

Villa Borghese

⊙ Sights
1 Basilica di Santa Maria del Popolo	A2
2 Basilica di Santa Maria in Montesanto	A3
3 Chiesa di Santa Maria dei Miracoli	A3
4 Giardino del Lago	C2
5 La Galleria Nazionale	B1
6 Museo e Galleria Borghese	D2
7 Museo Nazionale Etrusco di Villa Giulia	A1
8 Obelisk	A3
9 Piazza del Popolo	A3
10 Piazza di Siena	C2
11 Pincio Hill Gardens	B3
12 Via Margutta	B3
13 Villa Borghese	D2
14 Villa Medici	B3
15 Villa Poniatowski	A1

⊗ Eating
16 Al Gran Sasso	A3
17 All'Oro	A2
18 Babette	A3

19 Fatamorgana Corso	A3
20 Gelateria Dei Gracchi	A3
21 Il Margutta	B3

⊙ Shopping
22 Artisanal Cornucopia	A3
23 Fabriano	A3
24 Gente	B3
25 La Bottega del Marmoraro	B3

⊙ Drinking & Nightlife
26 Canova Tadolini	B3
27 Locarno Bar	A3
28 Stravinskij Bar	A3

⊙ Entertainment
29 Piazza di Siena Showjumping Competition	C2
30 Silvano Toti Globe Theatre	C2

⊙ Activities, Courses & Tours
Hotel De Russie Spa	(see 28)

Symbols & Map Key

Look for these symbols to quickly identify listings:

- ◉ Sights
- ✪ Activities
- ✪ Courses
- ✪ Tours
- ✪ Festivals & Events
- ✪ Eating
- ✪ Drinking
- ✪ Entertainment
- ✪ Shopping
- ✪ Information & Transport

These symbols and abbreviations give vital information for each listing:

- 🌿 Sustainable or green recommendation
- **FREE** No payment required

☎ Telephone number	🚌 Bus
⏱ Opening hours	⛴ Ferry
Ⓟ Parking	🚊 Tram
⊝ Nonsmoking	🚆 Train
❋ Air-conditioning	🍴 English-language menu
@ Internet access	🍴 Vegetarian selection
📶 Wi-fi access	👪 Family-friendly
🏊 Swimming pool	

Find your best experiences with these Great For... icons.

 Art & Culture

 Beaches

 Budget

 Cafe/Coffee

 Cycling

 Detour

 Drinking

 Entertainment

 Events

 Family Travel

 Food & Drink

 History

 Local Life

 Nature & Wildlife

 Photo Op

 Scenery

 Shopping

 Short Trip

Sport

Walking

Winter Travel

Sights

- Beach
- Bird Sanctuary
- Buddhist
- Castle/Palace
- Christian
- Confucian
- Hindu
- Islamic
- Jain
- Jewish
- Monument
- Museum/Gallery/ Historic Building
- Ruin
- Shinto
- Sikh
- Taoist
- Winery/Vineyard
- Zoo/Wildlife Sanctuary
- Other Sight

Points of Interest

- Bodysurfing
- Camping
- Cafe
- Canoeing/Kayaking
- Course/Tour
- Diving
- Drinking & Nightlife
- Eating
- Entertainment
- Sento Hot Baths/ Onsen
- Shopping
- Skiing
- Sleeping
- Snorkelling
- Surfing
- Swimming/Pool
- Walking
- Windsurfing
- Other Activity

Information

- Bank
- Embassy/Consulate
- Hospital/Medical
- Internet
- Police
- Post Office
- Telephone
- Toilet
- Tourist Information
- Other Information

Geographic

- Beach
- Gate
- Hut/Shelter
- Lighthouse
- Lookout
- Mountain/Volcano
- Oasis
- Park
- Pass
- Picnic Area
- Waterfall

Transport

- Airport
- BART station
- Border crossing
- Boston T station
- Bus
- Cable car/Funicular
- Cycling
- Ferry
- Metro/MRT station
- Monorail
- Parking
- Petrol station
- Subway/S-Bahn/ Skytrain station
- Taxi
- Train station/Railway
- Tram
- Tube Station
- Underground/ U-Bahn station
- Other Transport

Our Story

A beat-up old car, a few dollars in the pocket and a sense of adventure. In 1972 that's all Tony and Maureen Wheeler needed for the trip of a lifetime – across Europe and Asia overland to Australia. It took several months, and at the end – broke but inspired – they sat at their kitchen table writing and stapling together their first travel guide, *Across Asia on the Cheap*. Within a week they'd sold 1500 copies. Lonely Planet was born.

Today, Lonely Planet has offices in Franklin, London, Melbourne, Oakland, Dublin, Beijing, and Delhi, with more than 600 staff and writers. We share Tony's belief that 'a great guidebook should do three things: inform, educate and amuse'.

Our Writers

Duncan Garwood

From facing fast bowlers in Barbados to sidestepping hungry pigs in Goa, Duncan's travels have thrown up many unique experiences. These days he largely dedicates himself to Spain and Italy, his adopted homeland where he's been living since 1997. He's worked on more than 30 Lonely Planet titles, including guidebooks to Rome, Sardinia, Sicily, Bilbao and San Sebastián, and has contributed to books on food and epic drives. He's also written on Italy for newspapers, websites and magazines.

Nicola Williams

Border-hopping is way of life for British writer, runner, foodie, art aficionado and mum-of-three Nicola Williams who has lived in a French village on the southern side of Lake Geneva for more than a decade. Nicola has authored more than 50 guidebooks on Paris, Provence, Rome, Tuscany, France, Italy and Switzerland for Lonely Planet and covers France as a destination expert for the *Telegraph*. She also writes for the *Independent*, *Guardian*, lonelyplanet.com, *Lonely Planet Magazine*, *French Magazine*, *Cool Camping France* and others. Catch her on the road on Twitter and Instagram at @tripalong.

STAY IN TOUCH LONELYPLANET.COM/CONTACT

AUSTRALIA The Malt Store, Level 3, 551 Swanston St, Carlton, Victoria 3053
☏ 03 8379 8000,
fax 03 8379 8111

IRELAND Digital Depot, Roe Lane (off Thomas St), Digital Hub, Dublin 8, D08 TCV4

USA 124 Linden Street, Oakland, CA 94607
☏ 510 250 6400,
toll free 800 275 8555,
fax 510 893 8572

UK 240 Blackfriars Road, London SE1 8NW
☏ 020 3771 5100,
fax 020 3771 5101

 twitter.com/lonelyplanet
 facebook.com/lonelyplanet
 instagram.com/lonelyplanet
 youtube.com/lonelyplanet
 lonelyplanet.com/newsletter